A MATTER OF
DIGNITY

Books by Andrew Potok

A MATTER OF DIGNITY

MY LIFE WITH GOYA

ORDINARY DAYLIGHT

BANTAM BOOKS

New York Toronto London Sydney Auckland

A MATTER OF

DIGNITY

Changing the Lives

of the Disabled

by Andrew Potok

362.4048
P864m
2002

A MATTER OF DIGNITY:
CHANGING THE LIVES OF THE DISABLED

A Bantam Book / February 2002

Book design by Laurie Jewell

Chapter 6 ("Internal Music") appeared initially, in modified form, in *DoubleTake*.

Library of Congress Cataloging-in-Publication Data

Potok, Andrew.
    A matter of dignity : changing the lives of the disabled / Andrew Potok.
       p.   cm.
    Dogs: Pete Lang, guide dog school manager of instruction and training—Rights:
Mary Lou Breslin and Chai Feldblum, teachers, activists, social-policy thinkers—
Bodies: Dave Loney, prosthetist; John Fago, photographer, teacher, prosthetist—
Jaws: Ted Henter, computer engineer and entrepreneur—Scholars: Adrienne
Asch, professor of bioethics; Rosemarie Garland Thomson, professor of English;
Paul K. Longmore, professor of history—Internal music: Connie Tomaino, music
therapist—Neighbors: David Werner, biologist, health educator—Brothers and
sons: Jay Neugeboren, writer; Mona Wasow and Anne Larkin, teachers; Sam
Tsemberis, agency head.
    ISBN 0-553-80215-1
      1. Handicapped—Rehabilitation—Biography.   2. Handicapped—
Services for.   3. Handicapped—Rehabilitation—Technological innovations.
4. Handicapped—Attitudes.   5. Disability studies.   6. Quality of life.
    I. Title.

HV1552.3 .P68 2002
362.4'048'0973—dc21

                                                          2001043275

Published simultaneously in the United States and Canada

PRINTED IN THE UNITED STATES OF AMERICA
BVG   10   9   8   7   6   5   4   3   2

FOR LOIE

who makes everything possible

CONTENTS

A MATTER OF
DIGNITY

PREFACE

Recently, on the edge of a quiet Vermont lake, some twenty of us were whiling away a perfect late-September afternoon. We had all paddled from the boat landing to this spot in a half-dozen kayaks and as many canoes. Birds were calling from every direction as a gentle breeze rustled the yellowing leaves. There was Danny, telling jokes, some of which he had already e-mailed around. Knowing him, he was in shorts, the struts and flanges of his new prosthesis gleaming in the sunlight. Probably a couple of streamers with lightning bolts were hanging from the socket. Steve and Claire sat by themselves, smoking, getting ready for fishing. Geoff and Peggy were playing Go Fish with their nine-year-old. Etsuro, who was blinded in a car accident in Japan and emigrated to avoid ostracism for his bad karma, was posing à la some oriental martial art, his white cane aloft in place of a javelin. My guide dog, Tobias, watched intently at Etsuro's heels. The rest of us were lying about, sunning and schmoozing. Hard-boiled eggs and peanut butter and jelly sandwiches were being shared or traded for some newly concocted Vermont cheese.

After an hour or so of lolling about on land, I folded myself into a one-person kayak and pushed off, leaving my wife Loie, my friends and my puzzled dog on shore. As I began paddling, I relished the surge, the wantonness of my water freedom. The pleasure of being out there, where there is no fear of collision or danger or embarrassment, had few parallels in my earthbound life. The feeling was delicious. I picked up the pace and shot out into the middle of the lake. I hit nothing for there was nothing to hit, no shoes or chairs to trip over, no half-open doors, no wineglasses at the edges of counters to sweep away. My friends' voices, like the late-summer buzzing of flies, became indistinct, then wafted lazily into earshot again. Geese were honking high above. I heard someone calling my dog's name, followed by squeals of laughter.

On this glorious day, in perhaps the final third of my life, I found myself taking stock. What had brought me this freedom and this comfort? How to plot the rugged terrain I'd traveled to get here? Derailments and detours have nudged and shoved me off center in the course of my life, some as a result of war, some via disability. Of the more recent dislocations, who among the friends on shore, some blind like me, some not, had traveled a similar route to mine? And who had made the trip easier? I pondered living in this country, at this moment in time, pondered how technology, a privileged position in the world and evolving attitudes toward disability enabled me to have this much independence, accessibility, mobility and dignity. But I knew that in spite of that privileged position, to be sanguine about disability and attitudes toward it was simplistic. I knew very well that even here, in well-endowed America, the disabled are grossly unemployed, unequal, untended.

For much of my life, I gave no thought to this. Like most people, I had grown up with the accepted pathological definitions of disability as conditions that limit human motor, sensory or mental activity. A vague noblesse oblige attitude defined my occasional encounters with anyone outside the scope of my trajectory. I should have known better, but, though a refugee from war when I was a little boy, I had been quickly and thoroughly Americanized. I thought that there was no limit to my possibilities, and my responses to others who seemed less fortunate were often bounded by conventional stereotypes, by sentimentality, by the familiar inclination to dismiss and marginalize those who were outside the tribe of "the normal." Only recently have I begun to see disability politically, as another form of ethnicity.

Drifting in my kayak, I felt a powerful urge to explore the quiet ways that people embrace work that lies outside the sanctioned selfishness of the times. And some of those people doing this work were picnicking on the shore of this lake, the tech specialist, the rehab teacher, the counselor. Starting in my own backyard, I resolved to let that surge of energy lead me elsewhere, everywhere. I wanted to go off to meet them all, disabled or not, those who engaged in work and thought, technology or public policy, prosthetics makers and trainers of guide dogs, people who were devoted to independent living and civil rights. I wanted to learn what motivated people to make better tools, to take better care, to help change laws and attitudes. I knew a little about some people's need to be rescuers, about others' religious or ethical imperatives for service, not heroes or saints but those engaged in what I had come to think of as an honest day's work.

A breeze must have blown my kayak toward shore for I was brought back to the present by a voice to my right. "Watch it, Andy," Carolyn yelled. "You're drifting toward the waterfall." Just to be sure, she had posted herself mid-lake to keep an eye on the kayak antics of those of us who thought we were utterly safe.

When I was back on shore, Scott, a mobility instructor, said, "I never see any of you like this. It makes me think of sea turtles, so graceful and elegant in the water and so clunky on land." Tobias jumped onto my kayak and licked my face, then ran to show me his new friends. Happy to be temporarily off harness, off leash, this smallish sable-colored shepherd is one of the joys of my life.

But not all of my blind friends want a guide dog. Some are revolted by the idea. For Joe, a cane user, who has pulled out his new ukelele to strum the "Ode to Joy," dogs simply don't fit his compulsively neat lifestyle. A woman I know in Boston dislikes the sentimentality dogs evoke in others. "I hate it when they think the dog is brilliant and the blind person a hopeless klutz," she said.

The world is organized for a kind of average person designated normal. When this vision of ourselves is nudged off center by disability, the new, skewed picture undermines our established expectations and values. We must figure out all over again how to be and how to face others. We were once quick and deft, rich in potential, and now we are becoming fragile, diminished, even repellent to some. Roles are reversed, friendships come undone, loves bend and break, confidence is lost, ideals erode. We begin to live in a new reality.

But what a diverse population we are, as different from one another as from the ablebodied, different not just inside our disabilities but in what we bring to them. We can be rebellious, obnoxious, proud or combative. Our disabilities may feel comfortable, isolating, challenging, infuriating or ordinary. And how differently we respond to one another and to the informed or innocent entrance of nondisabled people into our lives.

According not only to the ablebodied but to many within the disability community, people with disabilities have a certain obligation to be docile, unprovocative, undemanding. If an ablebodied person crosses over into disability space, he expects a warm welcome. "No one likes to be blown off by a nasty blind guy," a friend once confided. Though no one likes being insulted by a sighted person either, the blind guy elicits certain deep, perhaps primordial responses, unmediated by complexity or wonder, arising from cultural expectations of how humans should look and act. Perhaps avoiding the disabled runs deeper than simple social ineptness or lack of empathy. Perhaps this one is zoological, based in the laws of natural selection, a built-in evolutionary tactic of favoring what most resembles us, with every body part functioning, every system quivering with static energy, ready to spring.

In fact, not all disabled people are nice. I take a perverse delight in my own and others' anger, entitlement and rebelliousness. I know a quadriplegic who prides himself on mowing people down with his wheelchair. At airport elevators, he nudges his way toward the front, knocking people about. He reports that often they are ready to scream at him until they look down to see his pitiful condition. "Oops, sorry," they nearly always end up apologizing. "I feel like a little kid," he says, "testing to see what I can get away with." Once, though, as he forced his way toward the front of the elevator line, he smacked a blind guy and had to pay. "Can't you see that man is blind?" a pregnant lady in line yelled at him. And then he understood that even in the disability world there was a certain hierarchy of entitlement.

I wondered about the very definition of disability: who was disabled and who was not. The thought of disability elites seems ludicrous in spite of a kind of blanket permission in the air these days for most anyone to take the role of victim. Nonetheless, the blind have long been considered, perhaps unjustly, to be on top of the disability pile, receiving more services and perks than any other disabled category. Perhaps this is because being blind is most people's worst nightmare, perhaps because everyone loves the idea of Milton or Homer or Stevie Wonder. But a wise elderly man with post-polio syndrome commented that to him it seemed clear that, in the final analysis, hierarchies among the oppressed don't mean a thing. If the eugenicists or other racists come upon us to decimate all the

5

blacks, all the Jews or all the disabled, lightness of skin color, the percentage of Jewishness or the category of disability will not matter much.

When Penny Marshall, the Hollywood director, was considering making a movie of my book *Ordinary Daylight,* which chronicled the early stages of my blindness, she came to Vermont to check me out. After dinner, we sat in my living room sipping brandy. "My friends say I can't keep making affliction movies," Penny Marshall said, weighing the issues. "They also say I don't know a thing about blindness but they are dead wrong. I just got my first pair of glasses and suddenly I became middle-aged. I can't see a damn thing without glasses. Flirting isn't the same," she said. It took me a few moments to regain my composure, yet it is true that our possibilities slip away with age and its decrepitudes. I know as well as anyone that the best flirtation is nimble, unencumbered, subtle and quick, and most likely isn't helped by peering over spectacles. Among the litany of losses that had once caused me grief, flirting had been near the top of my list.

A few years after Penny Marshall's visit, the wearing of glasses happened to be the salient issue in a case before the Supreme Court testing the scope of the Americans with Disabilities Act. The court was asked to decide if a woman denied a job as an airline pilot because she wore glasses was covered by the antidiscriminatory provisions of the ADA. Even though she didn't consider herself disabled for wearing glasses, she had been refused employment on the basis of a perception of disability. The Supreme Court, interpreting the ADA narrowly, denied her claim, drawing a distinction between workers whose disabilities can or cannot be mitigated by corrective equipment or medication, squeezing the definition, narrowing the circle of disability. Thus the ADA's safeguards might well vanish when individuals make themselves more employable through ways of overcoming their limitations. Here were a new bunch of catch-22s. If disabilities do not include conditions that are correctable with medication, prostheses, hearing aids, insulin, perhaps even guide dogs or wheelchairs, then people with these conditions may not be granted "reasonable accommodation"—any modification in physical access necessary for employment—one of the more interesting and forward-looking concepts of that amazing piece of legislation, the Americans with Disabilities Act.

Inclusion or exclusion of people who wear glasses in the perception and definition of disability is a more interesting question than it appeared to be at first laugh. When lawyers were initially writing the ADA they assumed a very broad definition of disability, one that included anyone with any serious illness whether it could be fixed or not. They toyed with the subject of glasses, knowing on the one hand that without glasses a lot of people couldn't see a thing, and on the other hand suspecting that the general public would probably not accept such an inclusion, mostly because this country seems to feel a need to draw a clear line between "them" and "us." It is still difficult for most people to conceptualize a spectrum of physical abilities and disabilities that all of us are on. As for the ADA framers, they turned out to be wrong in thinking that people would not be discriminated against for wearing glasses.

But even defining myself as blind is not without some ambiguity. I have been legally blind and getting worse for some thirty years, yet now that I have only light perception and at times can detect some movement, I have begun to paint again.

"Your painting is a tour de force," a friend said to me.

"It is not!" I said with a shudder, imagining it hanging in the lobby of the Lighthouse, judged only among the "very special."

"A man who can't see, *painting*," she said. "What else can it be but *special*?"

"Forget I'm blind," I told her.

"But . . . but," she sputtered. "No one can forget you're blind, for chrissake."

It's a dilemma, wanting my painting to make commentary on, say, the human condition. I tell myself that diversity doesn't simply add superficial variety to the human mix. It can improve the mix, add new ways of knowing, of creating and interpreting the world. Some say that being different means being less, others that it has within it the possibility of a new synthesis, a new paradigm. And it can provide the joys that attend transformations. Philosophy or anthropology or psychology might well take on fresh meanings when viewed from some new, unique slant. Skiing blind or on one leg can be ecstatic, the sensuality of surrender unparalleled. And so, I tell myself, it will also be with painting.

A while back, I sat at a friend's dining table across from Oliver Sacks. I thought that now I had the perfect opportunity to add my bit of weird disability behavior to the lists of exotica he chronicles with so much gusto and imagination and insight. I'd not only eagerly read the tales of his neurological curiosities but I've taken a lot of pleasure reading elsewhere about artists who not only worked in spite of their impairments but probably counted on them as the sources of their artistic uniqueness. I reveled in Van Gogh's glaucoma, Renoir's myopia. I scavenged the literature for retinopathies, for uveitis, for retinitis pigmentosa, my disease. The writing or music of manic-depressives and schizophrenics holds a special interest for me. I'm beginning to belittle nice, normal eyes or brains going their dull way through the world, observing and commenting like Boy Scouts about sexuality.

I told Oliver Sacks that after a twenty-five-year hiatus, I was painting again. "It has required weird adaptations and innovations," I said, describing how I'd measured out the room to avoid collisions, the easel a bit more than an arm's length in front of me and, to my left, just below my elbow, a table spread with brailled paint tubes, jars and bottles of oil and turpentine. I told him how I wiggled my gloved left hand to locate the canvas, how I'd left pushpins in the canvas to mark where my brush had just been. He nodded and went on eating. I continued, telling him excitedly about the confusing role of intentionality, about accidents and unintended gestural clumsiness.

He was polite and seemed happy that I was doing what I wanted to do, and then proceeded to tell us about people with Williams syndrome, the color-blind of some tropical island, some high-functioning autistics who were obviously in a very different category than a painter trying desperately, perhaps foolishly, to keep on painting.

Tail between my legs, I went home to accept what was really going on. My painting was a private pleasure only and, aside from being a relatively old guy trying to recapture his youth, inhaling again the sweet smells of oil and turpentine, or perhaps acting out a previously unconfessed desire to be supercrip, I finally realized that painting might best be left to the sighted.

The afternoon was beginning to cool on our beautiful Vermont lake and we climbed into our canoes and kayaks again, heading back to the landing. We yelled across the water to each other with directions and jokes. We'd arranged to ski together in a few months. In our car, driving a couple of exits south on the interstate, I admit to Loie that, until now, I have shown only curiosity, not involvement, in disability issues. Now, I say, I want to understand what some disabled people mean when they talk of "disability pride." Personally, I don't look at blindness with a lot of good cheer, though there are the cheerful blind who are able to chirp their way through life, considering blindness an inconvenience only. "I just don't get it," I tell my wife. "Blindness, all serious disability, is so big, so life-changing. Still, given that we are stuck with it, I suppose it's better to claim the damned thing than to angst about it."

"If nothing else," she says, "not angsting probably prolongs life."

There is something else to it too. Will claiming it tie me to disability, making it the focus of my existence? How strange our lives, the turns that have made blindness and disability define us more than painting or architecture. Not only as definers but the main preoccupation, the career, the mark made, the thing left behind.

Claiming disability has other pitfalls as well. It challenges our insulation from others who are making equal claims. It pushes us into membership in a larger community of people like ourselves, and this has not always been easy for me.

Many years ago, in front of the doors leading into a Low Vision Conference in Boston, I watched a bunch of blind demonstrators march clumsily in a circle. Everyone who had business inside had to fight his way through them. My business, the first of such occasions for me, was to give a talk on low vision, in contrast to total blindness. Back then, that was a lively insider issue. I have no recollection of why the demonstrators were there, but watching them, I was horrified. They stumbled over each other's heels, knocking placards out of one another's hands, looking foolish, unseemly, pitiful. I was on the road to being blind like them, and they were more than threatening. They filled me with fear and loathing and shame.

Since that time, I've perceived my rejection of those natural ties as misguided. Even though I don't particularly seek the company of disabled people, I recognize more and more that there are now fundamental life experiences that I can share

with no one else. Sharing them, feeling understood in my differentness eases the loneliness that comes with being an outsider. In a similar way, I don't seek out other Jews, but sharing
stories, humor and a history brings me a deep sense of belonging.

But my feelings of terror before disability and incapacity
in the guise of a few clumsy blind demonstrators plagued me
for years. At the time, though, I weaved my way past them
and entered the spacious, marbled halls of the conference center. Exhibitors beckoned me with a dizzying excess of goods
piled high, here a table of talking watches, there talking car-
penters' levels and scales and adding machines. The screen-
reading devices for computers, still in their infancy, looked
essential to my future well-being. There were white canes
with sonar attachments to alert the user to the smallest obsta-
cle, braille slates, tapes and punchers, devices that transformed
printed letters into electrical impulses of brailled dots. There
were magnifiers of every kind, closed-circuit TV systems that
enlarged the printed word, monocular telescopes, infrared devices used for night killing by the army or night wandering by
the night-blind like me. This was a veritable blindness mall, a
low-vision theme park. And then, in a booth to one side, a
man was handing out leaflets about a guide dog school he
represented. His own harnessed shepherd lay quietly at his
feet. More than anything else displayed there, this got me,
really got me. I wanted one of those.

This cornucopia of ingenuity, these goods and services,
that dog, were enough to satisfy anyone's consumer addiction,
but I also remember the nausea that came over me, the mix of
revulsion and attraction to forbidden objects. Touching the
Talking Book tape machine that would, from then on, be my
primary reading source was like touching poisoned mush-
rooms, dangerous but inviting. I wanted to take it all home,
all the gadgets, like a new wardrobe.

As it turns out, I have benefited from almost everything exhibited at that conference, things magnified and voice activated, things projected, enlarged and transformed. Now I'm dependent on taped books and screen-reading computer software, while my mobility is tied inextricably to guide dogs, three so far.

In those early years of my advancing blindness, I did take care of myself by learning new skills but, while in the middle of a doctoral program, I also bolted the rational world to pursue an insane "cure" offered by a woman in London who claimed she could cure retinitis pigmentosa with bee stings. My attempt to obliterate my unacceptable limitations cured me of ever looking for "cures" again. Finally, I have come to realize that many of life's essential problems aren't soluble. Misery doesn't always lend itself to remedy. As a matter of fact, this kind of attitude, I have come to believe, misunderstands what makes life interesting. Being cured of one's disability, one's peculiar psychology, one's angst, though sought avidly, runs the risk of leaving a residue of dullness and uniformity. All of this must seem silly to a society intent on ease, comfort, normalcy, a desire not to stand out in nonconformist ways, as crazy, poor, disabled, loud, different. But just as tragedy is not due merely to error, every question is not answerable, every ill is not always curable, everything does not always come out well in the end. "Everyone who is born holds dual citizenship in the kingdom of the well and the kingdom of the sick," Susan Sontag wrote. We are all a little bit ablebodied and a little bit disabled. The degree to which we are one or the other shifts throughout life.

That afternoon on Waterbury Reservoir with friends and colleagues pushed me to want to explore the work and philosophy of people who do not consider disability a curable medical problem but a social one, people who train guide dogs and make computers speak. I wanted to connect with people who have shown up on the barricades, taught, written, reached others who seemed beyond reach, and those who have not only changed our domestic laws and priorities but have changed the lives of people in other parts of the world as well.

I realized that I needed to learn about the legislative and legal aspects of disability as much as I did about our feelings regarding wholeness, beauty and ugliness, about the state called normalcy, about liberating technologies and therapies, about the role of the disabled in history and literature. And what could better inform and enlighten me than contact with people who help to create access, who elicit change via care, support, teaching and study as their life's work? As it turned out, I have learned from them that, in spite of the American addiction to youthfulness, "normalcy," virility, activity and physical beauty, diversity in all its forms provides not only fascination but strength. Uniformity tends toward dullness and extinction, diversity toward higher forms. What could make more sense than to value all that is diverse, unexpected and exuberantly impure?

DOGS

PETE LANG

*guide dog school manager of
instruction and training*

PROLOGUE

For some, independence is not a disability issue. "It's a stupid issue," a blind friend said. "Why pick on disabled people to talk about independence? It's everybody's issue."

Even though the concept of independent living is at the heart of the disability movement, the word *independence* seems irrelevant only to those like the congenitally blind who learned cane technique and braille very early in life and could then get on with it, no longer straining to see. Retinitis pigmentosa, however, is a physical condition that is constantly changing, and there is no respite from preoccupation with adjusting to new losses. Like the clanging of a loose muffler under a car, it's a constant reminder of its own existence. There are times, of course, when I am unaware of my blindness, immersed in work or other pleasures, but the blindness is never not there, and the struggle for independence, the preoccupation with gracefulness and dignity, the self-consciousness of an identity in flux muddles the tasks of daily living.

"If independence or appearance or decorum are too simplistic as disability issues, what are the truly germane issues?" I asked a wheelchair-using activist.

She didn't skip a beat. "Universal health care," she said, "reliable personal assistants and attendants, community mental health, affordable, accessible housing, relief from work disincentives, better public transportation and broad enforcement of the Americans with Disabilities Act."

Obviously, independence is not an issue only to those who have solved or resolved it, just as learning to walk or ride a bike is not an issue five minutes after accomplishing what had once seemed so daunting.

In my evolution as a person whose blindness began in adulthood and progressed steadily, the concept of independence loomed large. All those counselors and mobility instructors urged me on. "The cane's your ticket," they said, "and if you don't learn it well, you'll be a hitchhiker forever, ashamed and enraged, hanging on to arms, begging others to take you for a walk." And indeed, without my dog I become a beggar for mobility, pitifully longing for my lost manhood, my humanity.

"My cane requires no loving or grooming," says my friend Joe, defending his choice to use it rather than a guide dog. "When I'm working at my desk, I stick my cane against a wall until I'm ready to use it," he says. "It's not panting at my feet."

I like the panting. And when we're out and about, Tobias deflects questions about my disability by standing in for those questions. Instead, people ask about him and are largely satisfied. Often this suits me. Sometimes not.

I was on the treadmill at the gym, earphones stuck inside my ears, listening to a book. Suddenly I became aware of some guy waving his arms in front of my face. I turned the machine off, unplugged an ear. I was trying to read a book on evolutionary biology, hard enough without the competing hip-hop blaring on the club's loudspeakers, but who knew, maybe this guy had something important to announce, like a fire in the weight room. Unplugged, I listened. "What's the dog's name?" he asked. I muttered Tobias's name and plugged in again, but the guy wasn't satisfied. He wanted more. He was windmilling his arms again. I pointed to the earphones but he wasn't having any of it. Disconnecting, I listened to his urgent words. "How old is he?" the man asked.

"He was trying to make contact with a blind guy," Loie told me later, at home. "Look, Andy," she said, "these people aren't necessarily bad. That guy wasn't used to seeing a dog tied to the bar of a treadmill. He's intrigued. He loves dogs. He's starved for dog talk."

I admire the people who have gone beyond self-consciousness or shyness or a silly sense of decorum, people who can't be bothered with whining about how hard it is to ask directions or to fumble for a door handle. "Get on with it," they say, "get on to what's important, to whatever is on the other side of that door."

I remembered a defining moment when my need for mobility help took on a life-and-death urgency. I was visiting in New York and trying to hail a cab to meet a friend downtown. In the early evening, I positioned myself at an insanely busy corner of Sixth Avenue and Fifty-seventh Street. I waved at every moving car and when something resembling a taxi stopped, everyone in the world ran in front of me to grab it. Caneless, of course, because only very blind guys use canes, and dogless, for how could I possibly bring a dog into my mother's Louis-the-god-knows-which dainty little apartment, I didn't stand a chance. After half an hour, I stumbled down the stairs into the subway, a direct ride downtown. The Fifty-seventh Street stop was relatively new and well lit. The train was nearly empty and I sat counting off Rockefeller Center, Forty-second Street, Thirty-fourth, Twenty-third, Fourteenth and West Fourth, where I got off. The long gritty platform was nearly deserted. Having no one to follow, I inched my way to a staircase and stumbled up to the next landing, which was dark and stank of urine. On the middle level, which connects the downstairs platforms with those above, I heard voices by a far wall. As my footsteps echoed off the cement, the voices were ominously stilled. I felt eyes assessing me. Agitated now, I crashed up the next flight of stairs. Though the platform was wide enough, I felt I was walking a tightrope between dropoffs to the tracks on either side. I found the long echoing corridor to the final stairs that led out to the street, the foul New York air smelling sweet and fresh. I worked my way to a corner where a couple of cars were waiting for the light to change. I was disoriented but it was strangely peaceful, the roar of traffic distant. Gingerly I stepped off the sidewalk and suddenly found myself inside a sea of headlights and blaring horns. I'd misjudged everything. I, who had escaped from a European war and survived blindness until now, was about to be mowed down by furious taxis and trucks roaring up Sixth Avenue from Houston Street. Car by honking car, they allowed me to get to the sidewalk, and when the angry pack sped uptown, I leaned against the lamppost, my legs too wobbly to move. I had lost my bearings completely. I didn't have a clue how to get to Washington Square. A gust of wind blew garbage at me. I walked slowly toward lights and, as accidentally as Columbus ramming Santo Domingo, I walked into a pay phone. I called my friend, who figured out where I was. "I need a dog," I managed to say when he came to save me.

For years, I'd been running into a Seeing Eye representative, with his dog, at blindness-related conferences. I never missed an opportunity to talk with the man and he, for his part, would urge me to file an application to the Seeing Eye, though I was pretty sure that I still had a little too much vision. Nevertheless, I liked fantasizing a life made perfect by a perfect guide dog. "Ralph," I would say, "I've got to take a leak," and Ralph would sniff out the men's room, then sit waiting by the urinal.

The dog belonging to the guy from the Seeing Eye always lay quietly at his feet and, at the end of the day, the two made their way easily to his hotel. Oh, how I wanted a dog, a dog like his dog who would lead me through crowds, through buildings and hotel lobbies, a dog who would navigate around restaurant tables, take me to the gate in strange airports, cross Sixth Avenue safely, allow me to say, "Excuse me, I have to go now," to the person who corners me at a party, a dog who would lead me through the maze of the health club where I work out.

I liked fantasizing a life made perfect by a perfect guide dog who, I thought, required nothing more in return than a pat on the head, a scratch behind the ears. As I was to learn, the combination of me and Dash, then Topper, and now Tobias required and still requires a great deal more than that. It takes patience, discipline, persistent determination, respect and endless love. Dogs smell, shed, get ill, revert to deeply ingrained beastly behavior. They can be picky eaters, take up an inordinate amount of psychological space, need playtime and fairly regular trips outside to relieve themselves, even if I am engrossed in conversation or in the middle of a fiendishly original thought or the last five minutes of a ball game.

Dogs have been domesticated for some twenty thousand years. About then, they seemed to have figured out that they would do well to attach themselves to bands of humans with whom they could negotiate an interesting reciprocal arrangement. In return for barking at strangers or finding dead carcasses in the bushes for all to share, they would be fed, loved and groomed. In their domesticated state, they seem to live to please and charm and generally amuse, but when trained, they can be superbly useful animals and are used for many interesting purposes, guiding the blind just one among them. They are fabulous sniffers, retrievers, pointers, and have recently been trained to help the hearing-impaired, epileptics and the physically frail and wobbly.

In a sixteenth-century Italian painting, a dog stands at one end of a long, loose rope, an old bearded blind guy in a togalike outfit at its other end. Nothing about that arrangement could possibly work. Dogs became useful guides only when someone had the brilliant idea of attaching a rigid handle to a harness strapped around the animal's body. Only then could the blind person pick up messages from the dog's movements and act on them quickly and efficiently.

The first time dogs were used as guides in the United States was 1929, when the Seeing Eye opened its doors. The oldest of American guide dog schools, the Seeing Eye last year matched 300 teams of blind persons and guide dogs. At this writing, they have over 1,800 working graduates in every corner of America and beyond. Since their establishment, they have made more than 13,000 working partnerships.

The Seeing Eye is a sizable enterprise, existing on a huge endowment collected over the years from private and corporate donations. All of its services are free to blind people, who are the sole beneficiaries of them. Not only the dog but all the equipment, the elegant three-week residency in Morristown, New Jersey, air fare to and fro, and lifelong follow-up training whenever the student happens to need it. Unlike some other organizations that serve people with disabilities, there is nothing patronizing here. In another age, this work might have been done by some kindly order of monks or doctrinaire communards. In our age it would more likely be done by social workers. It is a wonder to me that, in the midst of the sickness called individualism, one can point to this work and wish it to be a model for something more universal, something like health care and education. No social workers are involved, no sisters of mercy, only dog trainers. For a cynic and pessimist like me, the work done here is a cause for wonder.

Services to the blind have historically been at the forefront of disability rehabilitation work. It's possible that the blind have been seen, over time, as the most helpable or the most pitiful, the least demanding or the noisiest. Whatever the reasons, all blind people get an extra deduction on their income taxes and free mailing services for blindness-related material. Aside from these relatively minor perks, rehabilitation services, though not always pleasant or useful, exist to teach cane travel and certain other blindness skills such as braille and independent living. Because blind people have tended to be the most organized and have created a political voice, they have taken a leadership role, not always a welcome one, in the disability community. Some blind activists declare their needs to be different enough, thus special enough, to warrant a separate, strong list of concerns and demands. They feel that they would be held back by participating in broader coalitions. Others among them realize that coalitions breed greater power, as was certainly the case in the making of the Americans with Disabilities Act.

Neither cane nor dog is perfect. In the realm of absolute safety, neither is eyesight. For teams of blind people and dogs, any number of things can go wrong. At times, I mistrust my dog's decisions. He's just a dog, I tell myself as he stops, for reasons of his own, in what I am sure is the middle of a block. I urge him to go on but he is adamant. Only then do I realize that he is right and I am wrong. A car is backing from an alley into the sidewalk.

I have heard cane horror stories and dog ones. I knew a great cane traveler, who, walking quickly on a Detroit street, walked face first into the metal cab of an eighteen-wheeler parked across a sidewalk. His cane went under it, picking up no clues. His face was severely damaged. I've heard of lethal accidents to dogs and handlers in New York subways as well as on quiet residential streets.

As for me, I am right-handed, right everything. That side of my body—that hand, arm, leg, even brain—is better developed than the other. But my left hand now clutches a leash and harness and has become sensitive to every movement, every distraction, every thought that passes through the mind of my dog. My whole body has been extended to include his. When as a team we negotiate the tumult of the busy world, at our best we move and act as a single unit.

During one of my residencies at the Seeing Eye, a fellow student compared his partnership with his dog to that of Tonto and the Lone Ranger. The California lawyer on my right, toking at his pipe after dinner, added his view. "You know, Andy," he said, "this whole dog thing is a Zen experience."

DOGS

On a sunny day in early spring, Loie and I climb into one of the Seeing Eye's vans for the ten-minute drive from the elegant spread of the guide dog school to the center of Morristown. The Seeing Eye's main residence, its offices and kennels, are situated in the rolling hills outside of town, but the real action happens in the streets of Morristown, a city of nineteen thousand, nestled in a hilly, horsey part of New Jersey.

Though I have trained here with three different dogs, the third of them, Tobias, now at my side, I have come this time to rediscover the place from a nonstudent point of view, and, most particularly, to talk at length with Pete Lang, who has been with the Seeing Eye for thirty-five years, the last ten as training manager.

The town, as always, is pulsating with activity, the traffic heavy, the nearly half-million residents of surrounding Morris County driving in to work. Upscale clothing, coffee and chocolate franchises have moved into vacated mom-and-pop businesses. Several fourteen-story buildings have risen far above the rest and contribute noticeably to the commotion of downtown. The tree-shaded green, rich with history, lies in the center of the city, girdled by churches.

Everywhere you look, you see guide dogs, chugging along at breakneck pace or moving slowly, carefully, dogs being put to one distraction test or another, by a pizza slice left on a sidewalk, by a squirrel, pigeon or cat, or by an unruly barking pet tied to a parking meter outside a coffeeshop. There are dogs weaving their way through webs of scaffolding or police barricades, past spewing diesels parked across sidewalks, dogs picking their way around planters and trees, under flapping flags and low-hung branches, through puddles, ice and snowbanks, in hot weather and cold, from early morning till dusk. And clutching the harness strapped around each dog is the hand of a trainer, or the hand of a blind person learning how to do it for the first time or brushing up and bonding for the second or third. At every corner, nook and cranny of this bustling city, teams are pushing their way through real-life situations. They labor in traffic, on city buses, trains headed to New York, inside the labyrinthine corridors of the county courthouse, in malls, chugging through racks of suits and dresses inside Epstein's Department Store, one of the few remaining family businesses struggling to stay alive.

Everywhere you go in this town, you can hear a chorus of "atta boy" and "atta girl" as shepherds and Labs and goldens stop at every curb, then step cautiously into the streets where they are tested by distracted drivers making a right on a red or by choreographed, near-disastrous events imposed upon them by the Seeing Eye's own drivers.

Pete Lang inches the huge Dodge van into a large garage attached to an unadorned, turn-of-the-century boardinghouse on Mt. Kemble Avenue, a central city location owned by the Seeing Eye and used as a drop-off point for students and trainers. Eight vans are already parked, each with as many as seven dogs waiting eagerly to be harnessed by a student or trainer for a downtown trip.

Several trainers are putting their dogs through the deliberate, careful pace of obedience exercises. Dogs are asked to come, then sit, then fetch a leather glove or a key chain. A dog barks from inside one of the vans and Pete hushes him. Lee, who was my instructor with my second dog, Topper, is leading a pup down the metal stairs. "We built that staircase without risers to be sure that our dogs would not be afraid of open staircases," Pete says.

We leave Tobias hitched to the wall and, unimpeded by alpha-dog conflicts, we observe Pete in the streets of Morristown as he retrains Connor, a five-year-old yellow Lab. "I'm working Connor to get him ready for an elderly gentleman with lots of new health problems," Pete says. Connor's been out of commission for nearly a month and needs this daily work while his blind handler recuperates. Connor is careful and Pete slows him down even more. "I don't get to do this as much as I'd like," Pete shouts back over his shoulder. "It's a young man's job. I told my wife Jane the other day that I'd give up being training manager in a heartbeat if I could get back to this. Being out in the street training dogs is the work I love."

"A couple of years ago the Seeing Eye celebrated its seventieth anniversary," Pete tells us as we take a break inside a coffee shop, Connor now relaxing under the table. "It's sort of amazing for me to realize that I've been there for half its existence."

Pete knew early on what he wanted to do. There was pressure from his family to find a calling that would make him as financially secure as his accountant father, who provided handsomely. Not rebellious by nature, Pete studied business administration in college, hating every moment. The certainty of a sedentary business life went against his still largely undefined longing for a deeper meaning, not to speak of the outdoors. He knew that there was something spiritual out there, something beyond helping one's self, but he didn't yet know what that something was.

"A decisive moment came in a class in which the professor asked which of us was concerned about the problem of world hunger. To my amazement, mine was the only hand that shot up in the air. I was disgusted and began looking for books in the college library which had nothing to do with business administration. Of all things, I found Morris Frank's *The First Lady of the Seeing Eye*. It grabbed me in a way that nothing had until then," he says. "The fact that dogs could be trained to lead blind people made me gasp for breath. Just then, I happened to see a blind man working a German shepherd in the streets of Cincinnati. And, Andy, I couldn't stop gaping at the man. I was moved to tears and I wrote a letter to the Seeing Eye, curious to learn more about the process. By return mail, they invited me to come have a look. Two months before my graduation, I went east for the first time in my life. I arrived in Newark the day before my Seeing Eye appointment. I was terrified of the city, found a Y, locked myself in, wishing the night would end quickly, and the next day I took the bus to Morristown."

We now follow Pete into the town green where he tests his charge for squirrel distractions. Connor seems admirably uninterested. Pete points out one of the historic buildings ahead of us. "I remember when they had a fire at this beautiful old church," he says. "It was gutted and took a long time to rebuild but it was good training for our dogs, who for months and months had to work their way through the construction site." For Pete, the real world of objects at rest or in motion must be nothing more than a testing ground for dogs.

Back in the Seeing Eye's town garage, Pete introduces us to Christian, a tall young man who had just been accepted as a new apprentice. "This fellow really moves me," Pete tells us. "He's the same age I was when I started and he's doing it for the same reasons." Christian is a skier who came to the Seeing Eye to try to do something meaningful with his life. "I need to do work for others," Christian says, "not just for myself. I feel ready for that. And here I can do it without giving up the outdoors."

In the package the Seeing Eye sent Pete thirty-five years ago, there was a pamphlet with the title *A Career That Counts.* As Pete recalls the moment of receiving the piece, he chokes up. He coughs and covers his face with his hands. "I had no idea I was going to react to the memory of that pamphlet like this," he apologizes, "but I am so incredibly lucky to have found my entire life on my first try." Pete is a gentle, shy man. "My mother was very supportive but my father was astonished. 'Four years of business administration and you want to be a . . .' He couldn't say it, Andy, 'a . . . dog trainer?' " Pete laughs. "With the pamphlet, the Seeing Eye sent an application, and now I felt I was at the beginning of a mission to do good work. I knew I wanted it more than I had ever wanted anything."

We go out into the streets again, this time with Tobias, and follow a trainer with a young dog on Maple, then a blind person from the current class doing her solo on the Elm Street route. "When I was Christian's age," Pete says, "one of my favorite books was Albert Schweitzer's *Reverence for Life.* It helped me realize that my own life didn't need to be about dollars and cents. I knew that everything was going right when I first walked into the vice president's office for my interview and spotted a bust of Schweitzer on the bookcase. That did it," he says.

Tobias is always happy but, as we walk, his tail is wagging more than usual. I am wondering how much of this place and these routes he remembers from his training. Often, when we pass a place we have visited even once, he will pause, look back at me to check—yes? no? you're the boss!—then, with no sign from me, he goes on. He does that now at the entrance of a coffee shop he hadn't visited for over a year.

"In Vermont, Tobias and I rarely see this much traffic."

"Great!" Pete says enthusiastically. "I'll supervise you on the High School route."

As a rule, I'm a self-conscious walker, too aware of how I think I'm seen. Blindness has contributed to my shyness and reclusiveness, a timidity of unnecessary contact. I often want only to blend into the landscape, embarrassed by the conspicuousness of blindness. Though there are those who avoid a blind person like the plague, I have been told that generally most people smile at Tobias and me. I believe that the sight of man and beast at work together makes more than a few people feel good, seeing this amazing partnership of inventiveness, synergy and love.

Now, as we charge toward the center of town, I feel particularly sure of myself and my dog, relishing the specialness of this occasion, being observed by the best of the trainers and by Loie. She sees me work my dog all the time, but here, in these circumstances, it seems like an intimate viewing, like sitting in on instructions given to novitiates of a secret order. Tobias and I are flying now, stopping inches from each curb, crossing at busy intersections, threading our way through crowds. For the two of them, I feel I am performing my best tricks, figure eights, loop-the-loops, belly rolls.

Now, at one crossing, Pete warns me that he wants to test my dog's ability to disobey and as traffic speeds left and right in front of us, he taps my shoulder. "Tobias, forward," I command and, remembering his lessons well, he does not budge.

"I don't think I can watch," Loie says. "Can I meet you in the coffee shop?"

Pete turns to her and laughs. "Andy's been doing it for years, and Tobias is doing great work."

"Okay, Andy, now," Pete says and again Tobias holds his ground. When the cross-traffic stops I tell him "forward" for the third time. He steps out into the street cautiously, and we cross safely. I choke up with pride and remember the first time I stood at a corner and was about to cross when Kris, my first trainer, said, "Today we are going to test Dash's ability to disobey."

"We are?" I had no idea what she was talking about.

"I'm going to ask you to give Dash the 'forward' command right into traffic," she said.

"This can't be true."

"If he does well, he will either not budge or he'll go only as far as the moving car and stop."

"And if he doesn't do well?" No response. "How many people die doing this?" I was pleading now.

"All right, Mr. Potok," she said, tapping my shoulder. *"Now!"*

Somehow we did it, everyone in our class did it, and, after that day in the streets, we sat around exchanging stories of our exploits like crusty old veterans of foreign wars.

Now, as Tobias and I continue on our route, one of the Seeing Eye commandos in his van nearly runs us over, his tires glancing the edge of the sidewalk. Tobias, hero for the day, yanks me back, but an ambulance full of young emergency workers pulls up beside me, outraged. "That drunk drove up on the sidewalk," one of them tells me. "I can't believe what he just did. We're going after the son of a bitch!"

"That's very nice of you, but he's one of us."

"One of you? But . . . but . . . Are you sure?" They need to be sure but they don't want to believe it. We all smile happily at them and finally they drive off, more than a little disappointed.

Pete has arranged with the cowboy driver of the van to make a turn toward us in the middle of our next crossing and, even though Tobias has stopped to let him by, the man reaches a hand out of the car window and smacks my perfect shepherd lightly on the nose with a rolled-up newspaper. Tobias jerks us back, yelping as if he has been stung by bees. I know that he is insulted by the impudence, for he must know that his street behavior had been exemplary.

"I can't believe he did that to our dog," Loie says, a bit shaken.

"It was a useful lesson," Pete assures her. "It'll serve as a reminder for Tobias," he says as I console my dog. "He'll keep an even safer distance from moving cars."

We drive back to the lovely rolling hills outside of town where the main Seeing Eye buildings are located. We talk for a while in Pete's office as we await the call for lunch. "When I first got here thirty-five years ago," Pete says, "they were just breaking ground for the construction of these buildings. It was beyond my wildest dreams that I could be a part of all this. Everything about it appealed to me. I knew I could handle this job and at the end of that day, they offered it to me. I took it in a flash. Let me tell you, I could have flown home without an airplane. I graduated on June 7, 1964, and began work at the Seeing Eye June 8."

The first time I went to the Seeing Eye to train with my dog, Dash, Pete Lang had already been working there for nearly twenty-five years. For me as for so many others, training with the first dog was a giant move, not only in shrugging off my natural fears about putting my life in the hands of a dog, but in being unequivocally identified from then on as a blind man.

All this pride in risk, this self-consciousness, this wanting to look good is, in fact, secondary to the principal reason for this immense effort. The reason different groups of twenty-four blind people show up for three-week residencies every month is to gain or maintain their independence. As sign language breaks the isolation of deafness, as the wheelchair breaks that of immobility, so the cane or the dog breaks through the limitations of one's reach, making everything available and accessible. Without my dog I control only what my arms can reach. With him I venture wherever his senses dare to penetrate. Without Tobias, I must negotiate with another person regarding when to do anything, I must be careful not to overstep a given number of demands, I must gauge how profusely and often to fuel the transaction with expressions of gratitude, how to reciprocate.

For me, as for most anyone, disabled or ablebodied, absolute independence is not the goal. Dependence is perhaps harder to learn, the balance of dependence and independence a subtle and crucial one. Nevertheless, just as I would negotiate with a person to use her arm as a guide to my travels, so I must temper the demands I make on Tobias with an equally important reciprocity, in his case taking the form of the kind of deep respect that Pete teaches, as well as the love and play and care, the recognition that he is the sweetest of animals and, for his animal reasons, wants with all his being to please me, at least when his other instincts don't interfere. When I am totally relaxed and trust Tobias to do the right thing, we race over sidewalks and streets crowded with pedestrians and car traffic. It can be as exhilarating as skydiving.

Being back here, as we file in to lunch, in these dining rooms, as in every nook and cranny of this place, there are vivid memories. Here magical things happen. Each time, it's like coming home again. On three different occasions, it has been a temporary haven, a three-week pit stop in the midst of busy lives. Each time I return to this club where my membership is lifelong, I am struck by how the place tugs at my heart. Nostalgia is woven into every smell, every explored corner, every sound, for in this building, intense, momentous things happen.

A cane-using friend once chided me for making a big deal out of training with a dog. "With you it's never the simple desire to find the tools, fix the problem and get on with it," she said to me. "It's never get a dog, then do what you have to do. No, with you it's how do I look, how does the new package compare with the old, how can I make my life grand, perfect? Jesus, Andy," she said, "nothing about it is mysterious or magical."

But part of the seductiveness of the place for me is its separation from my dramas, from the messiness of life, the theater of love and hate, of loss, loneliness, insubstantial friendships, the worries about children. The outside world disappears during the three weeks of 5:30 wake-up calls and feeding and meals, of the rush to "park" the dogs, the days ordered around first or second trip into town, around lectures and grooming time, around obedience exercises, around a stolen moment to listen to a book, another to take a quick shower. It is the temporary structure, a blessedness of discipline, the safety of being watched, taught, fed, gently manipulated.

At the lunch table, I have vivid memories of sitting together for the first meal with my class three dogs ago, the sharing of dog stories, the veterans there for their second, even seventh dog, the novices listening hard to every word, dreaming of their imminent freedom. And a couple of days later, sitting at the same tables only now with more than twenty bewildered Labs and shepherds, nose to nose, butt to butt, under the table, sniffing at each other's recently bathed, subtly perfumed bodies. Then, a week after our arrival, sharing aspects of our lives, though still feeling insufficient, awkward at best, the oldest handlers telling stories of unequaled bravery and unbearable cuteness.

Pete's wife Jane joins us for lunch. At her feet is her eight-year-old golden retriever guide dog, Matthew. Pete is preoccupied, checking on the current group of students negotiating the dining room. "Correct Beasley, Pat," he says. "That's it, lots of praise."

"At home, we have three dogs," Jane says. "We have

Matthew and Matthew's father, Finnegan, a retired breeder. When we go out walking, Matthew and I lead, Pete and old Finnegan follow. We also have Clancy, a retired yellow Lab who spent her life working in New York City."

I've known several Seeing Eye trainers and can hardly believe the number of animals they leave at home when they come to work. Lee, the woman who trained my second dog, Topper, maintained a household of one boyfriend and sixty-two creatures of every imaginable kind. Among them were goats and pigs and Newfoundlands, parakeets, cats and who knows what else. Kris, who trained Dash, then Tobias, describes the witnesses to her wedding ceremony in Maine. "We had a couple of friends looking on, together with one seal, two loons and six of our dogs."

"When I began my apprenticeship," Pete tells us over coffee, "I worked for two weeks cleaning up at the breeding station, then a month at the kennels. A couple of months after that, I began to train a string of dogs, all part of the three years of apprenticeship, which included instructing blind people on working the dogs I had trained for them. I loved seeing the dogs develop, loved the relationships I made with them. They were my dogs. They belonged to me. The very first dog I trained who made it into class was named Sabre, a German shepherd. I can't describe my elation when I saw how beautifully Sabre was doing with her new master. There are some dogs you never forget."

Another unforgettable experience Pete had during his first year was taking six old dogs from the kennels to the vet to be put down. "It was horrible," he remembers, "holding each dog as he died. But it gave me an appreciation for what each of our students has to go through every ten or fifteen years."

Remembering my own primordial fears on first meeting a lot of newly blinded adults like myself, I wondered if Pete had had to fight his own stereotypes when he faced his first class.

"My only anxiety," he says, "was about the performance of my dogs. Other than that, I was thrilled that finally I was about to do what I had only dreamed of doing before, teaching people how to use the dogs I'd trained for them. But, you know, I probably felt totally comfortable with blind people because I was so painfully shy. Come to think of it, I guess I had a harder time with people who weren't blind."

Pete met Jane during his second year at the Seeing Eye. "She was a student here for her first dog," he says. "We sat next to each other at a picnic. We talked and talked. I felt crazy, strange, confused. I'd never felt anything like it before. So this is love, I thought. I let a couple of weeks go by before I called her and then began to travel to Boston to see her, which I was able to do only two weekends a month. I took a crash course in braille and wrote her daily. On my summer vacation back in Ohio, I tried to explain this to my parents. They couldn't believe it. Not only was their son a dog trainer but now he was madly in love with a blind girl." He laughs. "I began pursuing Jane in July and married her in September. I proposed in the Boston Christian Science church. I figured she'd have a hard time refusing me there."

There are roughly 300 dogs on the Seeing Eye property, 40 on each of three floors of the older of the two kennels, some 180 in the new one with its quarantine areas, state-of-the-art surgical and treatment rooms. Both kennels are as elegant and pristine as the main building.

"The number-one thing about training a dog," Pete says, "is to respect the dog, a magnificent creature with feelings. From this underlying respect we build a relationship. We need to develop the dog's trust. It's essential that we get this across to all our trainers, who must have respect and reverence. They must treat the dog fairly at all times, never losing their temper, though we're only human and it isn't always easy."

When my first guide dog, Dash, smacked me hard into a

parking meter, my response was strictly from the Old Testament. "You son of a bitch," I cried, indignant, humiliated and bloodied. I snapped the leash back as hard as I could, cinching the choke collar tight around his neck.

"Good correction, Mr. Potok," my trainer said cheerfully, but when, five blocks after my meeting with the parking meter, I was still enraged because, well, I couldn't let it go, Kris instructed me with a wisdom given to these extraordinary trainers, from where? From Pete Lang, without doubt.

"Dash has no idea why you're still angry, Mr. Potok," she said. "You must learn to forget your anger right after you correct him." Ah, dear Kris, if only you could have followed me everywhere, my life's journey would undoubtedly have gone more smoothly.

"When the dog is taken from his mother and put into the new puppy-raiser's home," Pete says, "he begins an interesting and wrenching journey. The philosophy we thrust upon the family is simply to nurture and love the dog, as well as to subject him to lots of different social situations and experiences, lots of kids, lots of other animals. Of course the dog also has to be taught good manners. A year later comes another major trauma when the dog is wrenched from his puppy-raising family. On his return to the Seeing Eye, he spends three or four weeks pretty much without human contact, in our kennels. Some dogs come back showing a lot of resilience, probably affected internally but happy," Pete says. "Others suffer a lot more and show it. Typically, at this stage the dog is confused, worried, nervous, even fearful. This is a key moment and we want our kennel staff to be supremely sensitive to it, to give these dogs as much attention as they possibly can. Being pack animals, it's healthy for them to have this social activity."

Trainers, instructors and kennel workers begin their careful observation of how each dog interacts in the pack, which dogs are more submissive, which more dominant. The kennel workers keep an eye on all this and bring the overaggressive or fearful dogs to Pete's attention. Notes about behavior are passed on to the instructor once the dogs are assigned. "Each dog is really special," Pete says. "Each one needs to be treated differently, just like kids. We need to learn and appreciate those differences and adjust our training style accordingly. At this point, the dog begins to feel more comfortable with the kennel staff and with the other dogs. Each one is assigned to an instructor to begin the four-month training period. The weeks of feeling lost in the kennel pay off because now the dog latches on to the trainer, the new person in his life, the new leader. It's important for the dogs to find this alpha leader, otherwise they strive to be the alpha leader themselves. The dog begins to pay attention to the body language, the low-voice corrections, equal to the growls of an alpha dog similarly commenting on behavior. We need to establish that dominance in a fair way."

The first days of training are very light. The dogs know basic obedience, simple things like "sit" and "down" and "come." The instructors reinforce this learning right away. The dogs begin by simple walks down the driveway, fun walks during which they are urged to pull on the leash, then to stop at the various turns, to sit still in order to be praised and petted, the physical touch being very important. "We see a big difference in the dogs at this point, some getting too excited by the physical contact, some responding best to a very light touch," Pete says. "Gentleness is important, though some dogs are very tough and need firm handling from the beginning. We want the dogs to enjoy this, to like the cheerful voice on the instructor's part. After the walk, they are put in a yard by themselves and they can play. There, the dogs might go as far from the trainer as they can, all the time watching him. He doesn't force himself on them, and the dogs accept the instructor as a daily companion and teacher.

"Usually by the third day, the dog is entirely comfortable with the instructor and we become more serious about the training. We begin to put a harness on the dog, keeping a nice, even, positive tone of voice. The quality of the voice is terribly important, but now more and more discipline enters the picture, dealing with the dog's ever-present instincts, a very natural and beautiful part of the dog. I'm a strong believer in using the minimal physical force in controlling the animal. We try to get our best results from praise, from positive reinforcement. We teach, we do not bully. We should not expect 100 percent obedience. This is not what we want. We want the dog to make some decisions on his own, for instance, to refuse commands, as Tobias did this morning, to remember how to intelligently disobey. The willingness of the dog is so enormous, he wants to please so much, that he learns some pretty amazing things."

The instructors begin teaching the dog a number of new tasks such as directional commands, overhead clearance, traffic. Task by task, the dog learns what's expected, reinforced by praise or reprimand or correction. They have to get inside the dog's head, figure out how to motivate each one, how to get each to work. Some dogs need just a whisper or they get too revved up, while some, the low-key, mellow dogs, need a spark lit under them, need to be perked up with loud "atta boys" or "atta girls" so they don't become sluggish. "It's very subtle," Pete says. "With each repetition the dogs learn more and we step up the demands on them always in a fair way."

The trainer makes slight shifts from being sighted to acting more and more as if he were blind. The more he plays the blind part, the more he expects of the dog. Usually by the end of the first month of training, the trainer is putting most of the responsibility on the dog to guide. "At a crucial moment," Pete says, "we begin correcting for mistakes because we need to show the dogs that there is a danger with cars. We step up our discipline. If the dog leads us into a low-hanging branch we re-act as if we were truly smacked in the face with it. 'Pfuie!' we say and leash-correct, though never too harshly. We shake the overhanging branch, scold, go back, repeat until they get it right, then praise. You have to watch out for the intensity of the correction with most dogs. If you're a little too hard, he may not want to go back into harness. So we start with the lightest correction and gradually increase until we find the in-tensity which is ideal for that dog. Eventually the dog will ad-just to whatever the master's individual needs are."

One afternoon, Loie and I walk with Pete as he observes a couple of the Seeing Eye's veteran trainers, wearing blindfolds and working their dogs. Their supervisor walks closely behind them. "These sessions are incredibly important," Pete tells us. "The trainers are now totally blind for the first time of this particular session. They're scared but must put their faith in their dogs. On the other hand, the supervisor is there to keep them safe and to evaluate their performance." Dave and Drew are working with two dogs chosen to join an upcoming class. As we watch, Dave's golden walks him into a parking meter. He is corrected, then asked to pass that meter again. When he misses it by a mile this time, the dog is lavishly praised and, pleased with his performance, he squats to relieve himself. As this sideshow unfolds, the main drama is happening with Drew and his Lab, who has led him into the middle of the street. Looking after them, Walt, the supervisor, runs out to urge cars to keep going but with caution. On the sidewalk again, they discuss what went wrong.

I am struck by their total seriousness. None of this is a jok-ing matter, but I might have expected some ribald commen-tary on their mishaps. "They know," Pete tells me, "that what they are doing is a matter of life and death, not for them but for the eventual handler, who cannot take the blindfold off."

Pete still can't get over an incident that happened years

before in Virginia when a blind woman was killed by a garbage truck backing out of a suburban driveway. Her Seeing Eye dog was unharmed. "It happened before trucks were required to install backup beeps but I have a hard time not blaming myself," he says. "Was there something I could have taught that dog that would have helped him yank her out of the way? What did I do wrong? What didn't I do?"

Shortly after I had trained with Topper, I read a piece in the paper about a blind woman, a skilled traveler, and her guide dog who were walking their usual route to work. On the wide platform of the Thirty-fourth Street subway stop in New York City, something happened, no one knows exactly what. Was the dog startled or momentarily distracted? Had the woman slipped or tripped? Somehow she fell into the track and was crushed by an oncoming train. "This is as horrible as it gets," Pete says, "but it happens to sighted people as well."

Having been given a whirlwind trip through the spotless kennels, we walk back to the main building. Old oaks and beech trees provide a luxurious canopy on this foggy late afternoon. "Let me take you a little out of the way," Pete says and brings us to a grassy area where he places my hand on a bronze statue of a long-dead trainer, the man who introduced German shepherds to the Seeing Eye. My hand feels a beret on top of the man's head, a shepherd with huge stand-up ears by his side. To me it's a bit of kitsch. To Pete it's the Lincoln Memorial. Standing beside him, I am a bit ashamed of my cynicism. Then he guides my fingers over another life-size bronze, this one of a little puppy-raiser bending toward her Lab, as he reads aloud from a plaque honoring the families who socialize all Seeing Eye dogs during their first years. Under the flagpole, we are shown two gravestones, Buddy I and

Buddy II, the dogs belonging to Morris Frank, the first Seeing Eye graduate.

Standing now in the spacious hallway just inside the front doors, I recall the process from being dogless, clumsy and oafish to navigating this place, all places, with self-assurance and dignity. I remember the doglessness of the first couple of days, shuffling and stumbling to and from meals, some of us bouncing off walls, some using our dusty white canes, while trainers and staff lined the halls, directing traffic.

"Whoa there, Fred! A little to the right."

"Hold up, Katherine, there's a traffic jam ahead."

After breakfast of the third day, we were sent to our rooms. I paced, stuck a taped book into the machine but didn't hear a word. I squeezed my head out the window for a series of deep breaths. I knew that dogs were being escorted into the building, one by one, newly bathed and smelling as fresh as lavender. I heard my next-door neighbor leave his room, find his way down the hall. He returned saying sweet nothings to some bewildered Lab or shepherd. I waited an interminable minute, two, five, and then, on each of my three residencies, my name was called and I met my new partner. And inside this residence, near the end of the first week, we got our dignity back. The parade to and from meals quickly became orderly, even graceful.

At Pete and Jane's home, where every available place on the living room carpet is taken by a dog, Pete talks to us about his spiritual life. "At age nineteen I was in a spiritual desert. Something inside me said that there was more to life than what was on the surface. I didn't really understand it but it was a loud voice. Later, I came under the influence of a man at the Seeing Eye who turned me on to Quakerism. It talked to my spiritual yearning, my God hunger. It spoke to me. It seemed real. It led me to the warmth and compassion of Quaker meetings. I felt very comfortable with silent worship, with no altar, no symbols, encouraging us to seek within ourselves for inner light. This is a big part of my life, both at the Seeing Eye and at home. These moments of inspiration, short at times, are where my spiritual life is. These moments make it real. In sharing, there's a confirmation of an inner light, of love.

"I'm very goal-oriented, like this morning when I felt driven to get those dogs out into the streets to work them. The practice and service of the Seeing Eye is mindful, spiritual. It's all focused on the bond between the person and the dog, and that's where all my energy is channeled."

When I think of mindfulness, a concept that's become important to me, I am struck by all I've learned about it from the process of learning respect for these dogs. "Maybe that's why I feel the Seeing Eye is meditative, almost sacred," I tell Pete.

"Are you serious, Andy?"

"I don't feel that anywhere else."

"This is your place," Loie says to me. "It touches you more deeply than any other."

"There's another aspect to coming here. It's a bit like checking in with the National Guard."

Pete tells us that the place isn't as rigid with its rules and beliefs as it used to be. "When I first got here, all those years ago, they swore that they would never hire a female trainer. You're not going to believe this but they also wouldn't give a male dog to a woman student. I really like the way the place is evolving."

Pete is learning to take more time for himself and his family. Though I tend to romanticize his commitment and devotion as monastic, this is probably the wrong way of looking at his life. He vacations in Disneyland and, for a few weeks in summer, goes from baseball stadium to baseball stadium to watch his favorite teams. Last year, Pete took his sons on a five-city baseball trip. "It was memorable," he says, as we lament the end of loyalty to teams that once owned a piece of our hearts. "This year Jane and I are going alone. She's never had the chance to go and we're really excited about it." Pete owns his modest suburban split-level house, allows his car to fall into disrepair, loves to sit around the local cafe listening to neighbors talk mostly about the wonders of his wife Jane. Against one wall of their living room is a carousel horse, bigger than a couch, carousels being a Jane Lang passion.

"There are times when I feel harried," he says, "but I'm learning to slow down, take a deep breath. When I get home at night, I'm done in, totally exhausted. But you know, Andy," he says, "I don't know a more wonderful feeling than, at the end of each and every day, to fully comprehend that I've simply done an honest day's work."

RIGHTS

MARY LOU BRESLIN
CHAI FELDBLUM

teachers, activists, social-policy thinkers

PROLOGUE

Until recently, the question of rights for the disabled, like the question of rights for black people, did not even enter the lexicon of human concern. Sympathy and charity, yes, at least in some circles, at least at especially sentimental times. But throwing all who were seen as abnormal into institutions aroused little pause. There was no way to incorporate such people into benevolent thinking about "normal" humankind. The elevation of a disenfranchised group's status to a shared humanity, whether it be Jews or blacks, women or gays, the lame or the mentally ill, does not happen automatically. It happens as a result of huge shifts of consciousness, and only after intense labor and persistence.

Even among people who are themselves disabled, I've known many who are grateful for whatever crumbs are thrown their way. "Sorry," they—we—often say, "sorry for being here, for taking up space on the planet. Why make waves? Why put an extra burden on society?" Like the American Jews who didn't want to attract attention to themselves by speaking out about the Holocaust as it was happening, so do many who are disabled feel visible enough—with our canes and crutches and wheelchairs, our differentness—without the spotlight of added attention. The less we are talked about, the easier our passage through life. The less noticed, the less despised.

Nevertheless, many want not only to be noticed but to be actively recognized and supported as equals among fellow human beings. They want to be seen not as a population that is pitiful or unable to care for itself but, by law and attitude, a population that demands and is entitled to the same rights to health care, housing, education, transportation and communication as everyone else. If the disabled need modified or expanded accessibility in order to level the playing field, then that accessibility is their due, just as it is the due of the able-bodied who are given access via stairs or print or language.

Some disabled people are demanding, and the manner in which they demand is not always sedate and noiseless. An incident that I knew nothing about at the time took place in 1990, and hearing about it later, I began to question my instinctive lifelong sense of decorum. The action was called the Wheels of Justice march. On that day, 475 people in wheelchairs gathered in front of the White House, and another 250 by the elegant, curving steps at the base of the Capitol. "Access is our civil right," the crowd began to chant as they slipped out of their wheelchairs to crawl up the eighty-three marble steps to the Capitol, each of them carrying a scroll of the Declaration of Independence.

It was a chilling action, brave and focused, precisely to the point. But on being told about it, a friend of mine shuddered. "How awful," he said, "crawling up those steps like snakes." It would probably be a stretch to translate what evolutionary biologists consider our genetic dread of snakes into a built-in fear of the disabled, but the Wheels incident contrasted my own feelings about propriety with my love of oppositional politics, the sentimentality of romantic struggle, the uphill fight, the underdog. Perhaps this too is born of natural selection, some of us preserving what is, others stretching it, taking risks, skydiving.

After I learned about the march, I started reading about "the rolling quads" of the University of California at Berkeley, who in 1962—the year that James Meredith made his heroic stand in Mississippi—insisted on being seen, on not being invisible, on being given access to school and home and community. In Berkeley and in Mississippi, they made noise and turned it into music.

The disability community had to decide, one person at a time, whether their condition reduced them to feeling forever small, unimportant, peripheral, even nonexistent. For how does one dare to make noise from a wheelchair? From blindness? From stammering? From retardation? And who had given permission not to be nice, to break from conservatism, to find the courage to stir up wrath, break the bonds of civility and decorum?

Thinking about disability required major shifts of consciousness—from charity to civil rights, from sentimentality to a recognition of a wide spectrum of human possibilities—before laws could even be thought about. Moving from parents ending their isolation and mobilizing professionals by organizing around issues of their children's diseases to the creation of the Americans with Disabilities Act in 1990 represented a huge conceptual leap. Collecting money for "cures" or research sometimes helps, but to be considered fully human, with equal opportunity and dignity in every aspect of one's life, helps a lot more.

Businesses, legislators, courts and the public at large wrangle about the creation of disability laws and regulations not only from fears of getting an insufficient piece of the finite pie but from the fiction of a social contract that considers every citizen an independent productive worker, a competent adult assumed to be free and equal. Provisions for people who aren't part of the bargain—those dealing with disease, old age, accidents at birth or acquired during life—are not part of the basic institutional structure.

Discrimination began to emerge as a central issue as it became increasingly clear that lack of access to buildings, programs and transportation was more than an oversight. It was discrimination pure and simple, another kind of segregation. But as the disability rights community began to think about laws and legislation, they realized that barring discrimination solely on the basis of disability left several questions unanswered. In previous legislation targeting discrimination pertaining to race, gender, religion or national origin, those characteristics were to be ignored so that an individual could be judged only on merit. But in order to offer equal opportunity, disability required affirmative efforts. Though it borrowed language from race-oriented civil rights legislation, that language would have to change dramatically when its focus became disability. Disability had to be acknowledged rather than ignored. The concept was revolutionary. Before it could be accepted, people had to assume that the disabled were just as much a part of society as the nondisabled, deserving a legal offensive on obstacles such as stairs, inflexible work schedules and the lack of supportive devices. Though the struggle would never be smooth or easy, several factors were in its favor. The public was somewhat sensitive to injustices in society because of the previous successes of the civil rights and women's movements, and most of Congress perceived disability as a motherhood issue, a vote that cost nothing and angered no one, not much different from its sentimental and meaningless hire-the-handicapped resolutions of the past. But they were all to learn that disability rights would not be free, and several administrations fought hard to deny the rights that were to be provided by the proposed legislation.

In spite of the enormous difficulties ahead, the disability community had begun to coalesce into a powerful group whose ranks included representation from rich and poor, men and women, people of all colors, religions and ethnic backgrounds, as well as members of Congress themselves.

The sequence of eventual laws and legislation included the Architectural Barriers Act of 1968, which stated that all buildings receiving federal support had to be accessible to the disabled. As was to repeat itself in the future, people tried hard to weasel out of even the cheapest alterations, claiming high costs or the compromise of architectural integrity in spite of Department of Labor figures that stated that half of the legislated architectural accommodations cost little or nothing.

In 1973, in the second Nixon administration, the first civil rights law for people with disabilities, the Rehabilitation Act, was passed. It was applicable only to programs that received federal funding. Section 504 of the Act, a legislative afterthought, made it illegal for a federal agency, public university, defense or other federal contractor to discriminate against anyone solely by reason of handicap.

No one knew who had suggested adding civil rights protection. It was buried, seemingly innocuous, but the wording was clearly copied out of the Civil Rights Act of 1964, which had ruled out discrimination on the basis of race, religion or national origin. The powerful language of Section 504 was not subjected to hearings or debate of any kind, but luckily there were people in the nascent disability movement who recognized what had fallen into their laps.

Interpreting discrimination was an ongoing task in implementing the Rehabilitation Act. In race it meant to take the signs off bathroom doors, to level the playing field. With disability, proactive steps were necessary in order for opportunities to be offered. Things like architectural barriers, which would have to be remedied, didn't exist in race and gender.

Words like *reasonable accommodation* came from this time, words now fairly well known, meaning any modification in access, physical or programmatic, including support such as a reader or interpreter, that enables a disabled employee to perform a job up to the standards required by the employer. In one case, when a person in a wheelchair tried to board a bus but couldn't get on, a judge used the race analogy. "If the bus driver opens the door and says come in, that's enough," he declared. It took a smarter judge to realize that opening the door is not enough, that means have to be provided for boarding the bus, that the physical barrier served as the vehicle for discrimination. This was a new concept.

The Ford administration recognized the significance of Section 504, estimating compliance at billions of dollars and effectively stalling the issuance of final regulations. Though President Jimmy Carter had promised to complete what Gerald Ford had begun, his HEW Secretary, Joseph Califano, was so alarmed by the scope of Section 504 that he pleaded for time and effectively blocked its implementation, even claiming that alcoholics, drug addicts and homosexuals would seek protection under this law.

Demonstrations and front-line barricades, organized to demand that Califano make the law more than a hollow promise, took place in some ten cities in 1977. A quiet candlelight vigil of people in wheelchairs was organized in front of Califano's Washington home. They wanted him to sign the regulations immediately, without weakening them. Other demonstrations followed and three hundred people took over Califano's office overnight. Infuriated, he refused them food and phones, and the demonstrators left, defeated.

In San Francisco, however, the sit-ins endured, with demonstrators putting their lives on the line. Some two hundred people locked themselves in the Federal Building and, supported by the mayor and several community organizations, they persisted in spite of terribly harsh circumstances for twenty-eight days. This was one of the first times that people with very different disabilities recognized the benefits of working together.

From Washington, Califano again tried to cut them off but, because word had gotten out and many people outside smuggled in food and services, sabotaging Califano's efforts, he caved in and, in April 1977, signed the regulations without changes.

He had similarly stalled the implementation of the Education of All Handicapped Children Act of 1975—later renamed and rewritten in 1990 as the Individuals with Disabilities Education Act—but was now forced to activate this law as well. As a result, variously disabled kids began to be mainstreamed into public school classrooms. This act has helped not only to create a generation of people who have learned to live independently and to be active in pursuing the dignity that comes with civil rights but to demonstrate to ablebodied children that the disabled are not objects of fear and strangeness but rather ordinary people like themselves.

All of these actions required focused activism, a rethinking of the status quo, a reexamination of given ethical points of view. But even the Air Carrier Access Act, which allowed people like me to board planes with their guide dogs, ran afoul of the Supreme Court until it was strengthened by Congress in 1986. The resistance to many of these new laws was based on the perceived difference between disability legislation and the antidiscrimination laws regarding blacks. The latter was a financial saving. This was the opposite. How inclusive any new law had to be, how much money had to be spent, became the new balancing act, defining much of the relevant legal debate of the 1980s.

Particularly from the mid-1970s on, nationwide demonstrations and disturbances focusing on disability rights took place more and more frequently. There were sit-ins and crawl-ins, and in a 1988 uprising, students at Gallaudet University demanded, and got, a deaf president—which not only marked a great victory but was a television event, the disability movement's equivalent to Selma and Stonewall. Nevertheless, the culminating event of this era was the passage, in 1990, of the amazing Americans with Disabilities Act, unique in the world for its recognition of the rights of disabled people. Even so, many important parts, such as punitive damages for discrimination and making buildings and all transportation accessible, had to be bartered away to satisfy the heavy lobbying demands of business. Still, no business lobbies wanted to be actually seen as bigots, nor did they want to miss out on the huge number of the disabled as a source both of labor and of customers. Reluctantly and slowly, the business community complied, though it and others are constantly testing the scope of these laws.

Central to the critical legislation and to the politicization of a huge, previously little-heard-from minority of this period were imaginative and brilliant disability activists, academics and lawyers, some disabled, some not. There are times when thinkers are heroes, when self-interest is eclipsed by a drive for justice, when experience and thought join as wisdom, when the law, one word at a time, stumbles ahead and ignites real change. Why some go that less-traveled path and what they do once they find themselves on it was the drive behind my finding and exploring the lives and thoughts of two women, Mary Lou Breslin, an activist and social-policy scholar, and Chai Feldblum, a legislative lawyer.

RIGHTS

When I first talk to Mary Lou Breslin, I use the words *helper* and *helping* in describing the book I want her to be a part of.

"Helper?" she all but growls.

I hadn't given the word much thought and don't get what her problem is.

"I spent a lot of years trying to change the way people think about disabilities," she says. "I've put a lot of thought and effort into changing from a helping model to a more integrated holistic one that includes civil rights protections but also includes a postmodern paradigm." She wants to know how a civil rights component would fit into my "helping mode." Unmistakable disdain travels the phone connection from California to Vermont. "It's hard to think of helping as the solution," she says.

What am I getting myself in for? I wonder. What could be wrong with helping? Still, from the beginning of my contact with Breslin, I was intrigued with her defiance of familiar ways.

"Look," she says, "we're all intertwined in complicated networks. In disabilities we're intertwined with those who help but also with communities and our families. The trick is to get the analysis past the notion that helping is the fix. Sure, there is a need for facilitation and support, both integral to our having real choices, but helping as we have known it is not a piece of it. It's part of a model we've spent a lot of time trying to get rid of. It's important to analyze these interrelationships in a way that's contemporary. But another book about people helping people with disabilities? It may clarify motivations for doing one thing or another but it won't add anything to the movement."

It took Mary Lou a couple of long phone conversations to begin to trust my motives and, I must admit, it took me that long to feel comfortable with her academic point of view. Though she is indeed a brilliant academic and legal scholar, I came to delight in her thoughtfulness, her warmth, her ardent activism.

"The public is far from understanding what the movement is, what the real issues are," she says. "To understand disability in any sophisticated way is beyond most people. So the very notion of helper and helpee serves to reinforce the old models. The disabled can't be defined by their need for help. When you get a dog," she says to me, "you get trained and you leave. It's a tool on the way to things you have to do, that's all. The same with a car that needs fixing. It doesn't dominate or define your life."

I realize that I have to start nudging and replacing some of my ancient received notions about disability—hers, theirs, mine—to make room for all this.

"Before the civil rights laws were passed," she tells me, "the paradigm was mainly medical and paternalistic. It's a legacy of a few hundred years of the charity model. The by-product of industrialization was the marginalization of people with disabilities. Once people are marginalized, there needs to be social policy to deal with this isolated group, so large state institutions developed in the 1910s and '20s to isolate people from communities, a kind of eugenics movement to put people away so they don't contaminate the breeding stock. This longtime isolating of people has created the present feelings about disability, the public stereotypes. The government's re-action to this group of people has been to continue to leave them in a marginalized state, in spite of funding for social work or rehab counseling. Whatever can't be fixed with med-icine or rehab then remains the responsibility of the person. No more obligation after that. Thus, until 1975 there was no mainstreaming into public schools, only various segregated fa-cilities. That legacy is powerful in the way people still think about disabilities. The idea of helping triggers in me this whole picture of the pre–civil rights paradigm—and," she adds, "that may not even be the paradigm we're now living in. We may very well be, and I suspect we are, inside a wholly new paradigm."

Though I am the petitioner who knows damn well that I have found the controversies that fascinate me and the right person to take me deeper into the disability movement, I feel as prickly as she seems to be. Paradigms, paradigms, I spit on your stinking paradigms, I want to say.

"How independent are you?" I ask instead, knowing nothing of her physical condition. "Do you ever need help?"

"The reality of my own life is that I do need help," she says. "I'm a quadriplegic and need help even getting out of bed in the morning, but I choose who, where and how. The exercise of these choices is what the movement has enabled. It characterizes the shift from the medical to the sociopolitical model."

"Has any of this slowed you down? How are you lim-ited?"

"You mean in the global existential sense or literally?" she says, laughing. "I've nearly always been a quadriplegic in the diagnostic sense. I use a motorized wheelchair. Polio is com-pletely nondiscriminatory. It can get one arm, one hand, two arms, two legs, only legs, one leg, just the breathing, anything. I'm considered a quad because I have some muscle weakening

from the neck down. I have some functioning muscle in my
left leg and my right arm is pretty strong, which is really what
keeps me functioning with relative independence. I have a
very bad back and my stomach muscles are zero. I've had spinal
fusion surgery because I was so unstable in my trunk area. I
drive in my fabulous modified van. I mostly live alone. Physically, in spite of some pretty heavy joint problems, I fend for
myself, though I'm shifting to using more personal assistance. I
now have something called post-polio syndrome, pretty universal in folks my age. All my problems are biomechanical,
joint things that happen when you have a muscle working on
one side only. There's erosion, spurring, that kind of junk. The
attendant care enables me to keep working. I'll keep that going
as long as I can afford it. I'm really happy to have help. I'm not
resisting it in the least."

In the early 1980s, the Disability Rights Education and Defense Fund, Mary Lou's organization, was in a pitched battle
with the Reagan administration, which was advocating for
major revisions to the regulations of Section 504 of the 1973
Rehabilitation Act. DREDF was sending out press releases,
engaged in a major effort to make alliances with the Leadership Conference on Civil Rights. It had trained lobbyists to
go around and talk to various members of Congress to try to
get them to pay attention. This turned out to be crucial, as
Section 504 eventually formed the basis for the Americans
with Disabilities Act. It was impossible to see the formation of
ADA down the road but the idea was to keep Section 504
alive. DREDF had also made a good connection with the
Washington Post.

In this 1981 deregulation fever of the Reagan administration, Mary Lou, in her wheelchair, waited for a *Washington*

Post reporter who wanted to do a piece on disability issues. The office DREDF was subletting in Washington, D.C., was so tiny that she wondered where the reporter was going to sit.

"We're in the old cramped office," Mary Lou says, "and Chuck Babcock comes in. Before he sits down on the corner of one of the desks, we eye each other up and down. I know him from somewhere, I tell myself, and before we get going, we go through our where-are-you-froms. Well, it turns out we're both from Louisville, went to the same high school at the same time and then there's this 'aha' moment as we realize that he was one of the group of boys who carried me and my wheelchair up and down three flights of stairs every single day of school. It was a pretty profound moment," she says, "a little epiphany. His memory of hauling me and my chair gave him a deep, graphic understanding of our disability issues, of why these regulations were so critical. Without our shared experience, he might have written a good piece, but it wouldn't have had that personal component, his very own hands-on experience. In any case, he got it, he really got it. 'Why didn't we think of that then?' he asked. 'We were all smart people. What was the matter with all of us?' Anyway, it was a real parallax view for him, a light bulb that went off in his head. 'If these regulations had been in place when we were in high school,' he said, 'we wouldn't have had to carry you.' 'That's the idea,' I said. 'There would have been alternatives.' 'Yeah,' he said, 'like putting your classes on the first floor, not a big-money item.' 'And an interesting solution to the problem,' I said.

"This of course is the kind of impact that regulations have on people's lives," she says. "It was very useful to have this story on the front page of the *Washington Post* and to have it construed as a civil rights issue, rather than in charitable or health or entitlement terms. That was the goal."

In terms of legislation, it took a couple of years but,

eventually, during the Reagan presidency, the Regulatory Relief Committee was set up to review deregulation and found that the disability regulations were not overly burdensome and kept them in place.

"I came to the disability movement through the back door," Mary Lou tells me. "School and family didn't help head me in the right direction. I grew up in urban Kentucky, and after my polio my family had to figure out what to do with me, especially in terms of school. By the time I was ready for high school, I was using a wheelchair. If you needed any kind of accommodation, you were out of luck. Everything was inaccessible everywhere. My parents intuitively understood that home tutoring was the wrong thing for me, so they dredged up this high school in the suburbs, three stories up to the classrooms, no elevator at all. They talked them into letting me go there without any preparation, any real thought.

"I remember sitting just inside the front doors and the home room teacher gets the principal and they confab out in the hallway, beyond earshot, trying to figure out what to do with me. It's hard to recollect what I was thinking then, what any of them were thinking. I would so much love to get back to that moment, to recall what I thought as all this was happening."

She was thirteen, getting to the point when it was important to fit in, important to be out and about. After talking about it, the administration decided that older students would carry her up and down the stairs, wheelchair and all. During all the years she was there, about five minutes before classes, she would truck to that little hallway where her designated carriers, the four biggest boys in school, Chuck Babcock among them, would show up, and with everyone's books on her lap, they would haul her up and down the stairs. "I mean we flew up and down, unsupervised, unthought about, a nightmare of liability. I was terrified," she says, "but not humiliated. I was scared of being dropped, my attitude about all of it muffled, and unexpressed. On top of everything, I had my little girlish crushes on those guys."

Another horror of her school days was the lack of an accessible bathroom, which would have meant a door wide enough to get her chair inside. "Nobody thought about it," she says, "and no one even thought of asking. Honest to God, I was in my thirties before I could figure out what that was all about. I had no insight about it at the time and none of those smart adults even knew how to conceptualize the situation."

"A whole day without peeing? How did you do it?"

"I didn't drink anything for the whole day," she says. "The upside of it was that I got uncanny control of my bladder as well as getting a pretty good public-school education. The carrying part never got figured out. It really took getting involved with the disability movement to analyze it, to understand it as a response to the dominant social policy at the time. It had a tremendous influence on the way I think about the issues now. At the time, I never even came close to thinking about disability in civil rights terms, in individual rights terms. As a matter of fact, it pushed me the other way."

"Pushed you into hating yourself?" I ask.

"I wanted to squash myself into the 'I'm like everybody else' mold. The word *accommodation* was not in my vocabulary. I was feeling 'get out of my face, I don't want anything from anyone. I can do it, leave me alone.' "

In her Berkeley home office, Mary Lou, who spends most of her time thinking and writing about public policy, relaxes into reminiscing about those early days. "I got polio when I was eleven, almost twelve, and spent a year in rehab. Until then, I was doing everything upper-class kids get to do, playing piano, going to cotillions, all that junk. My father was a wealthy contractor. Home was privileged and racist. Black women helped raise me and became my best friends. Those early relationships got me involved with the civil rights movement at a time when my family's attitudes just about killed me."

She went to the Georgia Warm Springs Polio Foundation, which transformed her life. "This was rehab at its best," she says. "Their position was that you have no reason or excuse for not doing anything you want to do. Their approach was to enlist the family and everyone who cared into a model of cooperation. Philosophically, they wouldn't accept any kind of isolation or segregation. That place was the most influential in establishing in me the notion that I could do whatever I wanted to do. Between the age of twelve and eighteen, I went back there every summer for various rehabilitative fine-tunings."

When the Warm Springs staff asked where Mary Lou was going to college, she told them that she'd been accepted by several colleges that couldn't deal with her wheelchair so she had decided on the relatively accessible University of Illinois. The Warm Springs people urged her not to make any decisions based on accessibility. Nevertheless, she took the easier path. "Not many people at that time gripped the revolutionary notion of architectural accessibility," she says. "The folks at Warm Springs instilled in me the understanding that disability had little to do with whatever the outcome of my life would be. Everyone I know who went there went on to careers and family. All of them learned to support themselves.

"So Warm Springs, black women and my feelings of 'I can do it, get out of my face' in high school gave me the basis for whatever I was able to accomplish. It was a mix of stubbornness and social consciousness. What I really didn't get for a long time, though, and it was there in front of me, was the connection between my place in the world and my inalienable rights as a citizen. Can you believe it?"

At college she was with a bunch of people in wheelchairs

and was involved in every social issue, including the civil rights of just about everyone on earth except her own. The program at the University of Illinois was developed only for those who weren't severely disabled, those who were seen as capable enough to join the workforce. Students had to do everything for themselves. The only ones who fit that bill were young people with polio. "This made me feel I was the elite," she says. "Imagine, the disability elite. I had a bad attitude."

In this huge but very straight, engineering-oriented university, there were perhaps fifteen radicals, three of whom were disabled. "It was not your basic hotbed of radicalism," she says. The big political issues were about race. She hung out with political people and tried to understand what the options were. "I hadn't yet formulated the right concepts, the relationships between labor and economics, politics and activism and class. I didn't get it. It took me another ten years to understand the basic concepts in context. Maybe that's a maturation thing, maybe a result of growing up naive and protected. A crippled girl with privileges is not necessarily going to figure this stuff out."

All the disabled students were housed on the first floor of a dorm where the one adaptation was the accessibility of the bathrooms. Most of them had nondisabled roommates, primarily because it would have been impossible to have two wheelchairs in one small room. They had to enter buildings through back doors, take a series of three service elevators, find circuitous ways around the largely inaccessible campus. The college provided a lift-equipped bus that ran between all the buildings on a regular schedule, but the hydraulic lifts for the buses had no rails or flaps, no protection of any kind. "Getting ourselves on the platform just right was considered very cool, disability-cool," she says. "Even when, much later, I got a job helping disabled people find work, my reaction was, 'What am I doing with all those crips?' I didn't like it. I still can't believe I felt that way but I did. Until the light went on in my brain.

"Everybody thinks I'd give anything to not be disabled, but I never think that. Especially because I've been disabled since I was a kid, my entire existence has turned on these influences and relationships." She chuckles. "If I hadn't been disabled," she says, "I might have ended up married to a Kentucky dentist, taking Valium, drinking mint juleps, looking out over my sprawling estate. And utterly miserable. How could that begin to compare with the interesting life I have now?"

Mary Lou teaches at the Graduate School of Business at the University of San Francisco. Her students will go on to work with workmen's compensation, medical rehab, the insurance industry or corporate disability services.

In 1979, together with a couple of socially concerned lawyers, she co-founded the Disability Rights Education and Defense Fund. "At one time, we thought that empowering people to feel good about themselves could solve all their problems. I believed that for a long time. I don't believe it anymore. That simplistic approach was good twenty years ago but it's all gotten a lot more complicated now.

"One of the main things DREDF did was to teach people about the new laws, which at the time were Section 504 of the Rehabilitation Act and what was then called the Education of All Handicapped Children Act, the law that guaranteed public education for all kids with disabilities, kids who until then were either out of school or warehoused in segregated programs. We were able to shift understanding from ourselves and our problems to the role that discrimination has played in our lives. It doesn't matter what the medical diagnosis is. It's the same level of isolation and discrimination even for those who have coped with jobs and families. This analysis helped to liberate people. It made people realize that disability is the problem of the guys who design and build the steps, not the problem of the person in a wheelchair for not being able to walk. Once you shift the burden of responsibility to where it should be, it's a revelation."

Mary Lou had a hand in all the civil rights issues and legislation of the 1980s that led to the Americans with Disabilities Act, and the paradigm shift she talks about was involved in identifying the ways in which people were prevented from exercising their constitutional civil rights.

Disability is no longer defined as an insular entity but as it relates to the social, political and economic environment. It is no longer defined by the binary model, not on or off, but as a process that varies depending on what's going on in the culture, the society at large.

During the period of my conversations with Mary Lou, I was also talking with Chai Feldblum, a lawyer and teacher who was intimately involved in many disability issues of the 1980s and 1990s, including the actual crafting of the Americans with Disabilities Act.

Often, people who enter disability work are either themselves disabled or have someone close to them who is dealing with these or very similar issues. Mary Lou, in her wheelchair, resisted entering the field until relatively late in her life, while Chai Feldblum was drawn into it in spite of being a nondisabled woman. "For me," Chai says, "it was my involvement with the AIDS community and my passion for justice."

In 1986, when she was a law clerk to Justice Harry Blackmun, the Supreme Court heard the case of *Nassau County v. Arline*. Until then, the court had heard only two or three other cases under Section 504 of the Rehabilitation Act. The

Arline case involved a teacher with tuberculosis who was told she would not be allowed to return to teaching, even though she was no longer contagious. The lower court had ruled that it could not believe that Congress intended to cover people with contagious diseases and thus 504 didn't apply. The Eleventh Circuit reversed that decision and the Supreme Court took it upon itself to decide whether or not the woman was handicapped.

"As a clerk," Chai says, "I pulled this case, asking for it specifically for two reasons. One, I had done a fair amount of health-policy work on Capitol Hill in the three or so years between college and law school, and, secondly, more importantly for me, it was clear that this decision would affect people with AIDS. Being a lesbian, I felt very close to the AIDS issues. I knew nothing about disability law but I became very involved in this case."

The Reagan Justice Department argued that if someone was fired because of fear of contagion, no matter how unwarranted that fear, this was not discrimination based on handicap but discrimination based on reasonable fear.

"You don't usually lobby cases in the Supreme Court," Chai, a small, slim dynamo of a woman, says. "It's just not done. But I talked very deliberately to every clerk in every chamber, presenting my point of view, which was, of course, that Jean Arline should be covered. It ended up being a seven–two decision in our favor and I was very active in drafting the opinion, even though it came out of Justice Brennan's chambers, not Justice Blackmun's."

I ask Chai how she got into law in the first place, where her passion for justice came from. "I grew up in an orthodox Jewish home with a strong commitment to social justice," she says. "My father was an orthodox rabbi who taught Talmud, first in a rabbinical, then a graduate school. In spite of taboos regarding teaching Bible and Mishnah and Talmud to women, it was my father who instructed me. He is a Holocaust survivor who, during the war, lived in the forests of Poland. I grew up thinking about the extent to which injustice can be taken. He taught what was called the scientific study of Talmud, which uses tools like language and history, and uses the Palestinian version of the Talmud as well as the Babylonian. His work was very textual and very analytical."

Chai planned to get a Ph.D. in Jewish history and teach. She knew Hebrew, ancient Greek and some Aramaic, and spent the second year of college in a very religious seminary in Israel. While there, however, she decided that she no longer believed in God, and stopped being an observant Jew.

After college she went to Washington, D.C., where she discovered an outlet for her passion for justice and her desire to do interesting, intellectually stimulating work.

"Though I lost my religion when I was eighteen, my commitment to justice remained. When I discovered law five years later, it was like coming back home. I loved it, I loved figuring stuff out, I loved complicated textual problems. I wanted to do something with my life that made the world better. That didn't feel corny at all."

After her clerkship with Justice Blackmun, all she was sure of was that she wanted to do public-interest work, and unlike her own students today, who are graduating $100,000 in debt, she graduated owing little and could manage this. She started working on disability legislation because two days after the *Nassau County v. Arline* decision, Senators Robert Dole and Bill Armstrong put a bill into the Senate that would amend Section 504 to exclude all people with contagious diseases. Ordinarily that kind of legislation wouldn't have gotten anywhere in a Senate controlled by Democrats, as it was then, but that spring, the Senate was passing a bill called the Civil Rights Restoration Act (of 1988), which was meant to overturn a Supreme Court decision that had narrowly interpreted the terms *program* and *activity,* restoring their original broad meaning. Under Section 504, any program or activity that received federal funds couldn't discriminate based on handicap, so how those two words are defined is important.

By then, Chai had moved over to the American Civil Liberties Union's AIDS project. "People in the disability community recognized that the proposed amendment was an attack on the disability law itself," she says, "but there wasn't a real understanding yet in the AIDS community that AIDS was a disability because, like everyone else, they were influenced by the common stereotypes about disability meaning nonability. They were very focused on saying that they were living with AIDS, not that they were victims of AIDS. To the disability community, AIDS was still the new kid on the block. So it was an educational process and I was very active in it. This was the first time I worked with the more general disability community, understanding the wider range of concerns. And we successfully beat that amendment, not only in that Act of 1988 but later that year in the Fair Housing Act. Here was a definite convergence of the two communities."

All their legislative efforts were based on the original Civil Rights Act of 1964, whose Title 7 specified that there can be no discrimination in employment on the basis of race or sex. "Initially it was just race," Chai says, "and some Republicans added sex, figuring that would kill the bill, but it didn't." Title 2 of the Act covered public accommodation, meaning hotels, restaurants and recreational facilities. Originally it was much broader, covering all types of businesses, but in 1964 that couldn't fly politically. Title 6 of the Act specified that any program or activity that received federal money couldn't discriminate based on race. But housing was not covered under the Act. Then Martin Luther King, Jr., was assassinated, and the Fair Housing Act was voted into law in 1968.

The Fair Housing Amendment Act, designed to strengthen enforcement of the Fair Housing Act in race, religion and gender, was introduced in 1980 but wasn't passed until 1988. "The civil rights community generally wanted this," Chai says. "People with disabilities waited to jump on this train, though it wasn't the main focus of the bill but an amazing first step to prohibit discrimination in the private sector, 504 having applied only to programs and activities that got federal funding. And once this passed, nothing else was competing on the civil rights front. There was no other unfinished business. The civil rights community as a whole was ready now to work for all people with disabilities, not just in housing but in employment and elsewhere.

"I love figuring out legal answers," she says, "love being involved with the politics of negotiation. From the AIDS project, I went on loan to the disability community for about two years. From 1988 to 1990, I became the lawyer who researched, negotiated and held meetings with litigation lawyers around the country to figure out what they wanted in this new bill, the Americans with Disabilities Act. We had to figure out how to negotiate that in Congress. So instead of working on AIDS stuff, I worked on access problems in Amtrak double-decker dining cars," she says, laughing. "But the whole thing was a remarkable experience. It shaped what I was going to do for the rest of my life, making me create a new name for what I do in my clinic here at Georgetown Law Center, where I train students.

"I call what I do legislative lawyering. Litigation lawyers have a special perspective, which needs the law to say X because that's how they have to litigate it. But if the law says X, it may only get five votes. So I am the person who must understand why the litigation lawyers want the term X but also why X drives the senators crazy. You have to get both the law and politics in your gut, and when you do that you can come up with more creative legal and political solutions to political problems. If you're used to an adversarial position in court, the idea that you have to negotiate is tough. But on the Hill, if you don't negotiate, you won't have a law.

"Looking back on it, I had way more responsibility than I probably should have had, considering the short time I'd been doing it and how little I knew about disability. I do learn quickly. It's one of the things I do well. I'm a sponge. I learned disability politics from the people who'd been doing it for a long time. The law part came easily. It was a remarkable experience in terms of having an impact.

"So imagine," she says, "in my first three years on the Hill, I worked on three pieces of legislation, the Civil Rights Restoration Act, the Fair Housing Amendments Act, and the Americans with Disabilities Act, all of which passed. That's very unusual."

In 1991 Chai came to Georgetown for two years as a visiting professor, taught disability law and legislation, then decided that she was too much of an activist to just be in the classroom and was about to leave. The school then said it wanted to set up a federal legislation clinic but didn't really know what that would mean. "Oh, I told them, I know exactly what that would mean, and to create the clinic, I used the term *legislative lawyer* and created a theory to go with it.

"My clinic in the law school is like a practicum. I have twelve students each semester and four organizational clients. The students work for the various clients on interesting issues, such as trying to stop those localities who attempt amending the Fair Housing Act to get rid of group homes of mentally disabled people in particular neighborhoods. We've been working on medical privacy issues for the working group of the consortium of citizens with disabilities, and on restraint issues in institutions for another client, the National Protection of Advocacy Systems."

Usually Chai's students sign up for the clinic because they're interested in social policy, in changing the world. Only a few of them have a prior interest in disability, but by the end, several more are energized by these issues, even if they haven't been personally touched by disability. "When my students are given the opportunity to work with disability rights," she says, "they understand them, not instinctively but through engagement with the issues. That's the way it happened to me too. That's how we grow and what's so amazing about life."

She runs the Federal Legislation Clinic and teaches what she learned in the ADA process in a cozy wing of the larger academic law center. In her office, one wall is devoted to disability mementos, among them the framed first and last pages of the Americans with Disabilities Act and photographs with top ADA lawyers and legislators. Another wall is devoted to Jewish things, including the famous quote from Rabbi Hillel: "If I am not for myself, who is for me? If I am only for myself, what am I? If not now, when?" One whole bookcase is devoted to ADA-related literature, another crammed with books on gay rights. "I'm incredibly proud of the most recent addition to these walls," she says. It's a calendar on which she has devised a complicated system of colored dots, intended to regulate her unbelievably busy schedule. "When I've accepted a speech out of town, it's a blue dot," she says. "In town it's half of a blue dot. If I say no to a speech, it's a green dot, no to a writing project, an orange one. It took me a long time to come to this but it's a great visual behavior-modification system."

In her teaching, she and her students write and interpret legal texts. Chai made a motto for the program: "Changing the world one word at a time." "I love the intellectual challenges that I've created for myself here. I like twenty issues at a time. I'm sometimes amazed that they pay me to do this."

Mary Lou Breslin, on the other hand, does most of her work at home in the flatlands of Berkeley. Her home office, with its modified computer work station, its tables and bookshelves arranged just so, has enabled her to keep working. She can't stand or walk and she transfers from bed to wheelchair to toilet and shower with some help.

Outside, she tends a garden with large terra cotta containers at wheelchair level. Her modified minivan is equipped with electronic hand controls and she drives it directly from her wheelchair, an enormous improvement over having to transfer into the seat of a car. "The technology has kept up with my decrepitude," she says. "Now all it takes is money."

She seems to have paralleled her cultural and ideological journey with her geographical one, moving in the late 1960s from Kentucky to Chicago, and then to the eye of the disability movement's storm, Berkeley. "Getting to California was its own little saga," she recalls. "In Chicago, I was on a job search which was hideous in its difficulty. I was using a push chair and could transfer in and out of a car. I was pretty mobile— driving even though I had a lot more physical limitations than I was willing to admit. I pretended to be a paraplegic, but I was worse off than that, a lot worse than I looked."

Eventually she found a job as a psychiatric social worker, for which she felt completely unqualified. She had no special training or supervision, just her growing sensibility regarding injustice. While she worked in what she refers to as a snake pit of an asylum, she was also getting a graduate degree in sociology from the University of Chicago. It was 1968, and she and her close friends were involved in the radical politics of that tumultuous year. "I'm amazed that something terrible didn't happen to me," she says. "From my middle age, I look back on it with horror." A man she was living with was arrested and put in federal prison. She moved to Oklahoma, waiting for him to get out of jail. While there, she went back to graduate school and met another guy, moved with him to South Dakota, then New Mexico. She had a terrible time finding work and finally decided to change her life dramatically by moving all the way west.

"I remember sitting at a rest stop on the highway with all my belongings in the car, debating whether to return to Norman, Oklahoma, where I knew people and life was fairly easy, or to go on to California where I also had friends but where the access was completely horrible. It was a literal turning point."

At that time, she was able to get around fairly well, especially where the terrain was flat. But hills presented a problem, and her California friends lived in the steepest parts of San Francisco. "I knew that I'd constantly have to ask people to drag me up and down stairs," she says, "but in spite of it, I decided to go on to California. Not only was I in a high emotional state after the breakup of my relationship, but it was the first time I'd done anything like this by myself, where I didn't have someone around to call upon for help if I needed it." Once she got there, her friends quickly adjusted to her needs, with a flurry of ramp making and widening of bathroom doors. Finally, she got a job at the University of California at Berkeley, working with disabled students, and found herself appalled at being identified with other people in wheelchairs. "It took some doing to crank up my attitude around my job," she says. "I had this leftover attitude from the University of Illinois, a passive-aggressive notion about disability."

By then it was 1975, and the disability movement was already established and flourishing in Berkeley. The Center for

Independent Living had been around for three or four years. As soon as Mary Lou found herself employed in a place with even an ancillary role in community politics, she was instantly drawn into all of it, every activity, every meeting. In 1977, she was brought in to administer a federal contract charged with training people with disabilities in their rights and responsibilities under Section 504, which had just been signed into law. "The role of law and communities in changing social policy became apparent for the first time," she says. "I got my teeth into real legal issues. It was the most interesting professional time of my life because it was expanding so. There was a huge amount of stuff to learn, and it felt a lot better than going to law school.

"I had a little epiphany when I moved on from the university job to one at the Disability Law Resource Center, a program of the Berkeley Center for Independent Living," she tells me. "We had begun to realize that we needed to challenge restaurants and movie theaters that were telling us that we couldn't enter in wheelchairs, that no law existed to cover this, and after our people were trained, they ran workshops about the laws and regulations, the basic principles that eventually became the ADA."

The Disability Law Resource Center, funded by government money and staffed by young lawyers, grew out of those issues, evolving from zero to forty-five workers in four months. They brought in lawyers with lobbying experience and researchers in community issues. The new center had to be very knowledgeable about every nuance and interpretation of all the various policy issues, for its participants were teaching and litigating, garnering hands-on experience to bolster what they knew theoretically. They taught people how to use law libraries, how to do legal research. "I got an eye-opening jolt of what the opportunities were," she says. "Our lawyers didn't do disability, they did civil rights, and that spin influenced me in a profound way, and still does."

Before all this, if one thought about disability at all, one thought about it in terms of social welfare, rehabilitation and medicine. But the center wouldn't hire anybody who hadn't worked in civil rights. No matter how qualified in other ways, anyone who had an altruistic, paternalistic, medical or volunteer-oriented point of view didn't make it through the door. Theirs was a community law center where a person who was being discriminated against could come and tell his or her story. People became aware that discrimination takes place because of society's attitudes toward disability. They had to find a new language to address it, to understand that discrimination is generated by fear and bias and stereotype, not by anyone's being pushy or demanding. That organization became the Disability Rights Education and Defense Fund, which broke off from the Berkeley Law Center and found its own identity.

"I've been in that job in one form or another for about twenty years," Mary Lou says, "doing public policy development and litigation involving lawyers and senior public policy analysts, all of whom are disabled.

"I keep telling you this, Andy," she reminds me, "but it's still such a wonder to me that before this time, it didn't occur to me to connect race with disability civil rights. I got it in race but I damn well didn't translate it into disability issues. So thank God that I was in the right place at the right time. And I basically never left that job."

She says that it's easy for people to get stuck in old thinking, to lose track of new, relevant, burning issues. "There's not been a good collaboration or synergy," she says, "between the lawyers that do the rarefied theoretical work and the whole other world of academics who are thinking about disability as a social construct, about the role of technology, about the way we define disability from a social perspective, looking at it from the philosophical rather than the legal point of view. There's not enough cross-fertilization. On the other hand, I love the rigors of the law and the way that these lawyers consider these issues. The academics often don't even recognize that the lawyers exist and are sometimes way ahead of them."

When we meet for dinner in a Berkeley restaurant, I wonder where else in the world a quadriplegic could find so much access and feel so confident and comfortable as here. The management of the restaurant is neither shocked nor diffident about her in her mechanized wheelchair or me with my guide dog. They are not only welcoming but free of sentimentality and condescension. "That's true," Mary Lou says, "but architectural access and attitudes are improving all over the country."

Accessibility and attitudes are changing primarily, I am sure, for the more privileged, upwardly mobile middle class. With my first guide dog, I fought with airlines to allow him on with me. Now, attendants and pilots go out of their way to tell me what a privilege it is to have a dog flying on their plane, pulling dog treats out of their pockets. The other day, all the passengers on our flight were held up for ten minutes while a severely disabled man was helped to make the transition from his wheelchair to a seat. No one standing in the jetway complained, and when we boarded, people seemed to go out of their way to tell the apologetic man that he had discommoded no one.

At our table, Mary Lou tells me about having recently interviewed C. Boyden Gray, the senior Bush's general counsel when Bush was vice president and president. She was working on a project chronicling the history of the passage of the Americans with Disabilities Act and asked him to list his proudest accomplishments. "Like everyone who had anything to do with the ADA," Mary Lou says, "Boyden Gray put it at the top of his list. But do you know what the other things on his list were? Helping to get Clarence Thomas to the Supreme Court and pushing Bush into the Gulf War. I nearly fell out of my wheelchair," Mary Lou tells me, "but it does remind us that the ADA happened on Bush's watch. The sad thing is that though conservatives allowed it to happen, they are now trying hard to dismantle it, to take away what was given."

In fact, in 1982, Vice President Bush wanted to wipe out all of the hard-won disability rights laws of the 1970s. At the time, Reagan and Bush had a mandate for deregulation, and Bush was put at the head of a task force for regulatory relief. Both Section 504 and special education came under severe attack, but Bush not only began to understand that he was dealing with a hidden grass roots constituency, he also believed that it couldn't be that bad or even that costly, if it was true that disabled people merely wanted independence, wanted to make the transition from welfare to jobs, from bureaucratic entanglements to empowerment. Several Republicans who were themselves disabled leaned heavily on Bush, and by 1983 he dropped his objections to 504 and special ed. "I'm going to do whatever it takes to make sure the disabled are included in the mainstream," Bush said at the Republican convention when he ran for president.

Mary Lou confides that she is struggling to find new ways to teach. "You have to get it all together in your own mind beforehand. To me it's worth some energy to step out of thinking about public policy, which has been my focus for a hundred years, and try to think about things just theoretically. And one of the things that's clear is that we are in the middle of a new paradigm, and we need to define it and look at it to see what it is and where it's going and what its components might be. It's been an interesting exercise. In my classes, I try to teach the recognition of shifting paradigms because they're all in place at the same time. Some are dominant, and sometimes one is more dominant than the other. For instance, I've been rethinking the civil rights paradigm which I've been devoted to for the last two decades. I'm not abandoning it but acknowledging its limitations. For years I believed that if we could just advance this perspective through the courts and through education and enforcement, this would really solve some basic problems. I now have a better grip on what the limitations of that are, and realize too that there are other things that need to be factored in.

"We've been extraordinarily successful in this country focusing on civil rights," she says, "certainly more successful than anywhere else in the world. But we've been extremely unsuccessful dealing with social rights, which is done much better elsewhere. Twenty years ago, in order to make our case for civil rights, we put a high fence between them and social welfare, and now we're realizing that you can't separate the two."

Integrating institutionalized people into communities, for instance, and thus assuring their civil rights, can't happen without a lot of help. To make equal opportunity and free choice a reality, you need money and programs. "We used to insist that we weren't sick and thus didn't need social or medical services," she says. " 'It's not about medicine, it's about civil rights,' we said. Well, we need both."

As we talk more about the movement, I begin to hear a deep sadness in her voice. "I'm as ill-informed now as I've ever been," she says. "I guess that's a function of working at something for a long time, having felt intellectually in control, and suddenly realizing that maybe the world isn't where I thought it was. It feels like I have to start over again. I feel now the way I did when I first started in the movement. I've been going through some theoretical transformations during the last couple of years and I'm worried that whatever world-view I come up with will not make sense for the future. But, you know, a lot of other people are thinking about all this as well. I hope we can come up with a sufficiently meaningful vision."

After our dinner, I follow Mary Lou out into the parking lot where, with a remote control, she lets down a ramp in her van. "Go have a look inside," she says and Tobias and I prowl around the interior. The space behind the driver's controls is empty. "Feel the floor," she yells up and, on my knees, I finger the metal sockets onto which she will lock her wheelchair. "Pretty spiffy, don't you think?" she asks, laughing. When Tobias and I go back down, Mary Lou scoots in and locks her fabulous wheelchair into place. With her one good hand working the sensitive hand controls, she starts the van and, shouting goodbye, zips out into Berkeley traffic.

Chai Feldblum's work on changing the world one word at a time was in full swing in 1988, with two major acts, the Civil Rights Restoration Act and the Fair Housing Amendments Act, which linked not only the AIDS and disability communities but the disability and civil rights communities. This took some doing. People in the civil rights world had to become educated to understand that disability was a civil rights issue.

"That seems instinctive to me now," Chai Feldblum says, "but it wasn't instinctive then, not to me and not to others. I saw that change happen, and once that coalition was formed, we realized that it was essential for the passage of ADA.

"The civil rights leadership put ADA as one of its legislative priorities," she says. "That was key. Another key was a Democratic Senate and House and George Bush as president. This brings in the old AIDS story again, because when Bush was a candidate, the Reagan commission on HIV came out with its recommendation that Congress should pass a general disability-antidiscrimination law, an interesting recommendation coming out of an HIV-specific commission."

At that point Chai had been working on an AIDS-specific antidiscrimination bill, but a couple of people from the larger disability community thought that it made sense to be more inclusive. Since there is no law to protect everyone with disabilities, why, they asked, would it make sense to have a law to protect only people with AIDS? "Politically it wasn't so clear which was the better way to go," she says. "If you included all the other disabilities, you had cost issues, but if you did AIDS alone you didn't have the power of the full coalition. We came to the conclusion that from both an ethical and a political level we should not try to go AIDS-specific. Candidate Bush went on the record saying that there should be no discrimination about this, and his word on the record turned out to be incredibly important."

The first draft of the ADA was a great piece of legislation, fixing all the problems of 504, problems such as limits to the concept of reasonable accommodation, business having claimed that it was too great an expense, an undue hardship and burden. Under 504, retrofitting existing buildings or vehicles was not part of the statute, but this first draft required significant retrofitting. It turned out that the first draft was unrealistic politically, and four people—a staff member from Tom Harkin's office, one from Ted Kennedy's office, Chai and a lawyer from DREDF—worked for months to redraft that version of the ADA, still using 504 as a template. They introduced it in May 1989 and hoped that the Bush people would endorse it, but there were still a few unresolved issues.

After enjoying great bipartisan fanfare, the bill moved into hearings, where John Wodatch in Attorney General Richard Thornberg's office was a key player, negotiating on behalf of the Bush administration. Wodatch had begun his career in

1973 in HEW's Civil Rights office, when it got the job of writing regulations to implement Section 504. Like Chai, he had had no connection to disability before, but it was he who came up with the innovative and crucial idea of "reasonable accommodation."

Richard Thornberg, who himself had a child with a developmental disability, said he supported the bill in concept but was concerned about twelve or so minor issues that the business community objected to. Some bizarre negotiations then ensued in which people from the Bush White House and staff people from both parties in the Senate sat in a room together to carve out an ADA that the president would endorse. They hammered it out around the clock, producing reams of paper stating White House positions, then responses to each of these issues. Chai would then send these to a core group of litigation lawyers. This back-and-forth negotiation went on for about a month. As the process neared its coda, the two sides traded and traded big.

"We gave up getting money damages in employment and in public accommodation," Chai says, "in return for a broader definition of what a public accommodation is." In 1964, when the Civil Rights Act was passed, public accommodations only covered hotels, restaurants and recreation facilities. It did not include the corner grocery store, which they now wanted to include.

So their argument in this new draft of the ADA was based on two very simple messages: one, extending 504 to the private sector, and two, asking for equivalence, namely, the same protections for disability as already existed for race and sex. Their feeling was: "Whatever they have we should have."

Chai's group felt pretty sure that they would eventually get damages. They wanted the enforcement section in the ADA to simply be cross-referenced to Title 7 of the Civil Rights Act of 1964, which prohibited discrimination on the basis of race or sex in employment, and to Title 2, which dealt with public accommodation. They hoped it would happen and it actually did, in the Civil Rights Act of 1991, a year after passage of the ADA.

Late one afternoon, they thought they had a deal, but Bush's chief of staff John Sununu had a problem with elevators. "Can you believe it?" Chai asks. "Anyway, we cut an elevator deal at three A.M. Then they went to recess and, exhausted, I went to Hawaii."

When in the fall of 1989 the bill finally went to the Senate floor, there were fights about excluding people who used drugs, but not much else, because of the magic imprimatur of Bush having signed off on it. "It passed in the Senate," Chai says, "and it would have been nice had there been only one house of Congress, for unlike the Senate, where ADA had to make it through one committee, in the House there were four: Labor and Employment, Energy and Commerce because of railroads, Judiciary because of civil rights, and Transportation, which involved Amtrak. It was a bit like four different episodes of a sitcom," Chai says, "each with its own personality, with four different climaxes to the story."

In Labor and Employment, the business community was relentless, adding issue upon issue. Negotiating produced around twenty changes in the committee report and twelve more changes in the bill itself. For the next four months, the group moved into Transportation. Energy and Commerce followed and there Amtrak, which turned out to be everybody's client, produced endless wrangling. "We did horrific rewrites upon rewrites," she says. In April 1990, the last gasp of the business community was heard in the Judiciary Committee. The bill got to the House floor in May, where several amendments were offered. They beat down all of them except one that wanted to exclude people who engaged in food handling and had contagious diseases. That started two months of very intense lobbying, forcing the disability community to get together even more with the AIDS community. "It was wonderful," Chai says. "We stood strong, but what ultimately saved us was legislative lawyering, because we would not have won on a straight up-and-down vote without compromising."

A list now had to be issued about specific diseases that could be transmitted through the food supply so that only people with those diseases could be fired, which was consistent with the old Arline case and protected the people with HIV. That deal finally came through at the end of June. The bill passed overwhelmingly in the House and Senate and the president signed it on July 26, 1990. The only significant opposition to the ADA came from ultra-rightists led by Jesse Helms, who mustered only seven other Senate votes. "And I have never been so happy in my life!" Chai says.

When I talked about the wonders of the ADA and Chai's breathless voyage through it to a disabled friend involved with the Independent Living movement, he made a dour face. "It's better than nothing," he said, "but it's a law with no teeth. It's like the Montana speeding law. You can drive as fast as you like as long as you drive safely. What the hell does that mean?" He laughs. "Look, I'm an ex-cop and I know that the only kind of law that matters is: 'If you don't make your business accessible, we put a padlock on your door.' End of story."

Just as civil rights laws make little difference to blacks trapped in ghettos, large numbers of the severely disabled will not be helped by civil rights legislation. They need a lot more but there are many paradoxes. A person takes a job and is threatened with losing attendant care, health care, food stamps and housing subsidies. Some simply can't work. The homeless schizophrenic needs more than civil rights. He needs meals, a roof overhead, dignity and treatment.

The Americans with Disabilities Act is a great piece of

legislation. It has also produced a backlash of hatred toward the disabled, a phenomenon that accompanies any constituency's struggle for civil rights. In spite of 70 percent unemployment in the disability community, those who do work are often resented for taking jobs away from the ablebodied. Scapegoating knows no bounds.

The law itself, though seen by some as toothless, by others as significant primarily to the upwardly mobile middle class, is constantly being probed, often narrowly interpreted by the courts reflecting reactionary attitudes, by states pleading poverty and by the unashamed entitlements of business. In February 2001, the Rehnquist Supreme Court continued whittling away at the ADA, saying that state employees who suffered discrimination on the job because of their disabilities could not sue their employers for damages in federal court. This court held that Congress has no constitutional authority to subject states to such lawsuits under the Act.

The case arose out of the specific job-discrimination claims of Patricia Garrett, a nurse at a state university hospital who was assigned a lower-paying job after returning from breast cancer treatment, and Milton Ash, a security guard with asthma who claimed that he was treated adversely on the job after demanding accommodations for his condition.

The Supreme Court overruled Congress by holding that state governments can arbitrarily deny jobs to disabled people without violating the equal protection clause of the Constitution, even though a federal court of appeals had previously decided that the ADA prohibited such discrimination. The Supreme Court majority put cost accounting above the right to access when they wrote that it would be "entirely rational and therefore constitutional for a state employer to conserve scarce financial resources by hiring employees who are able to use existing facilities. If one is denied a state job solely because he or she must use a wheelchair, it seems a clear violation of the equal protection of the laws called for in the Fourteenth Amendment which extends universal civil rights to all Americans regardless of the state in which they reside."

The pendulum swings. At times, the words of the law seem lost in a din of markets, profits and greed. There are other moments, however, when one detects progress, an upward spiral, times when changing the world one word at a time actually seems possible.

BODIES

DAVE LONEY

prosthetist

JOHN FAGO

photographer, teacher, prosthetist

PROLOGUE

Appearance—how I look, how I present myself in public, what immediate gut reaction I provoke—matters. Even though I have been able to effect certain attitudinal changes, some because of the exigencies of the aging process, I can't entirely shake the earlier influences that are hardwired into my brain. Coming from the family I come from, all my behavior, all my dreams and desires were pointed toward a charmed life.

My family's business, in America as it had been in Warsaw, was producing beautifully crafted, exorbitantly priced furs that they sold to kings and queens, presidents and their wives, Hollywood stars, the fabulously wealthy. If I were looking for metaphors representing the distance between surface and substance, I wouldn't have to go far beyond the skins and pelts of their trade. Everything in that business depended on beauty and glamour. The only deviation from the norm that was tolerated was the egregious behavior of the rich and famous. But good manners were sanctioned and rewarded. Good looks and charm got you what you wanted. It didn't take a genius to extrapolate that disability was ugly, a pitiful state, worthy of invisibility. As a disability scholar has suggested, "Corporeal departures from dominant expectations never go uninterpreted or unpunished, whereas conformities are almost always rewarded."

Though pursuit of the beautiful, however defined, is not necessarily corrupt or exclusionary, it is often disturbing to the disability community. Americans cherish youth, virility, activity and physical beauty, not often associated with disabled people. Because of the addiction to such attributes, disabled people find themselves on the periphery, often feeling like supplicants to the fortunate mainstream.

As recently as the 1960s, statutes in some American municipalities known as "ugly laws" stated that the sight of disabled people was offensive. Such laws proclaimed that "no person who is diseased, maimed, mutilated or in any way deformed, so as to be an unsightly or disgusting object, is to be allowed in or on the public ways or other public places." How many generations does it take for sentiments such as these to be cleansed from consciousness? How many to find acceptance and even beauty in aberrance and deformity? In the mid-nineteenth century, Oliver Wendell Holmes, Sr., a physician and poet among other talents, felt that "for polite society the sight of the odious pegleg is simply intolerable." The man knew how not to pull punches. "Misfortunes of a certain obtrusiveness may be pitied," he wrote, "but are never tolerated under chandeliers."

When I talk to nondisabled people, they mostly identify me according to their learned and largely unthought-about attitudes and definitions. My physical disability, blindness, dominates and skews the ablebodied person's process of sorting out perceptions and forming a reaction. The relationship is often strained because of fear, pity, fascination, revulsion or merely surprise, none of which is easily expressed within the constraints of social protocol. Should the nondisabled person offer assistance? Acknowledge the disability? What language or expectation should he use or avoid? For my part, am I only or mostly my disability? Are other attributes worth checking out? Should I attempt charm or deference or humor? It's a stressful situation for both parties. Still, disability happens. It is not an aberration, it's a reality, not an anomaly or abnormality, and it is always complicated to face others with these masks, pretenses, repressions and blurs that influence if not totally define communication between us.

The human body is seen as a visible expression of human virtue. Different bodies, ugly bodies still signify unhealthy spirits, but now there are ever more possibilities for bodily transformations, including decircumcision and the creation of more appropriate genitalia. Passing from one group into another, from unacceptable racial origins or unacceptable disease into "normalcy," from the blatant vanity of nose jobs and tummy tucks to lifesaving grafts, the transformation of human bodies from bad to good, sick to healthy, unwanted to prized, is more deftly accomplished than ever before.

The philosopher Isaiah Berlin liked telling the story of Charles Steinmetz, the hunchback inventor, walking past Temple Emanu-El on Fifth Avenue with Otto Kahn, the assimilated Jewish financier. Kahn said, "I used to attend services there." Steinmetz replied, "I used to be a hunchback." Being a Jew was like being a hunchback, Berlin would say, with each Jew reacting differently to his hump, some pretending they had no hump, others glorying in theirs, while a third group, the timid ones, wore cloaks to conceal their contours.

In reminiscing about old times, a friend who had been connected to the original 1960s movers and shakers in the independent living movement in Berkeley remarked that most of them, having been paralyzed by polio only, were very attractive people. "I wonder," she said, "if the movement would have been as successful as it was if folks with gross deformities had tried to organize and to attract outside attention." Beauty is treated preferentially. Having it and flaunting it makes it easier to find sex partners, employment, more lenient sentences, helping not only to propagate the species but to ensure an easier life.

Posing, passing, comes easily to many of us. As a blind person, I struggled to pass until I could pass no longer, and even when I made the big move to define myself in public, I chose a dog rather than a cane, the appearance of the one being preferable to me than the other. Given the choice, I liked the image. As our instructors at the Seeing Eye were gearing up to match each of us with a dog, a woman who sat next to me dug her fingernails into my arm, anticipating their choice. "If they give me a Lab, I'll die," she whispered. "I need a shepherd!" she cried aloud to the room full of eager students and trainers. She whispered again to me: "A shepherd you can take to a good restaurant."

Recently, I sat in on a talk given by Mark Jeffreys, whose family is a living portrait of disabilities. His father had never walked without prosthetic support because of osteogenesis imperfecta, a congenital condition commonly known as brittle bone disease, which Mark inherited. Mark's youngest brother Jim was adopted from Korea as a legless orphan, his brother Clark had polio as a child and his brother Peter was born with spina bifida. Only his sister Alice was nondisabled.

Mark is small and frail, a young professor of English at the University of Alabama in Birmingham, a specialist in lyric poetry. His topic at the conference we were both attending was the cultural construct of disability, and he dealt poignantly with his family's deep need to pass. "After Jim was adopted," Mark said, "no sooner had my parents completed the medical surveys of the reality of his extraordinariness than they began to think how best to conceal it. The decision of the adults was to make Jim appear as 'normal' as possible, and the way to do that was to insist that he always strap on his prosthetic legs."

By the time Jim himself got married, he almost never wore the artificial legs. Yet the family's deep desire to create as "normal" a ritual as was humanly possible brought out all the old props. Jim's bride was unusually tall, and her dream of her wedding ritual demanded that her groom not make her look like a giant. If Jim got married in his legs, they could stand together in front of the preacher, just as she had always imagined.

A portrait taken at another of his family's wedding ceremonies shows a family posed to disguise the ordinary, daily realities of their bodies. "Someone took away Jim's crutches," Mark said, "so he stands there between us, shoulder to shoulder for balance, suited and propped like FDR for a publicity still. Except for the slightly odd forward lean of his counterbalancing torso, the illusion is perfect: the invisible cripple. Of course if any one of us weakened, the entire house of cards would collapse. Not that Jim's was the only illusion in that photograph, only one of the more successful. The least successful was probably Dad's, who had never walked without prosthetic support in his life. But here, he felt that if he stood still enough, somehow his bodily difference would disappear into the traditional patriarchal role of father of the bride.

"Oddly enough," Mark said, "even our ablebodied youngest sister Alice, who was coincidentally recovering from a broken leg, had her crutches taken from her and stands awkwardly, her weight on her good leg."

Other families pose with smiles to approximate whatever they believe a "normal" happy family should look like, disguising the frictions of their household. "We did too," Mark said, "but we also posed to disguise the realities of our bodies. We were used to being stared at, but we understood that if our disabilities were framed, our disabilities would frame us,

and we wanted to exclude them so we wouldn't vanish behind them."

In the replacement game, the reinstatement of function is often more urgent than aesthetic enhancement. But science and
human values are sometimes in conflict. Cochlear implants, a
fairly recent surgical technique, are being used to restore
hearing, albeit very imperfectly. It's a subject of great contro-
versy in the deaf community: Shocking though it may seem
to the hearing, many people who are born deaf don't want to
leave the culture of their deafness. They do not consider
themselves disabled or as having a tragic infirmity, but as belonging to a cherished linguistic and cultural minority. The
medical experts proclaim a great advance, yet the deaf community proclaims a dangerous setback to their interests.

From early on, at least from the time when medical science had advanced sufficiently that losing a limb was not real-
istically equivalent to losing one's life, people manufactured
crude replacements for lost body parts. Peg legs and hooks
were mostly functional, for it was easier to hobble on a peg
than be strapped with crutches, easier to gather something in
the good hand with a push from the hook. Still, even today,
hooks and all kinds of prosthetic devices are associated with
crookedness and evil in our literature and media. Even a limp
can signify an antihero.

Attitudes toward the making and the wearing of prostheses are, of course, culture-bound. There was a time when an
empty sleeve or trouser leg or a black patch on one eye were
badges of courage, while at other times they were marks of
emasculation, fear and loathing.

Replacement hands, feet, arms, breasts and legs, sometimes even penises, make enormous differences in an amputee's life, but some parts are more replaceable than others.

The actor Christopher Reeve and many others defend their militaristic approach to illness and disability, in which everything is potentially reparable, every wrong can be righted. Indeed, in the medical engineering business, it sometimes does seem that anything is possible. Even in the instance of eyes, scientists are beginning to implant crude chips that restore some primitive vision, hoping for a lot more, hoping for stem cell miracles, hoping to be able to lay down an infinitesimally thin layer of rods and cones and prod it to attach itself to the optic nerve. But waiting for cures for blindness or spinal cord injury or cancer, as many people do, not only instills false hope, a very cruel expectation, but loses sight of the pressing need for civil rights and ongoing care.

For some of us, "normalcy" stands for a hated average, another name for mediocrity. But it's lonely not to look or act normal. Not many of us are cut out for this kind of separation and aloneness. A great deal is at stake in struggling to be or to remain normal, to be noticed, if at all, only for qualities that reinforce our normalcy. The drive to "fix" disability in any way available is powerful.

BODIES

A short time ago, I was walking with my friend Danny toward an outdoor cafe on the Church Street mall in Burlington, Vermont, for a quick lunch. Danny is a rehab assistant and computer specialist who works with blind people. He is an above-the-knee amputee whose usual gait is graceful and easy, but today I notice a pronounced hitch, a tilt to the right with every step.

"You okay?" I ask.

"I need a new leg," he says.

"Just like that?"

"There's a lot of wear and tear on these damn things," he says, smacking the prosthesis and making a thud.

Apparently, every few years, with the body's natural changes, an amputee's stump gains or loses weight, the muscles tend to atrophy a bit, the connective tissue withers, posture shifts. "All of that happened," Danny says, "that plus the normal corrosion of bushings and axles and hydraulic valves. The socket is slipping. My left leg has to be refitted and remade."

Danny had lost that leg the summer of his graduation from high school. After a blowout of a party, dressed in shorts and a T-shirt and going like a bat out of hell on his motorcycle, he lost control turning a corner and hit a van head-on. He spent more than a year out of the next three in the hospital. He had a dozen operations. His other leg was also pretty well smashed and, to this day, it continues to give him trouble.

A week after our stroll on the mall, we drive down I-89 to New Hampshire, just across the Vermont border, where Dave Loney conducts his prosthetics practice. "This is the third leg Dave will make for me," Danny says. "I've had some pretty bad legs made by another outfit. With Dave, I know I'm with the best." Dave and his wife Georgia have restored an old brick factory, an oasis in a sea of car lots, malls and empty lots ready for the coming of Wal-Marts, Home Depots and Staples. Inside, they have carefully refinished the hardwood floors and exposed the brushed red brick, then pushed dark old furniture against the walls to make a light, airy, pleasing place to work. "The old arches were so beautiful," Georgia tells me, "that rather than destroy them when we had to enlarge the openings to conform to Department of Health standards, we dug down into the ground."

What they have done with this building restoration, I realize after a while, is what they do with the torn and broken body parts, replacing them as carefully and lovingly as they did the brick facade and arched doorways.

With Danny hobbling next to us, Tobias pulls me behind Dave and Georgia into a spacious examining room. Danny removes his prosthesis, leans it against a wall and hops over to a platform, where he stands on his good leg, his hands holding a railing in front of him. On Danny's previous visit Dave had made an initial cloth and plaster cast, which he now brings over to me to examine. Its walls are thin, even and durable, its topography a replica of the contours of my friend's residual limb. "It's just the first in a series," Dave says. Then, "Want to feel Danny's stump?" he asks.

My reaction shocks me. After a long pause, I say, "Danny?"

"Go ahead," Danny says.

Before I can take another breath, Dave thrusts my hand deep into the soft flesh of Danny's stump, his hands pushing my fingers farther, toward the bone. He begins explaining how he wants to distribute the weight but I hear next to nothing. "Push harder. Feel it? That's the ischial tuberosity."

I feel the bone that had been cut by a surgeon several inches above where the knee once was, the truncated end of a human thigh bone inside a smooth, soft sack, the now unmuscled thigh, once probably trim and firm. "It's like meat stuffed into a sausage skin," Dave says, a plain enough description, making me wince.

The intimacy of the act and my unexpected squeamishness stupefy me. It feels to me, though not to Danny, like a violation of his privacy, his disability space.

"Supersensitive, are we?" Danny asks as we drive back north. My feelings toward my friend are changed, the stump, his most private deformity, now shared. As far as I'm concerned, we begin to inhabit a new plane. But speeding back home along the interstate, we talk about anything but the privacy of residual limbs or residual vision. We talk about the Tragically Hip, his favorite rock band, we talk about the New York Yankees.

On our next visit, Dave takes the cast of Danny's stump upstairs to a workbench, where he changes its shape slightly.

There is a sweetness in Dave's frequent laughter, as ingenuous as his loping up and down his stairs with manufactured body parts. There is nothing holy about these replacement parts, nothing magical or symbolic or metaphorical. They are skilled workmanlike compensations, like a replaced shock absorber or axle or strut, as economically machine-tooled as a bushing under the hood of a car intended only to prolong its useful life.

Though this can't be a totally pain-free experience, Danny's body language tells me that he is comfortable here. He comes down off the platform and sits next to me. He stretches his leg out in front of him, his arms raised above his head as he yawns. This is the place where he knows he'll be well and tenderly cared for, where, after a few rather grueling sessions, he will walk easily and gracefully again, not unlike the role of the Seeing Eye in my own life.

"The first amputation they did on me after the accident was below the knee," he says, "and fitting that prosthesis was a misery. I spent more time on crutches than on the new leg. Everything went better from the moment they decided to do an above-the-knee amputation. By then I was reconciled to being an amputee and my prosthesis became totally functional."

"It seems not to have taken you long to get over it."

"No choice," he says.

"What do you mean 'no choice'? Some people take a lifetime. You should be proud."

"Proud?" He gets a little testy. "What were my options, for Christ's sake? You should know that. You either kill yourself or you damn well get on with it. If there's no real choice, it's not bravery." He jumps up from his chair. "I need a smoke," he says. "Come out with me." He hops over to his old, ill-fitting leg, standing in a corner of the room. He puts it in place and, not securing it properly, hobbles outside, Tobias and I following.

Out by the little brook behind the Loney building, a family of ducks quacks its way downstream. "My whole process led me in the direction of working with disability and the disabled," Danny says. "That whole progression really turned me on. As a matter of fact, were it not for my accident, my life wouldn't be as rich as it is. People seem more dimensional, more rounded when they have difficulties. There's a lot about it that sucks, sucks to this day, but the absence of a leg is just an inconvenience."

Danny's a good one-legged skier and now teaches skiing to blind people. Even though I have no preference for the supercrip, the inspirational hero, skiing blind or one-legged is a thrill, more sensuous, I think, more freeing, more satisfying to one's sense of adventure than it is to a daredevil two-legged or sighted skier. For blind skiers, hurtling down some icy slope is living life at an intense, crazy edge.

Dave Loney has another perspective. "As a Canadian," he says, "I've always laughed at Americans thinking that they can do anything they put their minds to. Well, that isn't true. I loathe that statement. I've learned from my patients that you have to be mostly aware of the abilities that are within your scope. I'm not thrilled when a patient who has lost a leg asks about running a marathon. That indicates to me that they're not accepting the loss. It seems silly. They should concentrate more on other things. Be realistic. Life is short. Rather than saying I can do anything I put my mind to, they should say, Okay, my abilities in this area have changed, so why don't I try to excel here now rather than there?"

Dave Loney's practice is doing very well. Nine people are working for him, including an orthotics specialist who makes braces and several workshop assistants. Upstairs in the workshop, Rob, the orthotist, and his apprentices, in green surgical garb, labor at a long workbench surrounded by tall windows. The smell of resins, glues and catalysts is pleasant though abrasive, like wood smoke. Plaster dust has left a coat of white on every surface. Plastic-forming equipment is crammed in everywhere, ovens with extremely accurate infrared sensors, heavy-duty sewing machines, vacuum pumps. Next door, in a plaster room, they work on molds, and in a grinding room, they route, drill and sand with their drum sander, consisting of a pair of motorized spinning cylinders. "It's hardly high-tech stuff," Dave says.

Dave makes changes to the socket, runs down again to try

it on Danny, then watches Danny's every movement with great care. Dave's wife Georgia, an ethereal being, warm and comforting, floats in and out. "She runs this whole operation," Dave tells me. There is nothing hurried about the work that goes on here. Dave is slow, deliberate, never annoyed. This doesn't feel like medical time.

"Are you ever squeamish about the wounded bodies you treat?" I ask him.

"I used to be a bit when I was young," he says. "What I had you do, touching Dan's stump, had a purpose. I always hand a prosthetic leg to someone who first comes into my place to talk about a prosthesis. They get over any squeamishness very quickly. If there is a patient around I ask them to touch the residual limb. Blood is pumping through that limb and they realize that it's a part of a living human body. Children especially adapt very quickly."

"I imagine that for some people having your stump touched or even looked at is more complicated than it is for Danny."

"If they're finished grieving, they usually don't care. And it gives me a pretty good idea what stage of grieving they're in."

For the most part, people who are disabled don't want to give cause for pity, don't tolerate statements like God loves crips or amputees or the blind. "Haven't you come across people who are afraid that they'll disgust someone with their stump?" I ask.

"Just today I had a woman patient, twelve weeks post-op, who very much wants her sisters to see her stump but they refused. It shows me that they aren't finished grieving. On the other hand, I just made a leg for a very pretty woman and she definitely doesn't want anyone but me seeing her stump. But then she wouldn't want them to see her varicose veins or her pimples either."

Dave makes a plaster cast from the initial mold. Then, in

order to best distribute Danny's weight, he works on the cast of Danny's residual limb with rasps and carving knives. From this, he makes a transparent plastic socket called a check or diagnostic socket. With heat, the inexpensive material of this socket is easy to mold and very fragile, thus lending itself admirably to this interim stage, rather than to the final socket that Danny will wear for years. As he modifies the shape of this socket, he doesn't simply try to reflect the surface shape of the stump, but presses it into places where Danny can tolerate more pressure, relieving stress from more sensitive areas like the groin.

"There are computer methods of doing this but I don't like them much," Dave tells me. "They work with the cast in three dimensions. They take the cast of the patient's stump, then digitize that cast. They also use lasers to scan the actual physical mass. The computer scan makes a topographical map of the mass, the skin, but not the structural interior. By hand, I can press in, feel the bones, and determine pretty closely where to put the person's weight. You need to do this with your fingers and your sensitivity to the individual patient, rather than rely on a computer grid. To me, this whole process is more art than science, even though all the materials and equipment seem complex."

He heats up a half-inch-thick piece of plastic, puts it into a metal frame, then into an oven at 375 degrees. The plastic droops into a bubble. While it is still hot, he flips it onto the plaster cast and a vacuum pump pulls it down, sucking it tight. This gives him a plastic model of the leg, which he glues to a block of wood and mounts on an alignment jig.

"I bet it was a whole lot easier when all they did was make a peg leg."

"As a matter of fact, sometimes a wooden leg is still preferable," Dave says. "I made one for a farmer because it was perfect for walking in furrows and plowed fields."

At Danny's next appointment, they try on the new check socket now attached to his old prosthesis. For Danny, putting the leg on is an exhausting process. He puts a big sock on over his stump, all the way up to his crotch. Then he takes a valve out of the socket and feeds the sock into the hole and pulls it through. The valve goes back inside so that his stump is held in place by suction.

"Do you have to go through all that every time you put the leg on?"

"Yeah, but the prosthesis stays in all day unless something breaks the suction. When I get in my car, one leg in, one leg out, that'll sometimes do it."

Dave Loney glides around Danny on a rolling chair, observing, prodding, reaching for a tool, adjusting. Danny walks all around the room, then up and down the hall. "It hurts," Danny says.

"Yeah," Dave says. "I can see it." He turns to me. "It's blanching right there and that's my clue. It tells me that the femur, the long leg bone, which was cut for the amputation, is pressing up against the side of the socket and all the blood is being flushed out. Sometimes, the weight of the leg pulling on it creates negative pressure. The socket's letting air in. And this," he says, "is one reason why the transparency of this diagnostic socket is so important." He fiddles some more. "You never get a very good seal with these check sockets."

"It feels a little short too," Danny says.

"That's easy to fix." He extends the rod. "Are you feeling pulling in the back? If I open it here, you'll drop in more and then I'll come back and tighten it."

Danny walks from one end of the room to the other. To me, the sound of his steps seems even. "It's a little snug," he reports. "It torques me counterclockwise."

"You have so much limb length that you don't need all this weight on the ischial tuberosity," Dave says. "Let's put in some padding. We also have to look out for too much weight on the pelvic bone and groin. If I get too low on the inside, then the soft tissue starts to spill out and that really hurts."

There is a comical edge to all this tailor talk. Instead of letting the pants out a little here, a little there, the next size up in a shoe, it's a matter of ischial tuberosities and the pubic ramus.

"When I was fifteen, I worked in a shoe store," Dave says, laughing. "I never saw the connection until now."

"Might you be more needed elsewhere rather than in rural New Hampshire?" I ask him.

"Of course. In war there is more need, but also among populations where there is more diabetes than elsewhere, as in the Indian populations of New Mexico and Arizona. Diabetes and other cardiovascular diseases are the biggest causes of amputation."

"Have you ever thought of going to a war zone?"

"Quite a bit. When we hire a third practitioner, we'll have a little more time off and I'd like to take a month or two every year to work in the field."

"Where?"

"Not in places where I might be fixing people up so they could be soldiers again. I would like to go to Vietnam to treat victims of land mines. In Cambodia alone, over twelve thousand people have lost legs for this reason."

I ask Dave if he could have easily done something else with his life.

"In hindsight, yes," he says, "because the older I get, and I am now thirty-nine, the larger the list of human activities that I consider as performing a useful human service, including people who are seen as greedy such as stockbrokers, financial consultants, all kinds of professionals, not just those who can more obviously be recognized as performing a service for humanity. I guess I should include artists and writers," he adds, smiling.

"How did you get into prosthetics in the first place?"

"My parents always taught us that there was no happiness in looking out for yourself—as a matter of fact, that it was the root of all evil. My father was a missionary. When he was older he pastored a church, then ran a retreat for burnt-out church people. My mother was very involved in all this. My oldest sister was a nurse until she bought a round-the-world plane ticket, went away for six months and came back to go to mission school. All the other siblings are more or less involved in the helping professions. My parents' philosophy was that if you want to save your life, you have to lose it, you have to give it away."

Originally, Dave wanted to go into medicine, but even though he was a good student, he couldn't bear the thought of that many years in school. He did a year in general science, then began to concentrate on human kinetics, which included classes in physiology, anatomy and chemistry. He particularly loved biomechanics, the study of human movement and the physics of motion. In his last year, he attended a lecture in prosthetics and orthotics. Even though it interested him, he realized that it required working primarily with his hands, and never having done so to any extent, he discounted it as a viable course for his life. Dave married in his last year at college and moved with Georgia to Oregon, where her family lived. There they bought and began to restore an old house and he discovered that he was not only good with his hands but loved using them. It was then he decided to go into prosthetics. "I apprenticed in a wonderful, old-fashioned place called the Oregon Artificial Limb Company. It was owned by two World War II veterans and one Korean vet, all of whom had lost limbs."

The prosthetists taught Dave an unforgettable lesson, namely, that to be really good at what he did, he needed above all to care, to really care. And if the job wasn't done perfectly, to do it over and over again, until it was.

Dave learned a lot about caring and community working in that atmosphere. In the facility, founded in 1911, everything happened in one big room. The patients, mostly veterans, would come in, often without appointments, sit down, take off their pants, take off their legs, talk, smoke or read while their limbs were altered or repaired at work stations all around them. "It was a great learning environment," he says. He then went on to do graduate work, moved to New Hampshire, pulled together various degrees and certificates and set up shop.

"During the first five years of my practice, I could really get down on myself. I felt very stressed until I figured out what I was doing wrong, which was promising people too much. I thought I had all the answers, that a new limb would quickly solve all my patients' problems. It turned out not to be so. For some people, the going was very slow. I had to learn to allow people to heal in their own time, their own inner schedule."

"What promises would you make?"

"I often saw patients who were not in the best of health and I would promise that they would be up walking without a cane long before they actually could. Usually their difficulties began when they neglected their stumps, never touched them. A stump really needs contact and pressure to heal properly. When I put a prosthesis on these patients, their pain was enormous. They wouldn't have had the pain if they hadn't ignored their residual limbs for so long. I got better at what I did. I learned what the limits were."

Before Danny's next visit, Dave had taken the corrected check socket and replaced it with the permanent one, made of a flexible, high-density polyethylene plastic, softer and more pliable and thus more comfortable than the one before. To accomplish this, he took the check socket and bolted the prosthesis into an alignment jig, a series of pipes and clamps on the workbench that can capture strategic placements or parts of the prosthesis in order to preserve the relationship between the socket on top, the knee and the foot below. The jig has a yoke that lines up with the axis of the knee and actually holds that axis. Thus, he was able to capture in every plane, x, y and z, the rotation, flexion, extension, adduction and abduction of the leg. The knee was then mounted in the yoke, which holds its height and its relationship to the socket.

After making the polyethylene socket with a hardened carbon fiber frame on the outside, he cut, trimmed and buffed all the edges and once again bolted everything onto it in the proper position. For those patients who want an approximation of a real leg rather than metal pipes and plastic, he would have pulled some foam over the outside of the prosthesis, carved a semblance of a leg in the foam, put the foot on and pulled a couple of heavy-duty nylons over the whole thing. And finally the leg would be done.

I have to fight a surge of envy as I begin to fantasize surrogate eyes, a dream I don't allow myself too often, partly because it's as improbable as replacement heads. But with prosthetic legs there is reason for good cheer, for as difficult as it undoubtedly is to lose a limb, the thing can be manufactured, fitted and lo, we are almost whole again, almost as if nothing had ever happened to interrupt the flow of life. Strange to contemplate, but at home Danny has spare legs, what he calls "parts legs." In his bedroom closet there's a pile of knee frames and hydraulic units he can tinker with.

As Dave runs up and down the stairs to the shop, whittling, filing, pushing and pulling, Danny and I talk about being found out in our disabilities, brought out of denial, exposed. "My first above-the-knee leg was liberating," Danny says. "I was good at it almost from the start. I have great balance, a good proprioceptive sense."

"Can you pass?"

"Unless I develop a sore, which always gives me away. It hurts and I limp."

"Is passing important?"

"Not anymore," he says. "Back then, it was. The legs I used to get back then were very different than now. They were all dolled up, cosmetic, made to look like real legs. You could almost not have told even when I was in shorts. Now it's all metal and plastic without a cosmetic cover so there's no question about what it is, but I'm cool with it. I prefer less weight, which means having the stark no-frills model."

"What's it like to wear shorts with all the rods and bushings and hydraulics in full view?"

"No problem."

"Do people stare?"

"Just kids, but I don't mind. They respond to it as it is, a special leg. I had Mickey Mouse put all over the last one to make it more fun for my nephews.

"If anyone had told me before the accident what was to happen to me," he says, "I wouldn't have wanted to live like that. Now, seventeen years later, I see the whole thing with very different eyes. My life has been strangely enriched by all this."

"What about women?"

"Ah," he says, "women. That's where it really hurt. Where women were concerned it was huge."

"They were turned off?"

"Sex is still an issue sometimes," he says, "but I think just one woman was revolted knowing I had a stump. Maybe there were others but I'll never know. At first, I dreaded being naked in front of a woman."

I had read in a magazine Dave Loney had given me about

people who call themselves "devotees" and are particularly attracted to residual limbs. The article warns amputees that sexual attraction is sometimes inexplicable. The very reason why many of the magazine's readers might be struggling with self-esteem problems, caused by the unsightliness of their stumps, is a turn-on to some others. What whips and chains are to a sadomasochist, so the remains of someone's leg are to these "devotees."

"Did anyone ever want a piece of you because of your amputation?"

"Nah," he says. "But this is Vermont."

Stranger still than the "devotees," I have since read about "pretenders," who mimic amputees, craving what they see as disability challenges and, weirder yet, "wannabes," some of whom seem to be driven by the kind of identity issues that make transsexuals feel that they were born into the wrong body. These wannabes feel that they can only truly be themselves with a limb or limbs missing. Some actually have their healthy limbs amputated.

Dave skips cheerily down the stairs with the altered socket. "Listen," Danny tells him, "I've decided that I want to be six feet tall."

"Okay, but of course only on one side."

"I saw a rodeo star on *That's Incredible* who lost one leg," Danny says, "and a couple of years later he lost the other one. His dream had always been to be six feet tall, and with two prosthetic legs, it was possible."

"I recently fitted a patient with two prosthetic legs," Dave tells us, "and I made him two inches shorter than he had been to lower his center of gravity. I figured that it would make it easier for him to walk and balance. But the man was miserable because he has one of those huge sports utility vans and he couldn't reach the pedals. Instead of getting another car, he wanted his couple of inches back."

These issues are of course different for everyone, because of people's anatomical differences, the different ways they walk, the ways their skeletal frames are aligned, their weight and height. But our bodies are constantly changing in one way or another. Diabetics are particularly difficult because of their frequent changes. "I have to try to be aware to make my most crucial fittings on an anatomically average day rather than an anomalous one," Dave says. "The easiest patient I can imagine would probably be Asian because he is usually short, lanky and active, say five-foot-six and at most 130 pounds. In America, we're giants and overweight and underexercised compared to this.

"If someone has just had a motorcycle accident, lost a limb," Dave says, "hey, those are the breaks. Those people are fun to work with. They get over it within a year and move on. But I see some people like a guy yesterday whose foot was crushed by a backhoe. When he first lost the front of his foot, he said he'd never go outside again. That's when the hospital called me in." He laughs. "There, outside his room, his girl-friend told me that he said to her that she wasn't going to think him good-looking anymore. Now, that's pretty foolish. It's hard for me to have sympathy for patients with an attitude like that."

"Isn't that the same kind of conceit as the person who doesn't want to be seen by his wife without his false teeth?"

"I don't understand that kind of thing very well," Dave admits.

"Our imperfections, slight as they are at times, can threaten our whole equilibrium," I say, perhaps a bit pompously, but from a wealth of experience on the subject.

"I do know that patients who have lost limbs face that," Dave says. "People who have lost arms are generally more distraught than those who lose legs. Your legs get you there but your arms make things. My contact with people who have been wounded has made me realize that we are all disabled in some way. Most of us can't do everything we want to do. We have our limitations. The losses my patients suffer seem to have nothing to do with their happiness. Sure, it does for a time, maybe a year, maybe less, but their capacity for happiness and unhappiness is the same as anyone's. Except for pain. That changes life totally and I feel terrible when I see pain." He pauses. "Sometimes I realize that I really need a sabbatical, a full year off. Today I worked on a diabetic who was losing body parts. He was on kidney dialysis. He'd already lost his left leg, his right hand, and now it looks like he's going to lose his right foot. He's forty years old and will only be with us for another year or so. I had to fight back the tears. All this reminds me how fragile we are and that this is all temporal, it has a limit."

We take a break. Georgia has made coffee and we sit in the large examining room, sipping it. The light is very bright. Even with my superdark sunglasses on, it's painful. Little by little, Dave and Dan begin working on some final adjustments, including the hydraulics of the knee joint. "We need to adjust the flexion and extension resistance," Dave says to me. "You don't want the foot to swing up too high in the back or he'll have to wait for it to come back down again."

A pneumatic unit resists the acceleration until it hits the back of its swing. It engages and keeps the foot from swinging out too fast and too far, and decelerates rather than having it hit a stop. The extension unit does the same thing, making the foot slow down, preventing it from clunking. Danny tries to walk again. "Look," says Dave, "now he's goose-stepping. His left foot is still swinging way too fast."

As Tobias sniffs at a few different feet laid on the floor not far from him, Dave and Dan get into a discussion of the available feet. One is high maintenance and also makes noise. One needs special tools to take it apart, making it hard to fix at home should it begin to squeak. "That's its only drawback," Dave says. "Otherwise it's lightweight and walks beautifully." Some are more springy than others, some have bumpers. They discuss the rebound quality of the natural foot and claims of stored energy in artificial ones.

Danny's current foot is called a flex-foot, designed as a high-performance athlete's foot, and it provides a significant amount of stored energy. "It's better if you still have your knee, the knee being important in controlling that motion," Danny says. "These are a bit stiff for just walking and they don't handle rough terrain as well."

When you run with your normal foot, you spring off the toe, while flex-feet act as the leaf spring in a car does. As you land on it, it flexes, and as you come off it, it provides a little bit of lift. "The new foot I'm getting will be better for me," Danny says. "I like spring on the heel, because that affects how I'm able to roll off the toe. Just as I'm coming off my foot, my good foot is ready to take the next step. With this new foot, the heel compresses really nicely when it strikes and there's enough stiffness in the toe. I don't run, and this gives me a nice smooth gait, which I like."

All the while, Tobias is considering chewing on one of Dave Loney's expensive feet. Dave notices and informs me that the feet cost as much as Tobias. This is not quite true, the price of the entire leg, all the visits and fittings, being about $15,000. All things considered, Tobias figures to be about $50,000.

"Hey, Tobias," Dave says, jumping up from his rolling chair, "I'll give you a couple of old feet to take home with you." He kicks over a foot that for some reason is no longer functional. "Tobias, it's yours," he says, and my dog puts a paw on top of it to begin his sniffing probes, eventually giving it a lick or two, then taking a quick snooze with his chin resting on it. We take the foot home, where Tobias stashes it among his other toys in a wicker basket in the kitchen and brings it out occasionally for me to throw.

Danny's exhausted by the end of the fitting but perks up again on our drive home. "When I sit," he says, "the leg is quite flexible. This socket is bolted to a carbon fiber frame that has an axle through the top, and the socket's attached to a plate that pivots front to back so that there's no torque."

It takes another couple of visits to make several small adjustments on Danny's new prosthesis. When he comes to my house with the end product, walking as smoothly as ever, he is like a new man, full of himself. "Feel this," he says, guiding my hand to the upper part of his new leg. "Feel that material? I had Dave laminate it. Know what it is? It's fake leopard skin."

John Fago, an above-the-knee amputee, a photographer and a teacher, travels widely setting up prosthetics workshops in Third World countries. There, he teaches local disabled people the skills necessary to make legs without recourse to the carbon fibers, steels, resins or hydraulics that are taken for granted in the United States. Where John goes, artificial limbs are more likely to be patched together with padded leather cuffs, scrap wood, car tires, PVC pipe in some countries, bamboo in others.

The replacement technologies available in wealthy countries are unimaginable to most of the rest of the world. Whether in Mexico or Cambodia or Uganda, legs and wheelchairs are ingenious adaptations made from available parts and accessories found on construction sites or bike repair shops or scavenged in garbage dumps.

John tells me about the time he spent in a famous leg shop run by a Dr. Sethi, an Indian orthopedic surgeon, where they make what is known as the Jaipur limb. This leg lends itself well to the regional lifestyles where one goes barefoot in homes and temples, squats at the toilet, sits cross-legged while eating. The best-known component of this leg is a cheap but durable wood-and-rubber foot that farmers can wear in environments such as muddy rice paddies. This leg costs less than a pair of Indian shoes. The Jaipur project is one of the best known of Third World programs, particularly interesting because it was developed by the local people as opposed to those prosthetic projects that are imposed by the First World. John spent time in leg shops in Mexico, in China, in Cambodia and Cuba. Aside from his work in prosthetics, he travels widely with a children's theater he founded in Colorado fourteen years ago, which focuses on social and environmental issues.

John Fago lost a leg to osteogenic sarcoma, bone cancer, when he was thirty. "The age you lose a leg makes a big difference," he says. "Young kids adapt so quickly that it's almost like nothing happened. It's pretty difficult if it happens in your teenage years or in your twenties, before you've figured out who you are. At thirty, the psychological part of amputation was easier to bear than the physical. When I got my cancer," he says, "I was given a fifteen to thirty percent chance of surviving at all, so the prospect of losing a leg became the least of my problems. When a doctor prepped me for my amputation, I remember thinking that this was going to be another way to keep me from being 'normal.' Being outside the scope of the normal always appealed to me. I liked being different, even weird, and now, with one leg, my weirdness would be assured."

He did feel vulnerable sexually, though, especially when, shortly after the amputation, he was with a female acquaintance, a friend of a friend. "I wasn't coming on to her," he says, "but she volunteered that the idea of going to bed with me disgusted her." Then, as he was getting chemo at Sloan-Kettering, having lost a leg, all his hair and a lot of weight, looking and feeling horrible, a woman he didn't know all that well came by to visit and fell in love with him. "Let me tell you," he says, "*that* helped!"

Because, like Danny's, his first two legs were terribly made, John began to think of designing and making prosthetics. He found a leg shop that let him help make his own leg. "After all," he says, "prosthetics was originally done by shoemakers. I loved the process and started looking for graduate programs in rehabilitation medicine." Just then, he got a job taking photographs of disabled village children for David Werner's disability program in the mountains of western Mexico. "David is a rare, rather impish kind of a saint who has devoted his life to initiating health and disability programs where none exist. I was so impressed by what this man was doing down there that I asked how I could help," John says. "David Werner's foundation put me through a six-month program at UCLA, where I learned the prosthetics craft. Immediately after, I went back down to Mexico to help set up a leg shop and train others to make prostheses. After that I made some twelve trips to the little mountain village of Ajoya in a six-year period. I felt that I had found the perfect outlet for my skills and my politics. The David Werner experience made me realize the necessity of this kind of work in the Third World."

After World War II, Congress tried to set up six regional prosthetics departments in the United States but private enterprise defeated the idea. As a result, John tells me, his first leg cost about $2,500, the second $3,500, the last one, just recently, $25,000. "It's true that legs have become very sophisticated," John says. "They're made of expensive components. But if some similar part were intended for a mountain bike, it might possibly cost $150, but because it's to be a part of an artificial leg, the thing goes for $3,000 or $4,000.

"Attitudes about the making of prostheses are very different in other parts of the world," John says. "The best I'd ever seen was in Cuba, where it was clear that they were trying to help people rather than make big money."

At his graduation dinner at UCLA, the director predicted that half the graduating students would soon not only have big-time leg shops of their own but within five years their net worth would be at least a million dollars. "That actually happened," John says, "though to me, only two of the fourteen of us were the least bit talented. The rest were obvious hacks." He remembers asking an ablebodied thirty-year-old guy in his class why he wanted to be in this business. The man told him he'd been the accountant for an artificial-leg shop and now wanted to get into real estate. He needed cash and didn't know a better way to make a lot of money fast than to open a leg shop of his own.

When I mention this to Dave Loney, he tells me of his meetings with the prosthetists he admires, during which they often talk of their frustration and disgust with the field. "We sometimes feel like slimeballs by association because of the preponderance of greedy hacks in the business," he says.

Previously, prosthetics work was in the hands of craftsmen, shoemakers, locksmiths and clockmakers, some of whom had never even finished high school. They devised wood and leather legs, rigged shoulder harnesses and complicated mechanisms for arms and hands, making prosthetics with the materials at hand and doing it well. Until recently, there were very few requirements in terms of education, so many of the children of the original craftsmen entered the field to make a killing. "For every ten prosthetists," Dave says, "there are nine we can live without. The whole thing makes me furious, but I'm hopeful that, little by little, those of us who focus on technique and clinical training will rid the field of hacks."

When the successors to the craftsmen took over in the

early 1980s, they could get away with shoddy work because, even though it requires some ingenuity to come up with artificial limbs that work, no one insisted on medical or anatomical training. Educational requirements were minimal and licensing has recently been made mandatory only by a few states. But as space-age materials, complicated torsion and myoelectric systems have entered the field, patients' expectations for comfort as well as function have been raised.

"The bad guys dominated the practice in Vermont when Georgia and I arrived on the scene," Dave Loney says. "People expected us to be vultures like the rest, here only to make a pile of money. It has taken all of the nine years we've been here to get respect."

Recently, Dave was invited to make grand rounds at Dartmouth Hitchcock Hospital as an expert in the field. "It was not only a great honor for me but it never would have happened unless they realized that there are a few of us who are in it for more reasons than the money."

"Who pays?" I ask. "Can anyone who needs a prosthesis get one?"

"Medicare pays, while the private insurance conglomerates pay only a small part. But there seem to be support groups out there that help almost anyone unable to pay. Plus, if you're a kid under eighteen, the Shriners' hospitals provide free prostheses."

Rather than greed or what some might call free market entrepreneurship, prosthetics programs in the Third World often reveal other serious problems. In 1990, John Fago was invited to spend a month teaching at the national prosthetics center in Cambodia. The country at that time had little experience with foreigners, and he arrived at the leg shop with his girlfriend on the back of his motorcycle. He was wearing shorts, his artificial leg in full view.

"Many of the local amputees lived in a dormitory at the

center," he says, "waiting for an artificial leg, though once they were fitted with one, only their mobility, not their status, would be improved. They needed a lot more than that to live like independent people. When I asked why there were no amputees working on making legs, I was told that none of them were qualified, which was totally wrong. As soon as I began showing them how to modify a mold for a stump, one of the amputees, watching me, grabbed the welding torch from my hands and started welding masterfully. I brought the guy into our class but this was a strange thing to do as far as my hosts were concerned. I thought it might help change attitudes but it didn't."

Aside from realizing that the status of disabled people in the Third World would not easily change for the better, he was shocked whenever he was witness to the behavior of the International Committee of the Red Cross. "With their huge budgets," John says, "and employees who are basically corporate executives advancing their careers, they hardly help empower the people they supposedly serve.

"One time, I was in a car, sitting next to a guy from the Red Cross who had just flown into Phnom Penh. We were off to a meeting to talk prosthetics in a small town. He told me that the secret of his effectiveness and understanding of what was going on in a country was built on excursions such as this.

"Typically, what these people do is to fly into whatever city, spend a night at the best hotel, catch a morning flight into the country, go to a meeting, get back on the plane to be back in the hotel by cocktail time. Here was someone with no experience of Cambodia, with huge resources supporting him, with a plan established beforehand by expatriate management rather than by the disabled people's needs.

"In that particular case," John says, "the man had come because a British company had begun to produce a new generation of prosthetic legs. The Red Cross was engaged in peddling the obsolete tools and machinery so that legs could be manufactured in Cambodia for Cambodians. You could argue that this would be an improvement but no one had checked it out with the natives. It was a corporate decision from on high and had nothing to do with a Cambodian delivery system, which among other things had to consider how to maintain production after the Red Cross was finished with them."

"What would have made more sense?" I ask.

"To identify those groups in the country who are trying to deal with the situation, then do whatever you can to support them financially and with training programs. You go from the bottom up, not the other way around. Whenever you bring in mechanical systems from the First World, especially if you're training nondisabled people, you give those people skills which they will undoubtedly take somewhere else where they can make more money. If instead you train disabled people, their personal needs are going to continue, as will their understanding and compassion for other disabled people.

"Listen," he says, "there are certainly a whole lot of dedicated people out there trying to help. But I've met too many who are living a colonial life, with servants and all the perks, and are interested mostly in continuing that life."

Though John passed on his prosthetics skills when he was in Cambodia, he's convinced that the best thing he did was to advance the concept of independent living by demonstrating that one can still live productively, not subject to karma, to God's punishment. "Though life is tough for amputees there," he says, "that trip was a lesson to me about how patronizing we from the First World can be. My being there with a positive attitude, my cameras, my motorcycle, my girlfriend, that's what was important."

Nearly twenty years ago, John was trying to repair his bike in a bicycle shop in China. By the time he had finished working, there were about three hundred people watching him, partly because in 1983 many had never seen a non-Chinese but partly because they'd never seen anyone with an artificial leg. "In China," John says, "most people who lose a limb don't get an artificial leg. They walk on crutches or stay at home. I love being out in the world because I'm not only seen as a privileged white American but as someone who has obviously had some problems of his own."

An accomplished sportsman and a daredevil skier, John translates his love of sports equipment into feelings about the appearance of his prosthesis. "Though in some ways, I couldn't care less about appearance," he says, "I don't want my artificial leg to be covered with flesh-colored foam. That's ghoulish. But I do want my leg to look like a piece of sports equipment, lean and functional, an athletic device, looking high-tech and cool.

"I do leg demonstrations for kids in schools, taking it off, putting it back on, showing the kids how it operates. I think it's important for kids, or anyone else for that matter, not to be afraid of a prosthetic leg or a stump. I wear shorts as much as I can. I want people to see that I have this disability and it's not stopping me from being out there or from doing things."

Aesthetics aside, a prosthesis that looks like the limb it's replacing isn't always desirable, as with the split-hook hand, which is easier to manipulate than a facsimile of a hand. Legs preferred by some amputee runners because of their flexion characteristics resemble a cheetah's legs or the suspension band in a pickup truck more than a familiar articulated leg.

"This design trajectory of a technology—from mimicry to modification and then to disassociation with the original—has happened many times in history," writes Katherine Ott, a curator at the Smithsonian Institution. "The first movable type resembled written script. Initially, railroad cars looked like horse-drawn coaches, and were pulled by horses along wooden and iron tracks. Early automobiles, the familiar horseless carriages, imitated buggies in design and suspension. Artisans of these technologies have long since abandoned any allegiance to their precursors." And thus, in the spirit of form following function, both Danny and John Fago prefer the brute honesty of transparency to an obvious imitation.

Because he limps pretty badly, John uses a cane, which his prosthetist doesn't like, but he feels a lot more mobile with it. When he was sixteen, he had a bad skiing accident, so he still has plates and screws in his stump, compromising his muscles and making his skiing feats even more astonishing.

John takes a lot of pleasure in describing the technology of artificial legs, talking about the way a foot rolls over, using stored energy, the way it flexes and extends, talking of knee joints, titanium cylinders with areas cut out of them, hydraulic pistons like shock absorbers in a car. He lovingly describes a little device called a rotator that lets the knee flex in one plane. If he's sitting down, he can actually push a button to rotate it, which allows him to sit in a full lotus position and get in and out of tight places.

He himself designed a prototype for a leg that is a big crescent extending to the ground to a point. The design seems radical, its application intended primarily for runners, the point of the crescent lending itself more to springy take-offs than standing still. "You couldn't even get pants onto this thing," John says.

John's present prosthesis is as high-tech as they currently come. For some years, he had a much less sophisticated leg, but, as he was financially able to do it, he was convinced that he owed himself a better one. "Not without some guilt, I got a high-tech prosthesis," he says, "and it made a huge difference in my mobility. The reality was that the Cambodia-type leg took a lot more energy to use and wasn't good for my spine.

"For people with disabilities," he says, "skiing is the most amazing thing because suddenly you're free and gravity is your friend, a welcome contrast to hopping around and being careful. Put me on the top of a mountain and I feel I can do anything." He arranges his life so that he can ski at least eighty days of every year. "Skiing on one leg is a very elegant thing," he says. "A prosthetist I know in New York keeps trying to develop a prosthetic skiing leg and I keep telling him that he's nuts. After all, I've got two outriggers for balance, and the idea of a heavy apparatus strapped to your body when you're flying down the hill just doesn't make sense.

"People sometimes say I'm skiing to get stroked. They yell down from the chair lift: 'Hey, that guy's not disabled,' then they tell me that I'm some kind of inspiration. But all I'm doing is having fun."

He talks about the logistics of disability. "Sometimes I feel guilty about calling myself a disabled person because all that's wrong with me is the absence of one leg. Especially because I'm very physically fit, I'm often hesitant to ask anyone to do anything for me. But say I'm in bed reading and want a glass of water. Do I ask my wife to get it for me or do I get out of bed, grab my crutches, get the water and spill half of it as I hop back into bed? I'm often confused about how independent I need to be."

He admits that he's always looking for discounts for disabled skiers. "There are people in the disabled community who think they should pay like everyone else," he says, "but as far as I'm concerned, screw that. When I first started skiing out in Colorado shortly after my cancer, little by little I realized that, even on one leg, I was as good as anyone on the mountain. I skied that first year free on a special pass, and at the end of the season I went to the director and said that I

didn't want to assume that I could keep on skiing free just because I was disabled. He opened his desk drawer and pulled
out a bunch of visitors' remarks about me, saying that as their
hands and feet ached from the cold and the trail looked
daunting, they'd see this one-legged guy whip down the
hardest run on the mountain and suddenly they were happy
to be there. The director said that I was earning my way.

"As amputees," John says, "perhaps as all disabled people,
we have to ask ourselves some crucial questions. Is the equipment we use intended to help our mobility or to hide our disability? Should we take risks, be models for others, an
inspiration, or should we stay out of the way, try for invisibility? Should we demand our rights or accept the status quo?
All these questions and a lot more become crucial when you
are suddenly dealing with new limitations, but involvement
with them tends, I think, to deepen our humanity."

When I visited Dave Loney's prosthetics shop a year after
Danny's leg had been finished, the practice was prospering.
Reimbursed primarily by Medicare, Dave was making some
hundred prostheses a year. He was closer to arranging to contribute his work to needy people in the Third World and told
me a story of one of his patients, an Indian man with an
above-the-elbow arm amputation. The man had grown up in
Singapore, moved to Canada, then come to Vermont. He had
never felt the need for a prosthesis before.

"Why now?" Dave asked him.

"Ah," the man said, "it is because I am going back to Singapore to start a new business and you know how they feel
about amputations. If any part of your body is missing, they
consider you an outcast, a beggar."

Dave fitted the man with a complex myoelectric arm and
hand. Before returning to Asia, the man practiced for months

with his new arm but its intended functioning proved to be extremely difficult for him. In Singapore, though, he wore the prosthesis for obvious reasons. As it turned out, his business venture failed, but, needing a job, he decided to spend his days traveling all over Asia speaking on behalf of amputees. He reported to Dave that not only was he changing Asian mind-sets about disability but was making good money doing it.

"I'm constantly astonished by people's fear of amputees," Dave says, "but I love this work. I love how quickly we can take a person who's been badly wounded and bring him back pretty close to where he was before."

JAWS

TED HENTER

computer engineer
and entrepreneur

PROLOGUE

Even though I'm an anxious and naive user of computers, I can now, not seeing the screen, log on to the Internet every morning and have my computer read me whatever I want to read in the *New York Times*. It's only my technological inadequacy, not my lack of eyesight, that keeps me from going further, from doing absolutely anything a sighted user can do to find relevant texts, research material, games or chat rooms. But my technological ignorance runs deep. My understanding of even television or, for that matter, the telephone, is minimal.

Nevertheless, for several years I've been using and taking for granted an earlier innovation, a more simply devised screen-reading computer whose voice reads the words that appear on the screen. Even that less complex technology had brought me into the mainstream in a way that had not been possible for blind people previously.

I'm quite sure that were I totally sighted and writing, I would still be doing it by hand, preferring that more human pace, like the awareness of a heartbeat in music. Still, I was very curious to discover how all these technological wizardries had come to pass, who had made them happen, and how. On hearing about my fascination with this, a disability activist friend reminded me that the disability rights movement prefers universal to particular design. This was unknown to me as a burning issue and I asked her to explain.

"How is this going to be used by the public at large?" she asked.

"I don't know." And I had no idea why she needed to know. Isn't it enough, I thought, that the program serves people who can't see?

"Take curb cuts," she said. My friend calls herself a quasi-quad, with limited use of her arms and hands. "People hated them at first but then they realized that they helped not just wheelchairs but strollers and just about everyone."

"It sure messed up the blind," I told her.

She paused for a moment. "How's that?" she asked.

"It used to be easy for a cane to feel a high curb. And how is a dog supposed to figure out where to stop if a sidewalk blends directly into the street?"

She let this pass and went on. "Take bathroom accessibility," she said. "It's for me, for my needs, for wheelchairs, but we can torque that idea into something called universal because in fact, everyone likes the bigger stalls. They can put their packages down or bring in a stroller or make it easier for older people or whatever."

"That's true."

"There are situations that are uniquely universal," she continued, "others that aren't. What I dislike is the idea that something is done solely because disabled people need special things. It's just too reminiscent of the old-style thinking about disability in society. It just isn't appealing when thinking of long-term movement goals."

"Aha," I said, still not totally convinced.

"The more universal something is, the more it promotes the idea of diversity and inclusion. The idea of a screen reader or an accessible bathroom has more to do with how we think about what humans as a large group with extraordinary physical differences need in a highly developed world."

I liked her certainty and began to see the validity of her point of view. I did recognize a healthy reciprocity between innovations developed for special needs and those that are useful to the mainstream. Just about anyone can have his e-mail messages read aloud by a computer voice as he drives his car, but this luxury comes as a result of blindness technology being adapted for sighted people. When the technology existed solely for the relatively small population of the blind, its price was astronomical. Since its development for more general use, the price has diminished considerably. A lot of techniques and equipment, some high-tech, some entirely mundane, filter down from their original uses. I read somewhere that carbon paper was originally invented for the use of a blind person who from that moment on would not have to worry if his or her fountain pen had ink, but its utilization by office workers turned out to be a noteworthy time-saving device.

Brilliant new technology is useful for some things, superfluous and useless for others. Screen-reading programs are irrelevant to the vast majority of the world's population with no access to computers. In some situations, sitting on a scooter board on wheels is preferable to the mechanized wheelchair, which is useless to those of the world's nonwalking population whose environments are sandy or muddy, or who, because of unusual circumstances, prefer crawling, as on the earthen floors of African huts.

Not only is advanced technology not always appropriate for cultural or geographical reasons, it sometimes also violates the "less is more" maxim, where the conservation of resources or lack of funds requires other imaginative solutions.

Alex Truesdell has for years made assistive devices, such as specialized chairs for severely disabled infants and children, out of cardboard, papier-mâché and glue. She plies her trade in New York as well as India and portions of South America. "I brought no tools or other equipment when I last went to Colombia," she says. "I had to figure out how to be resourceful. In considering their children, no one there thinks of things like developmental scales or tests. It's very much kids first, unlike here, where equipment and programming often smother the kid. When working with multiple handicaps, you have to adapt everything that's manufactured. You quickly learn that handmade is good. This teaches you that a solution can always be imagined and crafted, even by the totally unskilled. It may not be slick and shiny and sexy but it can work really well."

Here in America, just as access to print through braille or computer voice is essential for a blind person hungry for information, so are low-tech solutions, certainly not excluding the articulate human voice describing the visual world. Going to a museum can still be an immense pleasure if the person I'm with is an imaginative, informed talker.

Though hardly a technological breakthrough, descriptive videos are slowly being introduced to large-market television programs and some movie houses. In them, highly visual cinematic art is brilliantly narrated, filling the spaces between on-screen talk with a density of perfectly chosen adjectives and adverbs, expertly describing gestures, facial expressions, erotic activity and landscape. It's a labor-intensive, low-tech delight.

Retinitis pigmentosa, an inherited disease of the retina, has been picking away at my eyesight for many years. How actual sight is affected depends on the location of the dying rods and cones, at the periphery or in or near the center, but whatever the momentary configuration of the loss, the useful portion of the retina is constantly diminishing. Thus, just when I have come to terms with the vision I have left, the dying process continues and a new period of adjustment begins. The technology of print access seems to have kept pace for almost the entire period of my most difficult losses, and, over the last fifteen years, my friend Geoff Howard, a rehabilitation technician, has been installing ever more sophisticated equipment into and around my computer. He has introduced me to closed-circuit TV enlarging systems, then to computer magnification and, finally, to screen-reading programs.

Before the advent of Windows and the Internet, the technology of a computer's reading aloud whatever text appeared on the screen was impressive enough. But the injection of a mouse clicking on an icon somewhere in the vast desert of the screen made the translation from screen to voice that much more difficult, and nearly put blind people out of business after they had only recently been enabled to participate on a par with sighted computer users.

Many companies took on this challenge, and in 1995 the first crude graphics-reading systems came to the market. A few years later, as Geoff was training me to use a program called JAWS for Windows, he mentioned that he had just seen the man who created it on television. "The guy's blind himself," Geoff said. This got my attention. "And apparently a great water skier," he added. Though I've never been particularly interested in the exploits of the superblind, who tend to diminish the importance of the modest nature of most of our lives, my curiosity was piqued by Ted Henter. Was he on a mission to save the world? To make money? How did he do it anyway? Considering my technological illiteracy, I didn't have a notion how anyone, with or without sight, could solve the abstruse codes and symbols of computer language.

On the phone, Ted Henter seemed modest but self-assured. He is the founder and CEO of Henter-Joyce, a multimillion-dollar company whose only purpose from its beginnings in the late 1980s has been computer accessibility for the blind. He was quick to tell me that he doesn't dwell on his disability. "I got over feeling sorry for myself in ten minutes," he said, which made me even more eager to find out who this man was. Indeed, blindness and most other disabilities are not the end of the world, but which of us does not awaken at three in the morning, railing against the unfairness of it all? Getting over this makes sense, for not getting over it is as stupid as railing against death. On the other hand, there can sometimes be poetry in the railing.

I was soon to find out that, as upbeat and successful as Ted Henter is, he is a complicated man. Everything in his life has been a mission, and blindness was not about to drive him off course, nor intense competition, nor uncertainty. He's a brilliant entrepreneur whose significant engineering skills and fierce competitiveness, as well as his nagging personal needs as a blind computer user, drove him and his blind buddies to beat the odds in being the first to emerge from the bloody dogfights with the other companies racing to come up with this badly needed technology.

JAWS

While Ted Henter is held up in a business meeting, I drop in on Eric Damery, the vice president of Henter-Joyce. One of a handful of sighted managers in the company, he is settled in a pleasant, sunny office decorated with colorful wall hangings and framed photographs. Many of the other offices at Henter-Joyce are occupied by blind workers who are somewhat less interested in dolling up their environment. As I walk in, Eric is putting down the telephone. He punches a fist into his open palm. "Yes!" he says exuberantly. "Yes!" He springs up from his chair to pace. "I've been talking with a local UPS manager," he says. "We've been trying to access their computer programs with our screen reader and it's beginning to look great. UPS has ten major facilities nationwide with some eight hundred computer jobs in each. If we're successful, that translates into eight thousand jobs for blind people. It's a great opportunity."

Until JAWS for Windows became available in 1995, screen readers deciphered only text. The challenge was translating the icons and graphics of new, popular programs like Windows into speech. Without it, blind people were facing massive layoffs from well-paid, decent employment.

In the Windows environment, though everything starts out as text, as was the case before, by the time it reaches the screen it is no longer text. It's graphics on an all-over field that depends on the visual targeting of a mouse. In word-processing programs based on DOS, by contrast, there is a grid that is consistent with every program. Also with DOS, only one program can be open at a time, and it takes over the entire screen. With Windows there may be multiple simultaneous programs, all sharing one screen. While being able to use multiple programs was a benefit for many users, it created a nightmare for nonvisual access because it became almost impossible to navigate through all those screen layers. It was the equivalent of a sighted person being told to find a small object in a totally dark room.

Ted Henter's secretary comes into Eric's office to fetch me. She walks Tobias and me down a long hall and through a small kitchen where some of Henter-Joyce's more than fifty employees fix their lunches. A microwave oven is talking. "You have set the timer at two minutes," it says as one of the programmers grabs a cookie from the toothy mouth of a ceramic shark whose flippers clutch a half-devoured surfboard. Even though the JAWS name has nothing to do with sharks, standing rather for Job Accessibility With Speech, the company has adopted the shark motif throughout the building. It is everywhere. A shark mural, I am told, greets us in the entrance lobby, and the farther in we go the more sharks we meet: cookie-jar sharks, candy dishes, toilet-paper holders.

The walls of Ted Henter's office are full of his early patents, his multiple awards and certificates of service, photographs of his daughters in their various sports uniforms, of Ted and his wife Mel slalom-skiing on water and on snow. Ted tells me that he's particularly proud of a photograph of himself standing with six Navy SEALs beside a dugout canoe.

"From the early sixties when I was a Boy Scout in the Panama Canal Zone," he says, "I participated in this ocean-to-ocean canoe race. It's really neat, paddling through the locks of the canal next to huge ships."

"How did this one come about?" I ask him.

"A couple of years ago, those six Navy SEALs, a bunch of really buffed guys, needed a seventh for their canoe. Someone told them about me, a middle-aged blind guy, and they couldn't believe it." He laughs. "They were stuck so they took me."

"How did you do?"

"Well, we made it. Actually I kept up with them pretty well and they honored me by brailling *Slave Galley,* the name of the boat, on its side."

Ted had just recently returned from this year's race. "Parts of the course are really beautiful," he says, "but Panama is no longer what it used to be. Once, it was like small-town America, everything orderly and pristine, now it's a mess." Ted was with friends the whole time so he had only his cane with him, leaving his guide dog Lori at home.

"We were staying on the Pacific side of the canal so we loaded the boat on a trailer and drove across. I showed my friends the terrific sites, like the deepest cut from about five hundred feet high over the lock areas. There's a great view from up there."

Ted, like me, relishes his visual descriptions and judgments. Our unavoidable visual references come from our old sighted lives and emerge, irrepressibly, through memory and imagination.

"There were forty-two boats in the race," Ted says. "Plenty of reporters, plenty of old friends, a great sight. The weather was fine but real windy and rough, the wind blowing right off the ocean. Coming around the pier into the canal, quite a few boats swamped, blown over to the sandbars where the waves were even higher.

"I rowed up front, setting the pace. The others looked at

me and we'd do about one stroke every couple of seconds, switch sides every fifteen or twenty strokes. It was like running a marathon, except that we had no practice at all. The race was divided into several grueling stages over a period of three days. Overall, I think we came in fifth. I thought we'd do better, but that didn't really matter. We had the best time."

On the day in the mid-1970s that changed his life, Ted had been at the Brant's Hedge motorcycle racetrack south of London all day, having just arrived from a race in Venezuela where he placed eighth. Just before that, he'd come in fourth in Daytona. He was known in the motorcycle world but he wondered about his future. His passion for racing conflicted with his marriage and, being twenty-seven, he felt he didn't have a lot of time left to race.

"It was the beginning of the European championship season," he now tells me. "I had never been in England before, I didn't have a whole lot of support and I was working on a shoestring budget. I had a tough road ahead." Apprehensive about the whole enterprise, he nevertheless felt destined to keep doing it. "That day, I was preoccupied with the competition, with who could help, with who the important people were. From England I was ready to travel to Spain for the first race of my European tour.

"On the way home from the racetrack, in a rented car, on a narrow, dark, two-lane road, driving slowly but preoccupied, I saw the headlights of a car coming toward me. Not until we were very close did I realize that I was driving on the wrong side of the road. I swerved right and he, of course, swerved left and we hit head-on." He pauses to clear his throat. "In those days, cars weren't required to have shatterproof glass. I was sprayed by shards of windshield, which left me with minor cuts except for the glass that pierced both of my eyes."

"Did you lose all your eyesight at once?"

"I lost one eye outright, then had two operations on the other. The first surgery was a success but the retina didn't heal properly. When I woke up after the second operation, I was totally blind. I knew right away that it was essential not to be held back by the emotional part of losing my eyesight and approached it on two levels. One was the conceptual part. I got over that real quick, in about ten minutes. I was able to do that because of my faith in God. I realized that this was planned for me and it would end well. I just had to find out what the rest of the plan was."

The practical part turned out to be a little more difficult. He had to learn all the tricks, adjust to the mobility problems in getting around, to the very different way even well-meaning people treat the newly blinded person, and to the emotional impact when they treated him like a helpless idiot. "Unless you're pretty damn tough," he says, "their pity can have a detrimental effect. It bothered me but it didn't depress me. I know that it holds back a lot of people, those who get stuck in the 'why me?' phase. I didn't want to be that way."

"Did people fall all over themselves trying to rescue you?" I ask.

"My parents wanted to do everything for me. I had to push them away. I had to educate them. My wife Mel, like me, knew we would make it, blind or not. She was capable, she had a job, she took care of the family, drove me around. Not everyone has someone like that to help them build up their self-esteem. When a lot of people are treating you like an idiot, it's nice to have somebody who doesn't. But before the accident, we were probably heading for divorce."

"Blindness saved your marriage?"

"Hmm. I guess it did. It changed me a lot," he admits.

"You were a guy who loved speed, and, as we both know, a blind person is not particularly speedy."

He laughs. "Right," he says. "I guess that's why I still do

all this racing. But from the beginning, I stopped living in the sighted world."

The difference between losing eyesight in one catastrophic event and the endless adaptations required by gradual loss lends itself to interminable insider comparisons about which is easier to handle.

"How did you make the mental switch from a passion for big macho machines to the intricacies of computers?"

"I'm a pretty good engineer," he says. His grandfather was a machinist, his father, a hydrologist, both great mechanics. When Ted was in fourth grade he took apart the coaster brake of his bicycle and put it back together again. "My dad thought it was a miracle," he says, chuckling. He was able to translate his mechanical talents into computer skills. "Not only did I realize that I had a mind to understand computers but I recognized computers as an extremely promising field for blind people. I'm very fortunate," Ted says, "to be able to combine my disability with my career."

I ask him how the whole computer enterprise got started. "After my surgeries," he tells me, "a rehabilitation counselor went with me to check out the computer program at the University of South Florida. We talked to a professor and, to my amazement, he told me that he didn't want a blind person in his class."

"My God, Ted, I haven't heard a story like this since the bad old days."

"The professor said that he allowed a blind person into his class once before and the guy needed so much special attention that he held up the rest of the class."

"These days we could sue the bastard," I say.

"I had too many things going on emotionally at the time to make much of a fuss. Still, that professor's rebuff was almost inconceivable to me, too. After all, being an athlete, I'd been revered. When I was in the hospital in England after the accident, people would come to my room to ask for my autograph. So this hurt but I didn't want to fight it. I wasn't all that sure I wanted to go into computers anyway, and besides, I had too many other struggles in my life, mobility and braille foremost among them."

Unwilling to give up so easily, he decided to try a branch campus of the university. He managed to take a few computer courses and was hired by a friend who wanted to design a fancy computer program for his beach hotels. It was a foot in the door that allowed him to learn how to use a very primitive talking terminal. Maryland Computer Services, the company that produced it, noticed that Ted was becoming one of the few skilled users of its technology and the owners came down to Florida to check him out. "It was the middle of winter, so it wasn't a bad time to come south," he says, laughing. They asked him to come up to Maryland to manage a trade show and, seeing him in action, they hired him to make talking computers that were better than the ones he was asked to promote. Meeting a lot of great engineers, he got himself an on-the-job education, and ended up writing a new code for their computers as well as doing tech support, sales and marketing. Eventually he was involved with higher decision-making. "I was incredibly lucky," he says. "It was a fantastic way to learn."

But Ted and his wife were homesick for Florida, so they left Maryland and he continued to work for the company from home. Shortly afterward, Maryland Computers went out of business and both he and the screen reader he was working on were bought by another company. At the end of the first year, he met one of its clients, a blind millionaire from Chicago named Bill Joyce, who put up the money to start the Henter-Joyce partnership. Soon it was apparent that Bill Joyce had little time to give the new business, so, taking a huge risk, Ted Henter bought him out. "This whole progression of things reflects the wonderful breaks in my life," Ted says. "It was meant to be."

Ted and I reflect on how some of us fall into our lifework, how some lives seem preordained, on a mission. Some people stumble through the most unlikely, least expected doors. And then, who among us can stay on course? There must be folks who remain untouched by circumstances and end their days having lived in perpetual sunshine, but we agree that most of us face unexpected detours.

"Do you ever think of what life would have been like if you hadn't been blinded?" I ask Ted.

"I would have been a world-famous, world-champion motorcycle racer," he says, not skipping a beat. "Or I would have been dead."

In the late afternoon we sit on the terrace of his spacious suburban home overlooking a scenic canal off Tampa Bay, with blue herons that neither of us can see screeching overhead. Ted provides two mugs of beer as his wife Mel brings us a plateful of shrimp. "Taking risks in racing isn't that far from taking risks in business," he muses. "Certainly the competitiveness is similar. Everyone I know in both worlds is very competitive. We don't like to lose."

"When you suddenly found yourself blind, did you feel that your fate was entirely in your own hands or were there a lot of other folks who helped?"

"The emotional stress of learning to be independent while working hard to carve out a new career was difficult. Only when I got my first guide dog did a lot of the stress subside. I loved the freedom that dog gave me." Ted's dog Lori, an eight-year-old Lab, had once been attacked and nearly mangled by a friend's shepherd. Lori is now being very careful with Tobias. As a matter of fact, she and Tobias take positions far from each other, my dog's face resting on my shoe, Lori in a corner staring at the wall. "It took me years to begin to feel really comfortable with blindness," Ted says. "Still, though some people felt sorry for me and some talked down to me, almost everyone perceived me as a normal person, allowing me to do some powerful healing emotionally. And it was very important to have help. I could focus on what I was good at while Mel took care of the girls and the house, as well as helping in the business. My parents provided transportation and money when we needed it. Our whole family lives within minutes of here. There are quite a few people in my life, even competitors, whom I can trust. That's key. At the beginning, a lot of people talked down to me. They no longer do."

"What about you? Having been helped by others, do you now consider yourself a helper?"

"No," he says without a moment's hesitation. "Helping other people was never my motivation. This isn't to say that I didn't want people to get whatever benefits they could from my work, but I got into this to make money, not to help."

"Didn't you get help from rehabilitation people, folks from the Division of Blind Services?"

Ted sits up in his chair. This is obviously a hot topic for him. "From them, I primarily got mobility instruction. They also bought and paid for a talking computer and a braille printer. But when they tried to counsel me and give me advice, it was horrible. They wanted me to go to a class to learn to cook and sew. I'd never done cooking and sewing before and I wasn't about to start. I was twenty-seven years old, I had a wife, a college degree, and they wanted me to spend six weeks of my life in a rehab center doing nothing but learning skills I didn't want or need. Even though I didn't have a job yet, I didn't have six weeks to throw away. For a lot of people I guess that's perfectly normal.

"The rehab industry is built on the premise that the more

people in the system, the more funding they get. It's the natural progression of any bureaucracy. It's a great concept but it deteriorates as it goes. These counselors don't set high standards for the people they try to help. They themselves aren't successful, so they keep people down at their own level."

We both are veterans of the system, albeit very different people with very different politics. I tell him that, in my case, they gave me computer equipment, sent me to a rehab center, then to graduate school, all of it most useful at the time.

"What I object to," he says, "is the way these counselors go into our lives claiming to be saving any semblance of our self-esteem. What they do is commiserate with how horrible blindness is, what bad luck. I hate that. And it isn't true. So they tell you to sit back and relax, and they'll send you eight hundred dollars a month instead of really motivating you by saying: 'Look, you're worth it, you can do it, you've got to get out there and try.' If it were me, I'd offer people two thousand a month for a limited time, say four years, and tell them to get it together, to find a trade school or college or employment."

"And if they don't?"

"They can live the life of soup kitchens and barracks. My impression is that the motivational part doesn't happen as much as it should. The monthly money should be to get you over the tough spots and get you back into the game. When I was first blinded, I was looking for some vision of a future. What could a blind person do? What are the possibilities? They didn't have a clue. They couldn't find me role models of successful blind people. That's what I needed."

"But you were educated and motivated. Privileged. It's a whole lot easier to help you than someone without your inherent advantages."

"That's true, but a lot of very successful people come from that other side of the tracks—a lot more from there than from those who are born with a silver spoon. When tragedy strikes, it often ignites people and they become successful. What holds blind people and people with other disabilities back is the social system around them. If you pay people to sit on their ass, that's what they're going to do. You must give people a vision and a direction."

He tells me about being on the board of an organization called Abilities, which helps give disabled people a start. Recently, Abilities considered a case of a walking and biking path that cuts right through the city. Even though no one was allowed to put any business venture on the path, the board wanted to ask for an exception so that a disabled person could run a snack bar on it. "Just one other guy on the board besides me voted against this horrible idea," Ted says. "It's an example of pitying the disabled. I can take hatred but I can't bear pity. It's time to get rid of all the special privileges given to blind people. In America, if you're motivated, you can make it. I'm against handouts. Disabled people should not be special. If we are given special privileges or head starts in a business venture, nondisabled business people will have a right to despise us."

Even though there are many people in the disability rights movement who think somewhat similarly, wanting no special privileges aside from what they consider their absolute rights in the form of a level playing field, my views are softer, a lot more liberal. Ted himself is an avid follower of Rush Limbaugh as well as some of the religious right's radio evangelists, but in spite of his conservative political attitudes, he himself is a role model for a lot of blind people. A highly successful businessman, he helped create a very useful product that helps keep many blind people in the workforce. I suggest that making it happen must have been both exciting and challenging.

"We started in the late eighties," he says, "busy mostly with our DOS screen reader. By 1993, we realized that Windows had to be attacked. It looked formidable, but we knew it simply needed to be done."

Henter-Joyce had nearly gone bankrupt after unsuccessfully attempting to create an off-screen model, the essential data base, a memory list of every bit of text that exists on the screen, its location and pixel coordinates. Ted then hired Glen Gordon, a blind programmer whom he'd met earlier, a man who, like him, knew that without the move to Windows, he and many other blind programmers would lose their marketability.

The development process was arduous and at times somewhat comical. Because Windows was not accessible to blind people, it took all of Glen Gordon's ingenuity to juggle the possible options. "Imagine," Glen says, "I was flitting from the Windows help file to a primitive version of an existing screen reader, then back again. From there, I'd go into DOS, where I was writing the new program. Talk of pulling one's self up by one's own bootstraps," he says, laughing. "We gave that metaphor a new definition."

The wonder of the whole enterprise is that Glen had no visual access to Windows and thus couldn't truly know the screen configuration in order to determine how it should be represented verbally. "I could have had someone look over my shoulder and explain it but that would have been arduous," he says. For people like Glen and Ted, the challenge of beating the odds, no matter how daunting, was so seductive that they couldn't allow themselves what might have been an easier route.

The purpose then of running another existing program was to get a spatial concept of Windows. Glen used it and the Windows help files to understand what was going on, to understand that pressing a certain key would result in particular on-screen displays. The fluidity of text becoming graphics was a completely new concept and required learning how to store and quantify information in a new way.

In DOS, it is possible for a screen reader to read anything that is typed on the screen, to say aloud what any character is at any location. A lot of people had mastered this straightforward technology of intercepting the text and transforming it into words. But when Windows came along, the entire paradigm changed. It was no longer possible to say what the character in, say, row one, column six, was, because in Windows there is no such grid. Though most things start in Windows as text, by the time they're actually on the screen, they've been converted to graphics. "What we had to do," Glen says, "was intercept the text before it was turned into a picture and store it away so that it could be located later. Eventually, we would give it a number and a label, then a key on the keyboard that would make audible what to a sighted user was an easily recognizable symbol representing functions, letters, words, sentences and paragraphs."

But that wasn't the only problem. There are some things on the screen that don't start as text, like the picture of the recycle bin, which designates the place you're to put your deleted files, or the icon that says: Click on this and your text becomes bold. "We were able to determine that this was some sort of picture," he says, "and from that picture we computed a number and from that number a label, simply the name assigned to a picture.

"Intercepting keys can be complicated, because whatever we want to use for our JAWS program can't interfere with any underlying applications, but once we jump that hurdle, assigning keystroke equivalents to visual signs that appear on the screen is fairly straightforward.

"As a blind user, you don't care about the entire landscape of the screen. You care about the landscape of one application at a time. It's like a sighted person maximizing a program and not seeing anything else. A sighted person can rely on looking at a trash can on the screen, then delete his file by dragging it to the trash can. As a blind person you need more of a concept about how to perform this task. You won't get visual feedback which would give you a clue. You'll get audible feedback from the JAWS program that tells you where you are, asks you what you want to do and then tells you how to do it. So we have a whole bunch of keystrokes you might use that a sighted person can accomplish by simply dragging and dropping, doing something quickly with a mouse. None of this means that a blind person has to be less efficient, though a blind person who wants to keep up must learn all that is provided as an equivalent language in JAWS."

As the sun begins to set over Tampa Bay, Ted's youngest daughter's dog, an eight-inch-long miniature Doberman named Daytona, begins to run Tobias ragged. We hear a wicked splash. Tobias has been steered into the swimming pool chasing Daytona. Unsatisfied still, the little hotdog manipulates Tobias into flying headfirst into a glass sliding door. He seems unhurt but I bristle, mortified on behalf of my noble animal. Tobias, a little dazed and very wet, loves the playtime and, tail wagging, wants more.

I ask Ted about the dramas that must have accompanied the race with other groups attempting to solve the screen-reading problems.

"We were very concerned with beating a few key competitors to the market," he says. They scheduled a dealer meeting to show and release their product for the end of January 1995 though they hadn't solved many of the problems. There was an awful lot to do between September and January. They had to make an enormous number of choices about what to include, what to leave out. Nevertheless, they managed to release it in mid-January. "A lot of things that could have gone wrong didn't," Ted says. "It wasn't perfect but it was pretty damn good. Still, we were scared."

The trade show managers put all the developers of all the screen-reading programs on stage, six or seven of them with their products running, in front of a panel of judges and an audience. Then they instructed each of them to run Microsoft Word, open certain files, open a particular dialogue and load a different file. One at a time, each presenter stood behind his computer and tried to do what was asked. The computer talked, doing its thing, and the judges judged. "A pretty neat idea," Ted says.

"Things were going great for us but then this remarkably clever blind kid went up there representing another company. He really knew his stuff, outsmarted and hoodwinked the judges and audience by making them believe his product could do things it actually couldn't do. It was a terrific show. I really got off on that kid. Anyway, when he was finished, everyone cheered and his company won based on the kid's creativity. I realized what had happened but I also knew I had to be a gracious loser."

Six months later, the judges set a much more difficult task and Henter-Joyce did very well. It put them on the map. Technically speaking, JAWS could do more things, read more screens, get more information and present it to the user better than any of their competitors.

Ted gets up to get us another beer. In his home, he walks carefully but gracefully, not using his dog Lori. "I used to do a lot of traveling," he says when he gets back, "just me and my dog. A lot of trade shows, that kind of thing. Now that my company is big I do less. Other people do most of the traveling for me."

"Why did JAWS make it and the others not?" I ask.

"There are a lot of smart programmers in the world. Were you simply smarter?"

"Our commitment was urgent. Glen and I are blind. We needed a good screen reader. A couple of other guys on our programming staff were blind. That made a huge difference. We were driven. Most of our competition had sighted guys running their companies. Being blind, we have a very real commitment to making this stuff work and work correctly. We are the designer and programmer and user all in one."

"What a lot of stress. How did you survive it?"

"It wasn't easy. I wasn't sleeping, but then I always have a hard time sleeping, which has to do with being totally blind, not knowing the difference between night and day. My body's rhythms don't work that well. Blindness definitely adds to the stress."

"I also used to wonder why I was so tired by early afternoon every single day, until I figured out that blindness itself is exhausting."

"You said it. It takes a lot to remember where you are and where everything else is in relation to you. You have to do this every minute of the day. That takes a lot of organization and orientation skills."

Ted is a sportsman. As Geoff Howard had mentioned, he is a great water-skier as well as a very good downhill one. In 1991, Ted was the number one U.S. blind water-skier, winning seven national championships. Then there are those ocean-to-ocean races in the Panama Canal. But it isn't just Ted. The whole family thrives on competition.

At dinner, on the evening before his daughter Elizabeth's go-cart race, as we are finishing our locally fished amberjack, the telephone rings. Mel answers and shrieks with delight. Elizabeth's high school basketball team has just won their division in the state championships in Miami and she, a substitute point guard, scored five points. Emily, the eighteen-year-old,

was still at the state fair attempting to qualify in the cheer-
leading competitions. Earlier, eight-year-old Amber told me
about a string of horseback-riding ribbons in her room.
There are black and brown belts from every conceivable martial art, trophies, plaques and certificates. It's hard to keep
track of who got what.

The next day, a Saturday, Tobias and I meet Ted and his
family at the Sunshine Speedway, where Elizabeth is about to
participate in the restricted two-stroke light category of go-
carts. "This is how I started my racing career," Ted tells me as
Elizabeth, in her rose-colored space suit and helmet, gets into
a spiffy Yamaha, kept in tip-top shape by Ted and an old racing buddy. Tinkering with last-minute computer checkouts of
Elizabeth's go-cart, Ted tells me that the tension and excitement of the track sometimes erupt into unpleasantness, competitive fathers arguing and threatening. "Once," Ted tells me,
"one of these dads screamed at his son for being beaten by a
girl, my daughter. When the kid lost to my Elizabeth a second
time, they never came back to this track. I understand feelings
like that."

Suddenly we are all running for the grandstands as Elizabeth drives her preparatory laps. As the checkered flag is low-
ered, Elizabeth's cart is bumped and she does a full spin. It
costs her the race.

When Ted was a kid, he loved go-carts. He raced them
expertly until he was old enough to graduate into the motor-
cycles that became his life. "I had gone to college with the express purpose of designing racing machines," he says. "My
plans were to race for maybe eight years, then be part of some
racing-connected business." He was in the process of climbing
his way to the very top of his profession when he had his terrible accident.

Sitting on lawn chairs, with the drone of the afternoon's
contestants behind us, I remark that he excels in many

different things. "If someone had just met you, how would you define yourself?"

"Above all, I'm an entrepreneur," he says. "That's what I'm best at, not the smartest computer scientist by far. As a matter of fact, even though I was totally involved with the engineering of JAWS, other people did the real front-line work. I'm not the smartest businessman or business manager either, nor the marketer or salesperson. But I've been willing to take the risks essential to being an entrepreneur. To be a good entrepreneur you've got to know a little about all these things but you have to have a good feel for the market, what will sell, what folks will buy, what they need."

"Even though your motivation was largely money, aren't you proud of the effect your company has had on blind people?"

"Sure I am. I do think of the opportunities that blind people now have because of the effort we put into this. I'm sure all this would have happened if it wasn't us, but it wouldn't have happened as quickly. Our competitors have pushed us and we have pushed them. I'm proud of this, but we were neither the first nor the only. We didn't conceive of the idea. Others did. We learned from them and took it a step further."

On my last day of Florida blue skies and bright sunlight, I stop off again at the Henter-Joyce building, trimmed, I am told, in tropical teal, surrounded by pink hibiscus and bright red bottlebrush trees. Inside, Tobias's tail wags furiously. Many of the offices are occupied by employees with guide dogs. Chris, the company's development manager, is a fairly recent import from Cambridge, Massachusetts, which he wistfully remembers as the intellectual center of the universe. He is learning to enjoy the pleasures of sun and water and the malls of St. Petersburg. "We're not enabling anybody," he says, proud of the work they are doing. Chris is blind from retinitis pigmentosa. "With JAWS, we provide a tool," he says. "It's like putting a saw out there. A saw doesn't give a sighted person permission to cut down a tree. It's what is used to cut it down. The cutting is the important part. We don't heal. We're not do-gooders. We're very much a business, not a charity."

"I'll say," I tell him. "JAWS for Windows is very pricey. You certainly don't give it away."

"The company gets involved in charitable issues but we charge what the market will bear. What we make is a really valuable tool, not only to the larger blind community but to ourselves, half the company. JAWS gives us access to our work. It provides a tool which the rest of us transform into an education, into jobs, into poetry."

Back in Ted's office, I ask about Henter-Joyce's future plans. "We need to be broader," he says, "probably to merge with a bigger company, to have a bigger product line. In the blindness business we're one of the biggest, but if a big company bought us we'd benefit from a much larger sales, advertising and marketing force.

"Over half of our more than fifty employees are blind. The tech support is all blind, half the developers, most of the salespeople. We work on translating new programs and we work on making core, basic improvements in the ones we already have. It took about two years in all to develop the original JAWS for Windows, then we just kept adding features to it. It never ends."

Henter-Joyce commands the majority of the computer accessibility market, its sales larger than those of all its competitors put together. JAWS exists in ten languages, with the European market accounting for a quarter of its total business of more than 25,000 users. In some years, the company has grown by as much as 70 percent.

A few months after my visit to St. Petersburg, I call Eric

Damery, the Henter-Joyce sales manager whose excitement about the possibility of eight thousand good jobs for blind people underscored the importance of the enterprise beyond personal use. "Whatever happened to the UPS project?" I ask him.

"It got snagged with red tape within UPS," Eric says. "The way things stand, a lot of these companies have huge turnovers among their sighted computer workers. If we can set this software up properly, if it's perfectly customized so that their programs speak effectively, and if a company's training program to accommodate blind individuals is carefully crafted, then it'll work. Once they begin hiring blind people, those people have to be more productive than the sighted employees to be able to advance in these positions."

It could go either way, I am thinking. I can imagine a happy blind workforce, productive, satisfied, taking home good wages, but I can also see the potential for the old dismal sheltered workshops, scrambling for piecework, brooms and baskets replaced by the monotony of tracing packages. This is, of course, a familiar issue with minorities, who need to be better than the mainstream, who have to work harder, be more grateful. Perhaps this is the only way into the mainstream and perhaps even the best-intentioned openness works only in times of near-full employment and affluence.

As it turned out, the UPS project didn't materialize, but similar agreements with Northwest Airlines and Marriott World Wide Reservations did, both organizations having contracted with Henter-Joyce and its dealers to do scripting for their internal applications. Both organizations have many blind employees using JAWS for Windows.

JAWS for Windows was given a special award by the Smithsonian National Museum of American History, welcoming JAWS into the permanent research collection on information.

A year after my visit to St. Petersburg, Ted Henter and his

company merged with Blazie Engineering of Maryland, the leading U.S. manufacturer of braille hardware devices, a company owned by his old friend Dean Blazie. They formed Freedom Scientific, Inc., a new company dedicated to offering a broad line of assistive technology products for people with sensory impairments and learning disabilities. Henter-Joyce and Blazie Engineering plan to continue designing, developing and manufacturing their respective product lines in separate business-development units, but their sales, marketing, order entry and administrative functions will be combined.

"Dean Blazie was the man who, fifteen years ago, gave me my start in business," Ted says, "and we have been close friends ever since. Our teams have worked well together on numerous joint efforts over the past several years, and so we've often thought it would be a natural alliance to put our two companies together, but, until now, both of us lacked the necessary capital to make it work."

Shortly after this merger, Freedom Scientific acquired the business operations and product lines of Arkenstone, Inc., the leading maker of reading systems for people who are blind or visually impaired. When loaded into a personal computer, Arkenstone's Open Book system reads aloud any scanned book or other printed material.

For the first time in my nearly thirty years of listening to taped books, I can now take any book out of the library or buy one from my local bookstore, no longer dependent on whatever books others have decided to tape.

"The aim of Freedom Scientific," Ted says, "is to become the global market leader in the field of assistive technology."

"Things are going pretty damn well for you," I remark on the phone.

"Never better," he says.

SCHOLARS

ADRIENNE ASCH

professor of bioethics

ROSEMARIE GARLAND THOMSON

professor of English

PAUL K. LONGMORE

professor of history

PROLOGUE

I met disability scholars for the first time at a conference of the Society for Disability Studies. "SDS, our initials, are no coincidence," someone told me, referring to the Students for a Democratic Society of the 1960s. From my first encounter with the politics of this disability-oriented SDS, I felt very much at home.

"Disability studies?" a friend of mine, himself an academician, asked when I returned to Vermont. He thought he'd misheard. He tried saying it again. "Have they run out of categories of study?" he snickered, needing to tweak this thing further. "How about pedophile studies?"

In fact, scholars from all over the world had shown up. Some were disabled, some not. There were people from the arts and from the humanities, from English departments, from American studies, from philosophy, sociology, anthropology, law, political science and history, and though disability studies are not about cures, treatment, rehabilitation or the high-tech engineering of gene recognition, the disciplines of medicine, public health and rehabilitation were also represented. The papers presented were on views of the disabled in literature, film, the visual arts, on eugenics and euthanasia, on culture and identity, on epistemology, immigration laws, civil rights, accessibility, employment.

Throughout history, disability has been seen through varying lenses. Aside from the often sentimentalized mythology of disability stars, whatever history exists has come not from the marginalized disabled themselves but from ablebodied observers, anthropologists colonizing an exotic land.

Instead of viewing disability as a problem that needs to be fixed, disability-studies scholars are focusing on its social and cultural context. "Our society is based on the concept that everybody has to be normal," one of them said. "It's a view that defines disability not as a physical defect inherent in bodies, but rather as a way of interpreting human differences. After all, gender is not simply a matter of genitals. So disability is a way of thinking about the nature of bodies, rather than concentrating on what is wrong with bodies."

At the SDS conference, some of the audience, as well as some of the presenters on the many different panels, were in wheelchairs or wearing leg braces, were quads and partial quads, some mowed down by birth defect or accident or chronic illness, others with attendants standing by their sides, some talking with great difficulty, some fluttering spastically. There were the deaf focusing on the signers, the blind listening intently. This was my community and it moved me deeply. As a matter of fact, it was exhilarating.

In the mix, there were scholars pure and simple, clarifying distinctions, carving out turf, but many of them were also the warriors of this relatively new movement that had started with a clamor for independent living in the 1960s, continued in the '70s with demonstrations that resulted in the implementation of otherwise gutless accessibility statutes, followed up, year after year, by brave actions that led eventually to the passage of the Americans with Disabilities Act. "Many of us were academics to begin with," a disability scholar said. "As activism heated up, we became activists. And now, with activism firmly embedded, we're back to the academy again."

Though science and technology are often revered because we expect them to lead us to better lives, the presence of the disabled in society reminds us not only that precious resources need to be shared but that science itself has limitations. An extreme belief in scientists and physicians not only as surgical or pharmacological virtuosi but as the bearers of wisdom, the adjudicators of life, has penetrated deeply into our society.

Though the liberally praised human genome project holds some promise for important medical research, it also promotes our love affair with the image of ourselves as perfectly beautiful, healthy and brilliant, the tallest, blondest, whitest cancer-resistant athletes, the kind of people we have always wanted to be. Even though very few in this academic disability community idolize medicine and its drive to pathologize the human condition, it's hard to blame those who do. "The problem with people like the severely disabled matinee idol, Christopher Reeve, putting his celebrity in the service of cure rather than care," another scholar said, "is that he's not only highly visible but that he unfortunately echoes the wild expectations of the population. It's troubling because this attitude seems to dominate public discourse about what the response to disabilities should be."

When disability, as race and gender before it, is examined and illuminated, it can be seen beyond the personal misfortune it is often claimed to be. If it is perceived as deviant, compared to some prized norm arising from cultural expectations of how humans should look and act, it overwhelms a person's other, less visible aspects.

This is a lot more than an academic issue. It follows me around as it does most visibly disabled people, in the way we are seen, in the ways that our complexity as humans is often overwhelmed by the facile, single-focus stereotype. In literature too, the disabled are not subjects of art but its occasions. They are on the margins of fiction, exotic and uncomplicated, symbols and spectacles, eliciting responses, rhetorical effects, depending on disability's cultural resonance. As a rule, a few general strokes paint these characters, but blind is all you need to say and a host of images automatically comes up. Cultural assumptions fill in all the missing details.

"So how is anything changed by scholarship in this field? Why does it matter beyond the academy?" I asked Paul Longmore, professor of history at San Francisco State University.

"It matters a lot," he said. "Any social-change movement needs some of its members to do the analysis, the really hard work. That's what we do. For a movement to succeed it must precisely define what the problem is and how it must be addressed. There's a lot of entrenched thinking about all this and we, academic and nonacademic activists, have to change that thinking. Society thinks disability is a medical problem and that people need to be cured or corrected. This is not the case. Disability is a social problem and cures are rarely the solution. The solutions lie in social and political transformation, architectural and technological redesign. We need to examine all this in great detail."

"How will this happen? How will your work trickle down to affect us all?"

"One crucial way is through influencing public policy. For that to happen, we must analyze how cultural values shape policy regarding the disabled. Cultural representations of disability in literature or movies are not entirely separate from cultural representations in public policy or professional practices. Part of a scholar's job is to explore those inner connections. Our critical analysis must be both current and historical. How did things get to be this way? How does the present situation compare with the past? Was there even a concept of disability in earlier eras or is this a modern invention? If there wasn't a concept, how did it come into existence?"

Another way scholars try to effect change, aside from

analysis and reform of public policy, is through the examination of professional practices. "Some people mistakenly want to distance disability studies from rehabilitation and special education," Paul Longmore said, "because those professionals are seen as oppressive. They *can* be oppressive, but disabled people are always going to have to deal with those professionals, so disability studies must generate reform in the process of their training and thus influence how they practice. It's already happening at the University of Illinois in Chicago, where students in occupational therapy are coming into graduate courses in disability studies and some of them are going back out into their fields as missionaries."

The field of disability studies has met with resistance from some traditional academic disciplines. From these and from nonacademic orthodoxies come reactionary views that see these studies and this political awareness as cranky and wrong-headed. From both the political right and left, a self-satisfied criticism has been leveled against what is sometimes perceived as squawking about one's rotten luck. Thus, the ADA has been attacked by the right as too expensive, too softhearted, a costly crutch, the attorney's dream act, a dumb use of resources, even an abomination.

The political left has different reasons for neglecting the disabled. Even though the reality for most of the disabled community is extreme isolation, rampant unemployment, poor education and continuing discrimination, even though it is the most marginalized sector of society, there is a growing conservatism within the progressive movement, for whom race, class and gender are the overarching considerations. Disability rights hold a curious position within the social-change movement, even though disability is often a class issue and frequently is a direct effect of capitalism's excesses: of war, repression, poverty and backward social priorities.

Because educational institutions are the guardians of cultural memory and meanings, the existence of scholars in disability studies in the humanities is crucial. The subject matter of disability studies is not simply the variations that exist in human behavior, appearance, physical, sensory or cognitive limitations, but the meaning we make of those variations.

"As scholars, we're dealing with issues that have to do with experiences and social standing of people with disabilities," Paul Longmore said. "We're addressing all the traditional questions that the liberal arts had always addressed, such as what's the nature of manhood, womanhood, sexuality? What makes a person human? What is justice, equality, community?"

It seems clear that all of this can enrich learning for students and scholars in every field and therefore has implications for how society faces basic issues—issues such as differentiating between the normal versus the pathological, the insider versus the outsider, the competent citizen versus the ward of the state. Academic studies teach us that the very term *normal* is historically specific, arising in a particular moment as a part of the notion of progress.

Precision in the use and understanding of language itself also defines the academy. Though in times such as ours, this may lead toward politically correct euphemisms, words such as *challenged* or *unsighted* or *otherwise abled,* for the most part it leads away from them and toward a linguistic and conceptual honesty. It stands to reason that the use of certain terms, like *victim, affliction, wheelchair-bound, suffering from disability,* should be pointed out not only as demeaning but as conditioning the society in discrimination and segregation and pity. Also, the proper definitions of disability-related terms, such as the differences between *disability, impairment, handicap* and insider words such as *crip* in the disability world or *queer* in the gay one, should be, and are, thrashed out by the group itself, in the academy and in the street. Language has to be precise in attempting to define oppression and in wresting control of words from their previous owners, from medicine, psychology and rehabilitation. A fresh language gives different meanings to the social, political and intellectual transformations that have taken place.

Attitudes, customs and laws change, and language often reflects that change. In the medical lexicon, for instance, the three diagnostic categories that existed in the first half of the twentieth century under "feebleminded" were moron, imbecile and idiot, hardly neutral terms. These words reflected ideology. Medical language, as medical practice, is not exempt from expressing social beliefs. It is hardly an excess of political correctness that identifies conditions and people without apparent condemnation.

On the other hand, academic language can be a barrier to understanding, even offensive, not only to the public at large but to disability movement activists. Big abstractions, esoteric language and incomprehensible jargon can be counterproductive in a field that hungers for the broadest possible participation. "We have to apply the principle of accessibility to our prose," Paul Longmore said. "On the other hand, what any scholar does is technical and difficult to access. Still, it would be a pity not to, because disability scholars can make real contributions to disability rights."

When I return to Vermont, it is hard to explain to my professor friend that there are disabled people who take pride in their disability.

"You've got to be kidding," he says. "That sure sounds like trying to rationalize an intolerable situation. I've got to tell you that every time I see, well, not you, but some poor guy in a wheelchair, tapping out messages with a stick tied to his head, I want to run. I think, 'Jesus, there but for the grace of God go I.'"

I can only hope that those are not the words that come

into his head every time he sees me. Still, I realize that it's not easy to convince ablebodied people that some among the disabled are not searching for cures, and that there are actually those who feel pride in their condition, no matter how debilitating and troublesome it might appear to the ablebodied. Bombarded as some among us are by negative meanings of disability in the law, in utilitarian philosophy and economics, in public discourse and in the seductive dreams of perfectibility, it seems an open question whether or not we can alter our attitudes to include and support all minorities, no matter how mired in old fears and hatreds, no matter how costly.

The trickle-down effect of scholarship, and the education of teachers and the subsequent education of their students, is a slow process, but it is one way that attitudes begin to evolve from the narrow and primitive, from fear and paranoia, into clear and humane ways of thinking. At best, it allows us to broaden views, to open ourselves to discourse, to enable shallow biases to dissipate. Although neither racism nor sexism nor homophobia has been eradicated by black studies, the women's movement or gay studies, these programs have at least shifted consciousness toward better understanding and tolerance. Thus, scholarly work in disability can give legitimacy to more evolved views, and help produce a history, language and civil rights perspective in the effort to create a new canon of beliefs and to delegitimize bigotry.

SCHOLARS

Often, disabled people are unwelcome in a culture because they are thought to deflect resources and attention from the group as a whole, invoking a lifeboat image of a society abandoning its weaker members. Responses to disability range from containment and control to abandonment and annihilation, but how one serves and treats disabled people is not based solely on resources. It's a complex policy issue, rooted in profound ethical considerations.

Shifts in consciousness have by no means been universally progressive. In some places, infanticide is still practiced and has even been suggested in the United States, perhaps not to rid the world of six-fingered infants as is the case in some parts of Africa, but for what certain individuals consider severe disabilities such as Down syndrome or spina bifida. Many religions still believe that a disability is indicative of wrongdoings in a previous life. In many parts of the world, families still consider themselves shamed and discredited by a disabled child, forcing them to hide or abandon the cause of their misery. Everywhere there is discrimination in housing, education and employment.

"The only reason anyone thinks that money spent on people with disability is wasted money is that the population as a whole assumes the disabled person just doesn't contribute anything," says Adrienne Asch, Henry R. Luce professor of biology, ethics and the politics of human reproduction at Wellesley College. "The life prospects of disabled infants are unknown. You have to look at life as a whole. Who's to say if it's better not to have a disability than to have it? Every life costs and contributes different things. We can't know what any life costs or what it contributes until it is lived."

Recently, the controversial academic Peter Singer was appointed the new chair of bioethics at the Center for Human Values at Princeton. He takes the position that if you have a baby or a fetus with a serious disability, you should get rid of it so that you can try to have a better one. And, he suggests, you should be able to do it in utero or at any time during the infant's first twenty-eight days on earth.

A well-known advocate of animal rights, Singer asks why it is worse to kill a human than a nonhuman. Why is it more tragic when people are gunned down by a murderer than it is when pigs are killed in slaughterhouses? He maintains that the argument can't depend solely on species membership, and, if it does depend on a being's self-awareness, its high level of rationality, its ability to think of its own future—"Well," Singer says, "those are not attributes of infants either." Thus, as he sees it, the killing of a defective infant is not morally equivalent to the killing of a person. "Very often it is not wrong at all," he says. "In an area riddled with uncertainty, choices still have to be made. Someone may have inadvertently terminated a pregnancy of a musically gifted child, but because there is no way to test for musical genius, we have to judge by the only thing we have learned from a prenatal diagnosis: a disability."

"Singer's ideas are often seen as outrageous," Adrienne Asch says, "but he's got a lot of company, including much of the bioethics community, the political left and the general public, most of whom have pretty terrible views regarding disability. Most people, if pressed, feel just the way he does or close to it. 'You're such saints,' people say to parents of the disabled. 'It would be better if your child had never been born, you deserve so much credit, you're a hero.' Or they say to a disabled person: 'Have you considered killing yourself, aren't you sorry you were ever born?'

"I think Singer is wrong on facts about people with disabilities, who can obviously have okay lives," she says, "and, to the extent that they can't, disability is probably not the intrinsic reason. A lot of the reason is how society is set up to not treat people with disabilities very well. Why does he think that the nondisabled life is automatically better than the disabled life?" she asks. "And why does he think that pregnancies and babies are fungible? They're not cars. The point is that you wanted to be pregnant then and you already started planning your life around the birth of this child. I'm absolutely pro-choice, but if you decide to have a baby, you should damn well have it."

Adrienne Asch spends a lot of her time pondering how many resources should go to people with disabilities, when something is a human "variation" and when it is an "impairment," whether the status of impairment should entitle people to different attitudes or services than some other human status does. She teaches various bioethics courses at Wellesley, courses on reproductive, ethical and social issues in genetics, assisted-reproduction processes, including sperm and egg donation, surrogate motherhood and cloning. Only when it has to do with prenatal testing or physician-assisted suicide does her teaching coincide with disability issues.

"I dislike prenatal diagnoses because disability is only one characteristic of a person's life, infant or not. There is a whole range of other characteristics. Disability is not a burden with no redeeming benefits or attributes, and how does anyone know that it would take more effort to raise a disabled child than any other child? That's an assumption which might be wrong. The public assumes that it's terrible and burdensome and tragic but there is no information corroborating that view. You can find claims in old literature that a disabled child is the worst thing that ever happened to a family, but the recent literature argues that families with kids who have disabilities do about as well as any other family on measures of happiness or stress or satisfaction. It's possible that my male child would cause more stress than my female child, or my third child more than my second or the other way around. What would be nice to know, and you can't ever know, is if the infant will be happy, if you'll enjoy it, if it will enjoy you. These are things you don't know, and the problem with prenatal diagnosis is that you assume you do know. You say, now that I know my child is going to have spina bifida, I don't want this child anymore, even though I don't know anything else about the child except the disability part."

Another piece of this question is the glaring lack of support from doctors, social workers and genetic counselors for the parents' decision to continue a pregnancy after a disability diagnosis. As things generally stand, these professionals are coercive, telling only the gloomy, negative story of disability, and the parents making such a choice are as stigmatized as the child will later be.

"Of course disabled people don't like the way they're treated," Adrienne says. "Society needs to adapt to all people, not to some people. Aborting in this case is misguided because it assumes there is only one standard of life. Given that, if the society thinks you shouldn't exist in the first place, it doesn't matter what kind of job discrimination laws you have, because with those assumptions you don't stand a chance."

Early on in her career, Adrienne Asch turned from an activist arena to a more scholarly one, writing for both academic and mainstream publications on the disability rights movement, on women with disabilities, on the psychotherapist's role in working with people with disabilities. "When I got involved with bioethics," she says, "I wanted to communicate with the field to change mainstream bioethics writing, the kind of thing that medical professionals and philosophers, influential people, would read so they'd think in a new way about disability in terms of health policy and resource allocation."

In the context of her interest in disability rights, Adrienne became fascinated by bioethics and the complex issues surrounding transplants, suicide, the ethics of withholding treatment. "I was a Ph.D. student in social psychology and a practicing therapist," she says. "I liked both things very much, but I came back from my first bioethics meeting ecstatic at the breadth and depth of the people I'd met, the passion with which they approached their work. I fell in love with a discipline. Bioethics is a field in which reasonable people can disagree, which is one reason I love it. These were people who were not in it for fame and glory. They really cared about the issues."

In 1987, she was asked to join the New Jersey Bioethics Commission as a social science staff member to think about surrogate motherhood. The commission took on the case of Baby Ann, in which a woman refused to give up a baby she had agreed to carry for a couple. One court said she had to give up the baby, but the state supreme court ruled that surrogacy contracts were null and void in New Jersey and that the state should make new legislation regarding surrogate motherhood. The commission was charged with thinking about this legislation and Adrienne was one of the people working on the project. She loved the work and eventually did her Ph.D. on attitudes toward surrogate motherhood, finished it in 1992, and began looking for academic jobs in bioethics as well as in social work and women's studies. "Then," she says, "a friend of mine told me about the opening at Wellesley. I

applied but never thought I'd get it. The Henry R. Luce professorship of biology, ethics and the politics of human reproduction simply sounded like it was meant for a very senior
person and my doctorate seemed much too recent. In my application letter I wrote that if someone was to ask me to design my dream job, this was it. I got the job and it truly is my
dream job."

She has taught courses on disability but also includes
disability-related issues in courses she teaches on other topics.
Among those issues is abortion after prenatal testing. "Not
everybody would teach this kind of thing," she says. When
she teaches a course on motherhood, she includes discussion
on single motherhood and lesbian motherhood, on welfare issues, on disabled women. "Not everybody would teach this,"
she repeats.

Given most people's ideas regarding prenatal diagnosis,
euthanasia and other difficult issues, I ask if she thinks she is
influencing the thought of students or academics or the population at large in a meaningful way.

"I don't feel enormously optimistic about my views becoming popular with either the professional community or
the general public," she says. "I think it's very difficult for the
medical profession or the bioethics world to imagine that disability is not a tragedy. But I have to believe that ideas make a
difference. Otherwise there's no point in being a scholar."

I first met Adrienne Asch in the ballroom of a hotel
where we were both attending a disability conference. She
was brought over to me by a retinue of followers and admir-
ers. "You wrote a book about blindness," she said.

"I did. Did you read it?"

"No." For some reason, we were facing each other like
warriors, she with her white cane nearly up to her chin, I
clutching the harness of my dog. "Are you a member of the
National Federation of the Blind?" she asked.

"No."

"Why not?"

I said something about having once been, then, not agreeing with much of their philosophy, I quit.

Even though we didn't know each other, she was not pleased. "You should reconsider," she said. At our first meeting and during each of our subsequent talks, it was clear that she had little patience for niceties. Her views, honed during some thirty years of involvement in disability issues, are passionately held. Adrienne Asch was born blind. The difference between the experience of a person congenitally blind and one like me who has seen well into adulthood is enormous. So is the place and importance of blindness in our lives. She is supremely focused on her scholarship, the complicated webs of her bioethical thinking, while I am in a constant quandary about the world, seduced by ambiguity and uncertainty. Her direction is straight ahead, mine wanders, is distracted, nudged off course, derailed into anxiety or panic. I long for what I've lost while Adrienne seems to be way beyond that kind of thinking, or perhaps has never visited this unproductive terrain.

For most of us who have once seen, the seduction of the sighted world never diminishes. On the other hand, the congenitally blind were born into the world whole, and only learn by being told that they are lacking a sense that others can't live without.

Adrienne Asch is unimpeded by my kind of grief. What this difference creates in terms of our personalities might be huge even though our other experiences—the joys of study, reading, thinking, contributing, the joys of human relationships, of music, food, sex—might be similar.

"Kids weren't taught cane travel until high school," she says, "so I got along without a cane until then. I was very happy to get a cane when I got it. I never even considered a dog because I don't like dogs. I thought having a dog was stupid. I like the idea that when I need it, I use a cane and when I don't need it, I put it away. Also, I despise the way the public treats people with guide dogs, giving graduation diplomas to the dog, acting as if the dog is a saint. I can't bear people saying that if I had a dog, it would act as an icebreaker. That's the wrong thing to say to me. If ice is to be broken," she tells me, "I'll damn well break it myself."

As prickly as Adrienne can be, I find myself warming to the rock-hardness of her positions, but when I make the mistake of asking how well she manages getting around the Wellesley campus or anywhere else for that matter, she lets me have it. "The next time someone comments on my being wondrously independent," she says, "I think I'll throw something at them. I'm not overly independent or dependent. I'm just a person trying to live my life. Casting issues in terms of dependence or independence is simplistic. Life is not like that.

"When it's appropriate," she says, "I speak out on disability issues on the Wellesley campus, but I'm not here to be a poster child for disability. I think I've made a difference to students but I don't think it's because I have a disability but because I'm a good teacher. I don't know if they think differently about disability because of me. I think it's good that students at Wellesley who have disabilities don't show up on my doorstep and see me as a disabled role model, though if they did, they'd be welcome. I've tried to persuade other faculty and staff with a disability to be more vocal about disability issues but I haven't been very successful at that. There's a great deal of shame for some people in acknowledging their disability. A lot of successful disabled people believe that their success depends on pretending that their disability doesn't exist and they don't want to affiliate with others with a disability. I think that's a mistake, but everybody has to figure out for themselves how to survive."

Adrienne Asch became interested in bioethics in the early

1980s when she read about a woman with cerebral palsy who petitioned a California court to end her life. She wondered what else was involved. Could the woman be helped out of a possible depression? Was she getting counseling about better strategies for staying alive and leading a less miserable existence? Should a court decide who is allowed to kill themselves, who not? And who, if anyone, is to do the killing?

At about the same time, the parents of Baby Jane Doe, an infant with spina bifida, asked the court to stop their child's hospital treatment and to let her die. Someone sued the hospital to prevent it.

Even though Adrienne is left-wing in her politics, she was surprised to learn that the ACLU and other left-leaning organizations were supporting the disabled woman's petition to be allowed to die. According to Adrienne, everyone seemed to be screaming that, were they in her condition, they too would want to die. The woman was leading a pitiable and degrading existence, they said, and as for the parents of Jane Doe, they ought to be able to end their infant's life because, after all, she wasn't going to have much of a life. "The Reagan administration wanted to stop it just because of their stance on abortion," Adrienne says. "They weren't interested in babies, just in being pro-life maniacs. It seemed to me that if the baby weren't disabled, the parents would be charged with murder. It was clear to me that bioethics and the left and the general public all had terrible notions about disability, even worse than I thought."

Though I personally find the view that only the healthy should be allowed to live appalling, I have never had to attend to anything more serious than the question of continuing the genetic line of retinitis pigmentosa and thus blindness. When I recently said those words to a friend, his momentary silence communicated his shock. "More serious than blindness?" he finally said. "What could be more serious than blindness?"

Though I realize that for most people, the possibility of genetically transmitting blindness is hardly appealing, my children's view of this would be shocking to the members of that chorus. They are not only glad to be alive in spite of my daughter's having inherited retinitis pigmentosa from me, they are also, to my surprise, not particularly concerned with the possibility of saddling their own children with it. "If I have to have a kid with RP, I'll take it," my daughter said. Though going blind over many years has not been easy for me, sometimes causing panic and depression, still I would be shocked if anyone aborted solely for reasons of retinitis pigmentosa.

Nonetheless, given a chance, most of the people I know would abort a disabled fetus in spite of acting and talking an enlightened belief in diversity. Diversity, like poverty or any other kind of oppression, is not only tolerated but deeply felt and understood, as long as it happens to someone else.

When I ask about her views of the human genome project, Adrienne is not pleased with my question.

"It's like asking when did you stop beating your wife," she says. "There's no simple answer. I'm not opposed to any kind of knowledge, but I haven't seen any great knowledge gained. Perhaps there are potentially good uses for it though I don't know what they would be. We've known about the genes that cause cystic fibrosis and Tay-Sachs and sickle cell anemia for a long time, and none of that knowledge has resulted in better treatment. It's not obvious that knowing which genes influence which diseases or traits is going to make social services or medical care better. It might, but it's more likely that people will just develop more and more tests for prenatal diagnosis and abortion. They're talking about prenatal diagnosis of fetuses that might develop breast cancer or early-onset Alzheimer's. Do we really want to be aborting every fetus that might have one of these diseases? What about diabetes or heart disease? Whom are you going to allow to be born?

We're all going to die of something. I'm not sure I want to live in a society that does more and more testing, more and more eliminating of people who aren't perfect or who don't have the proper IQ. What about predispositions for high cholesterol or hypertension or back problems? Are we going to keep people out of the workplace for those reasons, as opposed to making the workplace better for those people? It's not at all clear what they're going to cure or how. It also proposes that all those characteristics like aggression, alcoholism or adventurousness have genetic roots, but genes are certainly not the whole story. They are ignoring the interaction of genes with each other and with the environment."

In her book *Extraordinary Bodies,* Rosemarie Garland Thomson considers the written and pictorial representation of physical differences, including a wide variety of disfiguring characteristics, such as scars, birthmarks or unusual proportions. She politicizes bodily differences, identity categories, disclosing how the physically disabled are produced by way of legal, medical, political, cultural and literary narratives.

"Disability is a system that produces subjects by differentiating and marking bodies," she has written. "Furthermore, this comparison of bodies legitimates the distribution of resources, status, and power within a biased social and architectural environment. The category of disability exists as a way to exclude the kinds of bodily forms, functions, impairments, changes, or ambiguities that call into question our cultural fantasy of the body as a neutral, compliant instrument of some transcendent will. Disability is a broad term, within which cluster ideological categories as varied as sick, deformed, ugly, old, maimed, afflicted, abnormal, or debilitated—all of which disadvantage people by devaluing bodies that do not conform to cultural standards. Thus, disability functions to preserve and validate such privileged designations as beautiful, healthy, normal, fit, competent, intelligent—all of which provide cultural capital to those who can claim such status."

Thomson, an assistant professor of English at Howard University, teaches American literature and feminist theory. She integrates disability studies into that teaching but because of Howard's understandable preoccupation with race, her work in the disability field takes shape elsewhere.

"Howard University is a great place to work," she says, "because race is such an important category of analysis here. It's very useful to always be focused on that, but one of my frustrations is that at Howard, race is such a central category of consciousness that it trumps all other identity categories. We don't even have a women's studies program. There's an interest but it's hard to institutionalize it. There's also a long-standing conservatism in black colleges and universities, clearly a post-colonial phenomenon. If you get some power, you conserve that power. Disability studies seems to some people here not only as a negative community to associate one's self with, but a distraction from the primary issue."

Being a white person in a predominantly black institution is as replete with fascinating paradoxes as men talking of feminism or the ablebodied about disability. As a feminist and a disabled person, Thomson is an insider when talking to those groups, while being very much the outsider when teaching black literature to black students. "I never forget these ironies," she says, "and I hesitate therefore to make naive, oversimplified, reckless generalizations." She has learned that within disability studies and feminism, intellectual discourse should be open to all, meaning that no one should try to create an exclusive environment.

A dynamo in her field, Rosemarie promotes disability studies at every opportunity, speaking, organizing, editing and writing, making contacts and connections, motivating everyone around her. "I'm naturally very social and gregarious," she says, "the Mrs. Dalloway of disability studies. I love bringing people together."

She works mostly in her office at home, surrounded by totems and posters, mainly from disability conferences. She recently came back from Turkey with a little plastic statue of the Artemis of Ephesus, not the run-of-the-mill Greek goddess representing the hunt or virginity, but a fertility figure, not exactly deformed though her torso is covered with a pattern of imbricated eggs, her gown with bees. On one wall hangs a reproduction of a Mary Cassatt painting of two women having tea. "It's as if there were a place for me in that painting," she says. "My real professional self is having coffee or lunch or dinner with colleagues. I even love committee meetings." People at the National Endowment for the Humanities started her on collecting disability figures, four so far, including Barbie's friend Becky in a wheelchair, Becky as school photographer.

"My students don't have to accommodate my disability in any way so it doesn't come up," she says. "It just is what it is because it's so visually evident. Most of us who are disabled and consider ourselves capable in the world have had to identify against the disabled label," she says, "so to embrace that label is both liberating and scary. Like so many of us, I was raised in denial about my congenital disability, which was never discussed in my family."

"It's strange not seeing what a person looks like," I tell her. "I don't see a person's color or disability. How apparent is yours?"

She laughs. "I find a strange irony in my appearance," she says. "On the one hand, I think my appearance is very ordinary. I consider myself to be average-looking, middle-aged with gray hair and glasses, working really hard at not being matronly. Ordinary, I'd say, except that I have half my left arm and only four fingers on my right hand. In other words, you can really find me easily even though having an arm missing is not like having a head missing. Still, it's quite obvious and it can take people aback, sometimes freaking them out. When I was a teenager, I must have had my right hand on my face and a kid in my class blurted out: 'Do you know you only have four fingers?' I'm very aware of who is looking where and when, when they notice the absence of one arm. The book I'm now writing is about *the stare,* an important definer of the relationship of the so-called ablebodied to the disabled. Anyway, people sometimes become very uncomfortable regarding my arm, staring, then jerking their eyes away, and usually only later noticing the incomplete right hand."

In a speech on the way disability is portrayed in popular photography that she gives in different venues around the country, Rosemarie talks about staring. "In contrast with other forms of casual or disinterested looking," she says, "staring estranges and discomfits both people engaged in this awkward partnership. Starers gawk with abandon at the prosthetic hook, the empty sleeve, the scarred flesh, the unfocused eye, the twitching limb." She points out that in many societies it's considered rude to stare. The blatant stare of "normals" directed toward the disabled is considered aggressive, demeaning and unwanted, as is the lewd sexual leer of men toward women.

On the other hand, many disabled people's experience, including mine, of being fixed by a stare depends on who is doing the staring. A child's exploratory stare can express the innocent wonder of absorbing something new, while a sneering or disgusted gawk underlines the perceived difference between us, the dynamic of staring defining the starer as normal and the object of the stare fair game as an object.

"Will the staring book or any other of your books include your personal experiences?"

"Though I respect many of the disability memoirs I've read," she says, "I have no desire to write one. I'd never deny my disability but I have no need to personalize it. I have noticed, however, that if you're a denier, people cooperate in your denial. I don't want to be sentimentalized or patronized and I have a good nose for smelling that out, but by identifying myself as disabled, I open myself up to that kind of thing."

Having been born with her disability as Adrienne Asch was born with hers, Rosemarie defines the huge difference between those of us who have come into it later in life and those, like her, whose disability is congenital. "If you have a congenital disability you tend not to experience it as loss," she says. "I truly don't feel a sense of not being able to do things because the things I can't do I simply never did. A congenital disability creates a sense of one's self as complete, which works against a narrative of bodily transformation and catastrophe that I read in a lot of other people's disability stories. When I read disability memoirs whose problems occurred later in life, I realize how different those stories are from mine.

"When you have a disability from a very young age," she continues, "the way your parents frame it is important. The pattern seems to be that the parents say: You are not disabled, there's nothing wrong with you, you're as able as anyone else, which is, on the one hand, very positive and enabling. On the other, it requires you to identify against a group, so you become a kind of success story and your success depends on being different and better than those other people whom you really know you're like. I've found that this is quite common, not just my own family's neuroses."

"Did your disability lead you into disability scholarship?" I ask her.

"My life was shaped a lot more by being a woman than a disabled person," she says. "I was a late bloomer in terms of disability studies, having done marriage, children and all of that first." She had a master's degree from fourteen years before, and only after raising her children did she apply to a Ph.D. program at Brandeis. "The social constructions of disability are logical extensions of the theorizing of gender," she says. "I still use this as a template for talking about disability. Feminism politicized me, making me understand that my individual struggles, the personal liabilities, weaknesses and neuroses, weren't personal at all."

The notion that disability is not something that must be cured or prevented places disability scholars and activists at odds not only with physicians and genetic counselors but with a lot of feminists. "While feminists argue for reproductive choice," Rosemarie says, "society's prejudice against the disabled practically forces women to abort a fetus suspected of having a disability. That doesn't mean that all disability activists would say there ought not to be genetic testing."

When it became clear to her that no one else was talking about disability from the viewpoint of gender, race, ethnicity and class, she dropped her earlier intentions to write a doctoral dissertation on Yeats and to study romantic poetry. Instead, she decided to write about the way disability was represented in literature. Though a lot had already been written, it seemed to her to be entirely from an unpoliticized perspective. "Lameness was a metaphor for castration," she says, "another one of those worn-out, unchallenging views." She became very aware of characters as disabled people. No one else had talked about it. "It was exciting, heady and fun," she says. While still in graduate school, she wrote on the novels of Toni Morrison, each of them replete with disabled characters. Many critics had detected a literary gold mine in terms of gender and race in Morrison's books but no one had seen it in terms of disability. Rosemarie put together an analysis of how these characters operated, and when this caused a stir, she began to understand that she needed to do more than her individual work. She needed to create a field that would give the work a context.

"I learned that disability studies existed in sociology and anthropology, in rehabilitation and government. My task was to bring it into the humanities. But I discovered that it's hard to work where there is no institutional framework, because there are no conferences, no academic positions defined in this way. So I had to create an institutional context. By using the structures of our profession, calls for papers, for conferences, calls for published collections of essays, I began networking via the Modern Language Association, the American Studies Association, the Internet listservs and bulletin boards, and thus I discovered the few others who were also doing this work in isolation." They began to infiltrate the profession, running on their instincts, proposing panels at conferences, editing books.

One of the major interests in the humanities is identity, another the relationship between the body and the word. Disability was a good fit into those categories in fresh ways. For twenty years academics had been talking a lot about race, gender, ethnicity and sexuality. Disability now entered the discussion for the first time.

I ask her views of identity politics, adopted by some groups, vilified by others.

"Identity is a little bit like nationalism," she says. "It's highly problematic theoretically because it can produce separatism, based as it is on the idea that somebody is different from somebody else. But when you press the concept of identity hard, it's fragile and problematic, women obviously being more than just women, a disabled person a lot more than just that. The nonintellectual argument against identity is 'we're all Americans, so why take it further?' It's disruptive. The more intellectual and sounder argument is that identity can be a very coercive category, leading to political fragmentation and division. Also, identity is almost always conferred from the outside. If you're stereotyped into the disability identity, you have to reimagine what it is to be a person with a disability so as not to accept societal definitions."

She tells me that she used to have to beg to be on panels in conferences. Now she gets a lot of invitations, even as a keynote speaker. Recently, the National Endowment for the Humanities funded an institute where she and historian Paul Longmore trained twenty-five academics from around the country. "One of these scholars was an anthropologist," Rosemarie says. "Several were philosophers who wanted to fold disability into the way they teach ethics. We had historians and scholars of religion, several literary critics, a couple of people from performance studies, some from women's studies. They ranged in rank from full professors to relatively fresh scholars. Some had disabilities and were coming out for the first time. By studying disability as a historical category, it opened the way for people with disabilities to enter the academy just as gender studies opened the way for women, race for blacks."

A couple of months after Rosemarie's institute had run its course, I talk to Paul Longmore again. Post-polio syndrome affects his arms and lungs and vision. He uses a ventilator to help him talk. "If it hadn't been for the disability rights movement and all that it has accomplished," he says, "I would be in a nursing home rather than teaching history and co-leading the institute." He tells me that the National Endowment for the Humanities had sent a program officer to see what this institute they had funded was all about. Their fear was that the participants were concerned solely with identity politics, that they were trying to get legitimacy through the Endowment's academic credentialing.

"The NEH officer sat in on everything," Paul says, "and after a couple of days, told us of his amazement at the intellectual seriousness of what we were doing. He realized that we were dealing with a set of issues that not only have to do with experiences and the social standing of people with disabilities but issues with vast implications regarding cultural analysis and social arrangements. We were addressing all the traditional questions that the liberal arts had always addressed. This kind of study via disability has implications for all disciplines."

While their institute was still in progress, the *San Francisco Chronicle* ran a piece that, in trying to achieve balance in their reporting, found a man in a conservative think tank who admitted that he had never heard of disability studies but accused them anyway of being nothing more than another group seeking to be pitied as victims.

As we talk about the importance of not only the topic of disability on campus but the presence of disabled people there, Rosemarie tells me a story of a recent job opening for an English professorship at another university. "There's a very structured way that a department conducts a job search, following certain guidelines," she says, "but one thing a school has to do is provide accommodation." In this case, a blind candidate applied and had to decide how much and when to disclose. At her campus interview she gave them a list of accommodations she needed. The department interviewers realized that they had many nondisabled candidates so they asked themselves why they should mess around with anyone who is blind. How can she do the job, who's going to meet her at the airport, how is she going to find the bathroom? They decided that she wouldn't be happy at their university. Six hundred fifty people applied, fifty made it to their short list. Why bother with the complications of this blind woman? How would she fit in? And what about the extra expense? So they decided to leave well enough alone and go on to another candidate.

Rosemarie says her belief is that if there is some awareness, if disability has been established as an issue of integration and an inclusion priority, then the administration would have gotten the point, understanding that the person would be the only blind person in the department, making an interesting diversity issue, even a draw for students. Perhaps she would be a person who could teach disability studies, fitting right into the way they teach gender and race. Maybe she could really offer something new and different. Maybe it would actually be a privilege to have her. "The point is that if you reframe disability as a diversity issue or a category of difference or inclusion," Rosemarie says, "and they see it that way rather than wonder how this is going to work, well, it becomes a matter of consciousness-raising. It's so easy for them to stop at thinking: My God, if it were us, we wouldn't know how we would teach if we were blind, and then they start thinking of it not only as a confusing and unsolvable problem but an expense. The fact of disability studies on campus helps solve this problem.

"I'm an optimist constitutionally rather than in terms of the evidence," she says. "The ADA, its logic and its presence, is basically transformative. I think the country is ready to look at disability as a political issue, though just like feminism, there's a backlash, meaning that things will go slowly. There's a lot of work to be done and there'll be a lot of resistance, but I think that most people are of good will. Even so, I think it's very important to be evangelical about it. It's very hard to explain that the ADA is a matter of political right and integration, not charity, not inspiration."

A powerful example of the academy as a force in identifying cases of exclusion and blatant discrimination is the teaching of the history of American immigration, which chronicles the policy of automatically turning away everyone who was sick or disabled as they showed up at Ellis Island and other entry ports. Obviously, they were expected to deplete the treasury, spread misfortune into the breeding stock and probably not contribute much of anything. Through disability studies, the knowledge of the existence of such policies will seep into the consciousness of American historians, and will work its way into the classroom and the general population just as race and gender did.

In the academic culture, the opposition maintains that the academy should be about objective learning, literature about aesthetics. Politics, they say, has no place. These old, entrenched elements are the worst adversaries of disability studies, seeing disability as the straw that will break the camel's back. "First we had the women coming in," they say, "then the blacks, the homosexuals, and now we've got the cripples. When is it going to end?" There is also an unfortunate competition among other minority groups, who say that in an economy of scarcity, disability is going to take a big piece of the pie from them.

"Thinking of the parallels of the older race and gender movements," Rosemarie says, "what is happening in the newer disability movement is reaping the benefits from the excesses and oversimplifications and naiveté of feminism at its beginnings. Using feminism as a model, we have the experience of feminism becoming more sophisticated, more self-aware. We don't have to go through that long, evolutionary period."

As for me, I must admit that there were times when the morass of identity politics, immersion in the literature of disability scholarship, a feeling that disability was the sole focus of my existence, threatened my equilibrium. In the midst of this crisis, I began late one evening to read Samuel Beckett's novel *Malone,* which washed over me like nectar, sweeping away everything that was bogged down by scholarship, theory or ideology, everything that was tinged with sincerity or correctness, humility or goodness. Just in time, I was swimming in Beckett's sea of purity, the absurdity of existence, the art and dream that underlie not just the pedestrian struggle for sanity but all anguish. I was awash with relief at drifting ecstatically in the inner logic of irrationality.

In talking about the role of feminism in her development, Rosemarie says that when she first found it, feminism was liberating because it showed her the systemic way that gender operates. It had an effect on her life and it wasn't just a shortcoming of her particular situation. She says that she wasn't blaming gender, but gender gave her a way to figure out who she was, what her strengths were, what about her womanhood was useful, what was a liability.

"Younger women today think they no longer need feminism," she says. "They think that the patriarchy has been defeated, that there are no more issues. They benefit from the gains without understanding that it's an ongoing situation. Feminism seems redundant to them because their lives aren't that different from the men they know. But in a black college like Howard, there are tremendous rifts between men and women. The women strive for internal validity and empowerment. The question for them is: Which comes first, womanhood or blackness? Is your allegiance first with women, which includes white women, or is it with all black people, both men and women?

"Part of the notion of representation is how we define things. It's not exactly finding the right words for reality, it's creating a reality by using the words we want to use. We're more aware of that than we were twenty years ago, feminism having done this embarrassing thing, having been overly paranoid, not open to understanding diversity within the group. If we can understand that there'll be a lot of conflict within disability studies, it can be a productive conflict. Taking in other forms of identity is something feminism didn't do a very good job of."

Her next book project when she finishes *Staring* is *The Cultural Logic of Euthanasia,* about the use of euthanasia to eliminate a spectrum of human differences and create a standardized human model that will be achievable through tech-

nology, as in the human genome project, and will then ideologically triumph under the banner of eliminating disability.
"It's a highly problematic ideology," she says, "going against
what is fundamentally human variation. I want to examine the
historical elements that have led us to where we are."

Rosemarie feels strongly that activism can come as effectively from the academy, in spite of the belief that the university is an ivory tower, as from nonacademic sources such as
the law. "Teaching is unequivocally an activist pursuit," she
says. "We prepare students and teachers to go out into the
world, so ours is an important act of dissemination, determin-
ing what will be taught, what books used, what ideas considered. If, for instance, the notion of disability studies is
introduced in freshman writing courses, it will have a big impact. If in history class you have a teacher who shows that disability is one category of analysis, attitudes will be affected. I
love this work, investigating, analyzing and examining the
ways that disability is represented in the culture, with the notion that the personal is political, that images and representations have a tremendous impact on the ways that the world
operates."

INTERNAL MUSIC

CONNIE TOMAINO

music therapist

PROLOGUE

I used to have little battles with Loie, my therapist wife, part of whose therapeutic arsenal is a technique called sand tray, an art therapy in which children and adults create worlds with objects that Loie stores on dozens of her office shelves, as crowded with these knickknacks as the cabinets of the Victoria and Albert Museum in London. She calls it art therapy, while I in my snobbishness would retort that art is art, therapy therapy.

On the other hand, who's to say that the impact of art is more sustaining than the impact of therapy? Still, I thought, therapy is art's enemy, as is politics or sociology or scholarship.

But when Oliver Sacks, the neurologist and writer, suggested I get in touch with Dr. Connie Tomaino because of the fascinating work she was doing with music therapy, I had shed almost all my skepticism about the entire category known as expressive arts therapy. It had finally occurred to me that some of us, I very much included, expressed ourselves better nonverbally. So, why not use any technique at all to draw out of us whatever is stuck inside unexpressed? I realized that my difficulty is not with the idea but with the language, with the use of the word *art*. I have an equally hard time with the art of cooking or of motorcycle maintenance or of lovemaking. To snobs like me, art is resistant to easy comprehension, it is cryptic, self-referent and hard, hard, hard. When you dig deep for its meanings, you come up with more than improved self-esteem. But because I had only the breeziest of notions about the role of music in healing beyond the obvious "soothing of the savage breast," Sacks piqued my curiosity.

I had read Oliver Sacks's *A Leg to Stand On* and now thought about the epigraph he used to begin his chapter on the role of music in his recovery from a shattered leg: "Every disease is a musical problem, every cure a musical solution," quoting the dark, brooding romantic writer Novalis. With the return of his own personal melody, Sacks said, he could walk again. Walking's natural rhythm and melody came back to him, like remembering a familiar but long-forgotten tune.

Music plays a central role in my life as well. It has given me powerful pleasures. When I feel scattered, confused or in a lazy, dull mood, the sequences of musical lines can not only soothe me but order my thoughts, regroove and make sense of them. Or they may transform simple sequences in my brain into more complex ones, modifying them and enriching them. Its complexity and resistance are among music's special allures.

A few years ago, during a hospitalization for depression, I turned to music and it did indeed play a part in defending me from ongoing panic. But when the hospital first offered various art therapies, music among them, I balked. Still a snob about art, I resisted slopping around in buckets of clay or listening to easy music. But we were asked to lie down on the carpet to listen to music, relaxation music. I was horrified by the crashing of waves on sandy beaches, the mournful airiness of pipes, the maddening chime of new-age bells. "Relax," the man on the tape said in the syrupy voice it took no time at all to hate. "That's it. Good," he continued, his deft tongue flicking his palate like a butterfly landing on a kettledrum. "Good," he said again.

The function of that music was to numb, to soothe, to give momentary respite to our whirring, obsessed minds, and, if not for my near-allergic reactions to those treacly sounds, I might have profited from them. On the other hand, when I watched Connie Tomaino work with patients, I realized that this was another realm entirely, the realm of maintaining or restoring humanity to those whose humanity was hanging on by a thread. "Music is not a luxury but a necessity for such patients," Tomaino said. "It acts as a Proustian mnemonic, eliciting emotions and associations that have been long forgotten, giving patients access to moods and memories, thoughts and worlds that seemingly have been completely lost. Music opens doors to the entire thought structure and personality of the past. For some, playing or even imagining music, even the mention of an opus number, fires the brain's mechanisms of memory and allows small restorations or transformations."

It seems that our bodies can often remember what our minds cannot. Music provides a gateway to lost function. Spontaneous movement as a response to music seems to happen as a matter of course. In other words, the potential for movement may be there, as in people with certain motor dysfunctions, but the ability to initiate movement is lacking. Aside from this, a song can, of course, encapsulate an entire period of a person's life, and hearing it can restore the essence of that reality. Everyone has a hundred examples. A Frank Sinatra tune brings me back to an adolescent summer on the beach, a Mozart quintet to a fabulous year in Paris, Benny Goodman's Carnegie Hall concert to the hip-swinging joys I associate with standing in front of my easel, painting.

Connie has written that the nervous system, often compared to computers, is in fact more like a symphony orchestra, in which everything must be synchronized, harmonized, melodized. It echoes the inner music of the organism, the silent music of the body.

Knowing little about the effects of music on people whose minds were dramatically changed or stilled by severe neurological disorders, I was awed watching Connie, accordion on her lap, playing "Auld Lang Syne" or "Oh What a Beautiful Morning," then witnessing severely impaired or comatose patients return to momentary or prolonged consciousness. I realized that when internal music has been disrupted, the need for external music is overwhelming.

Some people live full, productive lives without visual stimulation, some without music. But functioning eyes and ears and a drive to use them fully provides enormous sensual and intellectual satisfactions. Sight and sound soothe, stimulate and heal. They feed our imaginations and energize the neurons and synapses of our brains. So, perhaps, smell, touch and taste. I wondered if what is accomplished therapeutically by way of music could also be accomplished by a familiar touch, the sound of a foghorn, a perfume, Proust's madeleine. But when the brain's mechanisms are severely impaired by accident, illness or age, these formerly active processes need help.

Connie Tomaino's informed reach into people's lives, sometimes just for pitifully short contact, was not intended to numb or soothe. The lessons of her dramatic reach were profound. She took me on an intense journey, showing me an extraordinary kind of patience and deep love for people who at times were only nominally present. Still, they were people with long lives behind them, replete with fading thought and experience, lives that continued to be worthy. With infinite patience and love, she transported them, even for that instant, back to fuller, richer times. It was not only worthwhile but a deeply generous act, representing for me humanity at its best.

INTERNAL
MUSIC

Connie Tomaino is the director of the Institute of Music and
Neurologic Function at Beth Abraham Hospital in New York
City. She has just moved into her new office, still piled high
with unpacked boxes, CD players and tape recorders. We are
a little cramped as we sit facing each other, for the relatively
small space also accommodates a piano, all kinds of percussion
instruments, another keyboard and the accordion she uses
most often in her music therapy sessions. Through her windows she can see the Bronx Botanical Gardens, where she and
her colleague and mentor, Oliver Sacks, walk and talk during
his Wednesday visits to the hospital.

Silently fingering her accordion, Connie observes that for
her, a deep understanding of music came late, well after she
had become a good instrumentalist. She is probably one of
about four people in the country who are looking at the neurological aspects of music and the recovery of function. Most
other music therapy is psychotherapeutically oriented, while
her work is predicated on the assumption that our bodies can
often remember what our minds, when severely disturbed, no
longer can, and on memory being resilient enough to restore
lost functions through music. A specific piece of music can
help a dementia or an amnesia patient recall personal information. For people who can't process or sequence memories,

music brings back to life entire areas previously unreached and unreachable.

"So picture this," Connie says, her soft voice competing with some noisy announcement over the hospital loudspeaker outside her office. "An Australian film crew wants to do a segment on music therapy. They contact me and I'm delighted. It's supposed to be part of a series called something like Health Watch or Body Works or some such thing that was popular at the time, the late 1980s.

"I'd been running a group of five women with severe dementia and that's the group the Australians decided to film. They arrived on a very hot summer day and set up their equipment. When they turned on their incredibly bright lights, all five of my women fell fast asleep." Connie sits demurely, like a proper schoolgirl, her hands on her lap. Only her eyes betray the delight with which she recalls the scene. "So the subjects of the film were snoring away," she says. "The new PR man that the hospital had just hired was anxious, the film crew totally stumped. 'Don't worry,' I told them. 'I know these women well. They each have what I call a contact song.' 'A what?' the cameraman asked. 'Listen to this,' I said, and I played 'Let Me Call You Sweetheart' on the accordion and up popped the head of one of the women, totally awake, answering questions, singing along. The woman next to her was not only suffering from severe dementia but she was totally blind. Her head was thrown back rigidly and she was making disturbing gurgling sounds. So what did I do? I played 'When the Saints Come Marching In' and she snapped to, her head erect. She was awake and aware, telling us where she was from, one of the Carolinas, I think. One by one, these incredible women responded to the music that meant a lot to them. Afterwards, they retreated back into their dementia."

The picture of the five women sleeping under the klieg

lights is poignant, the resolution of the scene amusing, upbeat. But I wonder if being brought back for a matter of minutes isn't more of a game than a significant contribution to those women's lives.

"For me, reaching people who seem unreachable, even for a very short time, is momentous," she says. "I'm quite sure it is for them too."

Connie Tomaino is small and compact. Her curly hair sits up like a halo around her head. Alive with stories, observations and a most articulate knowledge of music and brain function, her words are spiced with a Bronx accent as savory as Genoa salami.

"There was never a question about helping others," she tells me, "it was simply what one did. I knew from the beginning that life only had meaning when you were helping other people."

All the kids in her family were expected to do work that served people. She and her siblings could be doctors, nuns, nurses or missionaries. "Even the brother who works in business spends every off-moment volunteering in hospitals," she says. Her father, who ran a fruit stand in the Bronx, worked hard six days a week, and on the seventh, he was running around doing things for others.

Connie worked with Down syndrome kids while she was still in elementary school, then, much later, in a small nursing home in Brooklyn, with Alzheimer's patients. "They were agitated," she says, "unaware of their surroundings, yelling, screaming, seemingly unreachable, yet I discovered early on that they responded to music."

In the mid-1970s, when Connie chose music therapy as her field, it wasn't the first time her parents had to find a way to understand her or her obsession with music. There was the trumpet. She would come home from school and run up to the attic to practice. "My mother used to cry, 'What are your children going to say about a trumpet-playing mom?' Once, when I was in high school," she says, "my mother and I got tickets to a show called *Dial M for Music.* We watched Dizzy Gillespie, a guest artist, blowing the trumpet with his cheeks bulging. 'See, see,' my mother cried, 'that's what's going to happen to you.' " She laughs. And later, her parents would say gingerly, "So tell us again what you're going to do. Play music for sick people?" Being the first woman in her family to go to college, this decision wasn't looked on with much hope or pride. "In fact," she says, "they thought I was nuts. 'If you're so smart, why can't you be a teacher or a scientist?' they wanted to know."

She knew no one in the field, nor was there much of anything written about it. The fact that there was no competition, no set path, gave her the impetus to try it. The hard thing was how to justify her choice. "People said that I was reading too much into this, that I meant well, but shouldn't be projecting my own hopes into terminally damaged individuals. They said that it was bad for me, that I couldn't be a good therapist if I were so totally involved.

"And every time I came home from college, my parents wanted more clarification. 'Say again what you're going to do, Connie. What is it called?' My father asked all his customers if they had ever heard of music therapy and they were as puzzled as he. Now, my mother reads stuff about my music therapy research and is proud of me, saying, 'Hey, this music therapy stuff is really catching on.' "

Music therapy began in this country about 1950, when doctors going into VA hospitals found they could reach fairly unreachable people in catatonic states with music. Music therapy associations and college programs were initiated as scientists began to delve into the reasons why, when and how music helped.

Still, as Connie points out, "When I started my dissertation several years ago, not much if anything existed in the literature on music and memory or on memory function. Everything then had to do with cellular processing. In the past couple of years, a lot of books have appeared. Brain research is now showing us that we have a lot of control over our destiny once we understand how the brain works, and how to take advantage of all these skills and abilities that we have and don't even know we have, like self-healing and wellness and pain management, processes that don't require outside analgesics. In fact, we are learning that, through music and guided imagery, we can stimulate our body's own opiates.

"Being here at Beth Abraham was a fortuitous circumstance," she says, "because this place gave me the chance to work with neurologically disabled people. The full impact of music in these people's lives first hit me because of Oliver Sacks. I joined him in observing and working with the post-encephalitic patients he described in *Awakenings*." The L-dopa awakenings happened in the 1960s and when she came to the hospital in the 1980s, there were very few of them left. "I was touched seeing the way he interacted with patients, taking their hand, talking softly, gently, with enormous compassion. I was working with one of the survivors, now an old woman," Connie says. "Her tongue was moving in and out of her mouth. She was babbling. She couldn't stop her weird tics but I was sure that she knew exactly what was going on in spite of being stuck in her terribly sick body and mind. I told Oliver that I couldn't bear the way people were treating her and that I thought she knew a lot more about what was going on all around her than anyone realized. That's when he gave me her old journals to read. In them, she wrote about what it was like to be in her condition, what it was like to be spoon-fed and to have the food drip down your face, to have the staff laugh about her. She wrote that just because she is the way she is doesn't mean she has no feelings.

"This was a momentous and defining moment. I was driven to find out how to reach people like her, how to find that part of them I could connect to. It became an obsession. There has to be some aspect of memory and personality still functioning even though the person can't exhibit this. The research I do now deals with music and memory.

"I'd always had a lot of respect for people but I became even more aware that no matter how debilitated somebody is, no matter how removed they seem, we can't assume that they're disconnected. Maybe it's my Catholic upbringing. Every life, no matter how limited, is worth sustaining. In this work, you have to have patience, and patience is an integral part of my personality. In this field, things don't happen very quickly or dramatically, but it is obviously incredibly poignant to witness any retrieval of memory."

In trying to reach each patient, she explores different types of music, different rhythms, different songs. "I find out from the family if there's any musical history, favorite entertainers, concerts, whatever. And then I look for responses. I sit very close, knee to knee, and I play the accordion. I do a lot of touching. I probe to see how far I can take the person and how much he might do independently.

"In the early stages of dementia, there might be some talking, but later, that stops and there's only music. In the initial stages, the goal is to maintain whatever memory there is, their awareness of the immediate present, who they are, some important parts of their lives.

"People go into rapid decline, a decline that can get a lot more rapid if we don't make any attempt to reach them. The decline is not so much based on the disease itself but because nobody is giving them anything. There is a potential for improvement of some degree and a level of awareness that's still possible. It's sort of like a balancing act. You want the person to be aware enough so that they have some quality in their lives, that they're not tormented. Besides, to deny somebody any enrichment activity is probably unethical, even though there's no funding for this kind of thing.

"One time," she says, "I was working with a young man in a coma. No one knew if he was responding to anything. He didn't even track with his eyes. We had no clues. He was Latino so we thought we'd try some salsa and other Spanish pop music. Well, his eyes started going back and forth. We called his mother and she said he hates that music." Connie laughs. "We got the music his mother said he loved. Of all things, it was Italian opera. We don't know if *Rigoletto* did it but he came out of his coma. He's in long-term care. Who knows if he would have been locked into his coma if the music hadn't been available to him."

Even late dementia patients begin to recognize where they are, their agitation and restlessness helped at least momentarily. Because they don't recognize what's on their plate, they can't feed themselves and become fearful of everything. Human contact can give them a sense of safety and familiarity. "To give someone even moments of real pleasure is worthwhile for me," Connie says.

Over ten million Americans, mostly over sixty-five, have strokes, Parkinson's, Alzheimer's. With no medical cures, their function is immensely improved by remedial and therapeutic nonmedical measures like art and music therapy. Music can also play a vital part in the rehabilitation of orthopedic patients, helping to restore former mobility. Often, where physiotherapy doesn't work in getting a patient walking or moving, music can.

Music connects to the part of the brain that processes

emotions. In people with neurologic damage, the higher processes have ceased to work, but the emotions are still functional and become the most salient feature of their personalities. With higher functioning people, the music Connie plays might be all improvisation, a creation of the patient and therapist, based on what symptoms the patient is presenting. This music can bring about remarkable synchronizations and entrainments of brain function. It can stimulate and organize lower functions in the basal ganglia but it can also heighten mental functions, as in aphasia, a condition where language is lost. With physical agnosia, an inability to make sense of the world visually, music can organize that world in a way that the brain cannot without it. And patients with Alzheimer's, who are in a state of agitation and confusion because their memories and powers to organize are failing, can find some help with music, because music is fundamental in its ability to help the brain restore identity.

"With early Alzheimer's," Connie says, "the sense of self is still pretty much intact. I'd like to believe that it is so until the end of the disease process. It's the detection of that self, the caregiver's respect for it, that can help people have a better quality of life. If we can provide them with some sense of who they are, they can maintain some sort of connection with the world around them. In my doctoral dissertation on four women with Alzheimer's, the one thing that came out loud and clear was that they wanted human contact, that they were in need of having these relationships. They held on to those couple of minutes for dear life."

When, days later, I think about my first meeting with Connie and her feelings of urgency about reaching people, I begin to understand the consequences of avoiding any person who is not easy to approach. The distance between ability and disability—between sight and its absence, a clear mind and one clouded by short circuits and corrosion of brain matter, between what is considered beautiful and what is seen as deformed or freakish or ugly—sometimes seems unbridgeable. But the reach is essential in preserving what is decent in the human condition.

"Easy for you to say," a friend tells me as I relate the nature of Connie's work. "I have a hell of a time facing a severely damaged person. Frankly, I'm scared." My friend, who is a scientist well-read in evolutionary biology, tells me that he's not proud of his atavistic attitude when confronting severely disabled individuals, but that there might very well be an inherited, genetic basis for his fear, a built-in tribal response to the unrevealed threat of "the other."

"It's easier to reach out to some people than others," I agree.

"I mean it's no problem with someone like you," he says. "You don't look blind. It's a lot easier to make contact with a cogent person than one who has trouble speaking, makes weird noises, has tremors, cognitive problems."

When I think of Connie's observation that most of her patients were once healthy people who got a virus or suffered head trauma or some other accident, which can happen to any of us, or that they simply got old, the abyss between us seems smaller and, while terrifying, very much worth attempting to bridge.

"That Australian television crew," Connie tells me the next time we meet, "came to the hospital while I was part of the recreation staff, doing music therapy half-time. About the same time, the hospital administration hired its first PR person. They'd never had anyone before who looked at our image, our outside contacts, things like that. The whole happening with our five ladies was not only remarkable for the film crew to see but also for our new PR person, who was totally amazed. 'This is really important work,' he said. 'How much of this are you doing?' I told him that this was the only group of this kind I was running because of my other job requirements. He said, 'Shouldn't you be doing more of this?' I said, 'Yes.' You see, I'd been doing it all these years and no one knew about it. So he said, 'Let me see what I can do.' "

What followed was a flurry of publicity that not only enabled Connie and Oliver Sacks to publicize their work, but enhanced Beth Abraham Hospital's image. The *New York Times* featured Connie in an article, she appeared on the TV news program *48 Hours* and was asked to be a consultant for a musical version of the play *Wings,* about a woman who had a stroke. And she had recently been named the national president of the Music Therapy Association.

"Hearing about all this," Connie relates, "the head of the hospital called me in and said, 'To tell the truth, I didn't quite understand what this music therapy was all about. I had no idea what you all were doing down there. Now that all these people are interested, I should know what's going on.' Everything was happening at once and the president asked me to speak to the board of directors to tell them some of the clinical stories. They were very taken with it and felt I should get more support and more leeway to do the work I wanted to do."

Connie notices that Tobias, at my feet, is panting. We decide that we all need air and find our way to the patio of the hospital, which is crowded with people, a multicultural garden party, the full gamut of race, age and disability. Tubes and bags hang here and there, feeding and emptying. There are loners, facing walls and staring or snoozing in the sunshine. Others are sitting in groups around tables, smoking, drinking coffee, playing dominoes. There are outpatients, day-trippers as well as those who will never leave, people with bandaged head injuries, with leg braces, in wheelchairs, hobbling on crutches or canes.

There are a lot of young men with shaved heads and tremendous skull scars, mostly from gunshot wounds. Many of the ones in wheelchairs are spinal cord injuries, a lot of inner-city young men caught up in the drugs and violence. Most of them, sometimes perpetrators themselves, sometimes innocent bystanders, come from dire poverty.

Lulled by the relative quiet of Vermont, I am a bit over-whelmed by the din of planes overhead, the garbage trucks outside, the chugging generators, the never-ending city noises that seem to bother no one else. The smells too are overpow-ering, garbage mixing with cigarette smoke. A young, hip physical therapist comes by, stops at a wheelchair occupied by a bandaged boy, slips the guy's glasses off his face. "I gotta buy these," he says. "I really want them." The kid's laughing. "Let me just borrow them for a half hour, I have to schmooze up a patient."

The kid says, "I can't believe he did that to me again."

When Connie first came to Beth Abraham more than twenty years ago, teeny pencil-sized wisteria was planted, and now its thick vines are dripping with flowers that give off only a faint scent. But the patio is planted with raised flower and strawberry beds, accessible to people in wheelchairs.

"I want you to meet Annie," Connie says. I grab Tobias's harness and we follow her. We stop at a table where a large, handsome woman is sitting alone. Annie suffered anoxia, a se-rious oxygen deficiency in the brain, as a result of a severe asthma attack. She was in a coma for three months.

Annie can raise her hands and spread her fingers a little but her hand is deformed. Not seeing this, I put my hand out to shake. Annie raises hers and we touch, my fingers grazing the back of her hand. We don't clasp because she can't clasp. "Well, we made hand contact," I say.

"Yes, we did," she says laughing, forcing the words with difficulty. Perhaps if I had seen I would have held my hand back, fearing the awkwardness of the touch, but as it is, there is no awkwardness, just a couple of innocents making contact.

"I remember the first sounds as you were coming out of your coma," Connie says to her.

Connie tells me that Annie is in her late fifties, very alert, a big woman with a big smile. She has rings on all her fingers, an ankle bracelet, brooches all over her sweater, decked out to beat the band. There is a sign she keeps at her side all the time. It says: "Don't forget to breathe."

Annie went through traditional rehab, got some movement in her arms, worked with the speech therapist. She learned to point to letters on an alphabet board and could spell out words. "About three years ago, we had a music therapy group and Annie started making melodies. We began working on exercises where she could match words to music." After that, speech therapy picked her up again, teaching her to breathe properly, to reinforce the sounds she could make. This got her voice to an intelligible level, then her tracheotomy tube was removed, the hole in her neck closed up and her speech became even better. "Now you speak all the time," Connie quips, making Annie laugh. "Music helped Annie control her sounds, change and modulate them," Connie tells me. "The music work encouraged her to turn the sounds into actual words embedded in song. She was very motivated." She turns to Annie again. "When you heard yourself, you realized you could do it."

"That's right," Annie says.

"In the spring of 1993," Connie tells me when we get back to our little table on the other side of the patio, "we planned a music therapy conference at the hospital. It was to be a way of introducing my work to the board as well as trying to network with some of the music industry people like the National Academy of Recording Arts and Sciences to see if they could help us. Until then, Beth Abraham Hospital had never put on a conference and now I made it happen. We had standing room only. It totally blew our board away. They had no idea.

The board of governors of the music industry group had also come and, at a brainstorming lunch with them, our president announced that we would start an institute. It was the birth of the Institute of Music and Neurologic Function.

"When the hospital realized how much we had going for us here, they decided that this music therapy work should be separate, a department of its own. At this point, they realized I was making less money than some regular staff. I was the lowest-paid person on the research team and the development person started advocating for me. We submitted a grant proposal to study music and memory, a grant that had not only been refused in the past but the refusal came with a suggestion that we never apply for this again.

"I was pregnant at the time. I gave birth in September. By then a very large grant had been approved, enabling the hospital to provide me with a huge salary increase, making life a lot easier for my husband and me. Up until that time we'd not been able to afford full-time day care and suddenly everything changed. I came back from maternity leave in January 1994 to a whole new ball game, a brand new institute and a hospital department."

We head back to Connie's office. The halls are packed with physical therapists and attending nurses. Blown-up framed articles from magazines and daily newspapers about Connie and Oliver and the music therapy program decorate the walls. They are the undisputed stars here.

The hospital is run by United Jewish Philanthropies and is religiously orthodox. On this Friday, there are services ongoing in the chapel. Six old men with yarmulkes are davening around a table laden with Manischewitz wine and cookies. In the hall, the candy machine has a large sign glued to the front. "Absolutely Not Kosher," it says.

Back in her office, as Connie looks through a couple of the unpacked boxes for a copy of her dissertation, I ask her when she uses music on a structural rather than a nostalgic level.

She tells me that music engenders movement of a specifically human type that goes to the roots of our being and takes shape in our gestures, in our deepest and most intimate responses. "The concept of movement to someone who has been left immobile by head injury or stroke is daunting," she says, "but spontaneous movement in response to music seems to happen as a matter of course. In other words, the potential for movement may be there but the ability to initiate movement is lacking. Thus, rhythmic cueing has the implicit possibility of initiating gait, anticipating and organizing the next step.

"In parkinsonians," she continues, "the affected parts are the basal ganglia, the organs of succession. If damaged, a patient has problems with sequences, with consecutive movement. Music can substitute for this basal ganglia function. It can become a template for organizing a series of movements. Because the music used must move the patient emotionally, it is the music particularly suited to the individual that works."

Connie tells me that there is new research coming out now that deals with auditory cueing, especially in Parkinson's and Huntington's chorea and some kinds of ataxia involved with involuntary function like balance, conditions where there's an unrealized connection between the auditory system and the brain stem. In such cases, there's a way of cueing and organizing movement, the musical rhythms driving auditory rhythms. To a metronomic beat, a parkinsonian who can't take a normal step begins to walk perfectly. Different people react differently to rhythm, some to the beat of a marching band, some needing an anticipatory loud beat to get started. For the latter, it's the anticipation of the beat that drives their motor system.

With Parkinson's, there is now evidence that the brain is setting up some sort of internal clock and responds to the cueing of a beat at a certain frequency. Neuroscientists who are doing CAT scanning also see this happening. This allows the person to anticipate when the next beat is going to arrive. That expectation cues the motor cortex, and here music can play a very big role.

For people who have had a stroke where the language areas have been damaged, or in the case of expressive aphasia, where comprehension is intact but the ability to execute language has been damaged, it now seems possible to enhance speech function by singing to their right brain. In aphasia, a person loses the ability to communicate verbally but can still sing songs, the centers of speech being dominant in the left temporal area while singing is in the right. There is clinical evidence that people start recovering the ability to use words, to use phrases, spontaneously. "I think that one of the things I'm best known for," Connie says, "is my studies of music and the auditory function. Everybody else is in psychotherapeutic treatment, early ed and special ed, but my work is really news to a lot of people.

"Nothing is localized to one part of the brain," she says of her patients. "There's constant cross-talk. Take the man who couldn't walk but could dance. It isn't just the motor cortex that's involved but a whole group of locations dealing with the subtlety of movement."

She tells me about a man who could do little, sat around all day, walking only with assistance. Suffering from extremely poor balance, he stumbled and shuffled, tiring easily. At one point, Connie played some upbeat dance melodies and the man jumped out of his chair and danced for nearly two hours. Later, his daughter told Connie that he used to dance at the Savoy Ballroom. His ability to dance was a lot better preserved than his ability to walk, and dancing eventually aided his physical recovery.

Neurologically, there are two different types of memory.

One is declarative, predominantly cognitive and fast, an exact memory of time and place, which can be declared or brought to mind as an image. Then there is procedural memory, slowly acquired over time from enactments of a skill or task, including motor skills, cognitive skills and simple conditioning. Most music responses can be attributed to this procedural memory. That's why people who used to dance can still dance, no matter what the neurological damage. Those who have lost their memories of other events in their lives can remember music well.

"My painting probably engages altogether different processes," I tell her, "but nowadays it's almost entirely based on gestures, which had apparently cut a groove in my brain. In other words, my arms and hands, probably my whole body, remember how I once painted a human figure."

"The body does remember," she agrees. "Neuroscientists are just beginning to do brain imaging technology, to map specific responses to music. By using various types of musical cues, they've begun to identify some of the pertinent networks in the brain for auditory processing."

For example, one group of scientists is investigating the responses to classical piano pieces compared to very rhythmic poetry. Both are rhythmic in nature but one is melodic, one verbal. They're beginning to understand properties in brain function that wouldn't normally be associated with music. This new knowledge concerning the connection between auditory processing, motor function and memory will lead to a better understanding of how the brain works and the role that music may play in enabling such responses to take place.

"One of the neurotransmitter dopamine's effects is to stimulate motor function," she says, "so if someone is lacking in dopamine, he may think about wanting to move but can't actually move. He can't switch on the execution of the function. Something about listening to the music and processing it, possibly through another neural network, may cause the release of enough dopamine to turn on the motor system. Brain mapping will eventually explain how it works. For now, we simply know through observation that it does work."

It has been shown that speaking lights up certain areas of the cortex, particularly on the left side. But with music, there are subcortical as well as cortical responses to rhythm, harmony, a key signature, instrumentation, range and frequency. It has also been noted that musicians exhibit a more analytical response, a left-brain process, when listening to music, whereas nonmusicians will show more activity on the right side of the brain.

One area of the brain, the reticular formation, is concerned with the regulation of cortical electrical rhythms. There are many connections between the reticular formation and the auditory pathways, and it may be that the rhythmical component of the auditory input has an impact on the entire cerebral cortex, responsible for all the higher intellectual functioning such as speech and vision. The auditory nerve does have an immediate connection to the midbrain, the limbic system, the brain's emotional center, whose action can be observed when a song makes a patient alert, making her smile or cry. First the rhythm helps focus the person's attention, then the melodic line and harmonies stimulate the emotional response. "If we can understand the pervasiveness of music processing in the brain," Connie says, "then we open up a whole different understanding of how the brain works."

She tells me of another client, a young man in his late teens, shot through the neck and spinal cord in a gang fight. Though he seemed totally unresponsive, his parents were convinced that their son was aware enough to warrant the administration of passive exercise, lifting and stretching him to prevent his muscles and joints from becoming rigid should he regain function. "I couldn't tell looking at him if he was aware or not," Connie says. "His eyes seemed to register nothing. His parents told me he'd recorded his own rap music just for himself and his friends. As we listened to his tapes in the music therapy studio, we noticed that something in him began to change, that his eyes moved and he began to perspire. Moments before we heard a gun fired on the tape—the song being about one of his brothers shot in a gang fight—tears began flowing down his cheeks. He knew what he was hearing, even anticipated what was coming in the song. The scary part was that he was aware but locked into a body unable to respond. But the music was getting in and registering even though nothing else was.

"As a person develops in childhood and throughout life," Connie says, "the neurons in the brain continue to form connections with various areas of the cortex and other brain structures so that the learned responses can be saved and recorded for future use. Our neurons develop a series of networks with other neurons to allow a response to take place speedily and faithfully. In neural network theory, there's a lot of interest in how the pattern and connection of these networks form. For example, does the sequential pattern of repetitive signals eventually develop into a stored memory? Because the auditory system has strong connections to subcortical neural networks, the signaling that hypothetically takes place when a person with dementia hears a familiar song stimulates these emotional and perceptual centers of brain activity, thus giving access to otherwise lost function. The time-oriented rhythm of our internal nervous system that allows us to remember how to accomplish a task next time around is a predictable sequence, and that's exactly what music is. When this very rhythmic, very well organized outside signal is paired with internal perceptions that need signaling to be activated, the brain is enabled to make sense of it all. The two processes reinforce each other, music and emotion having always been connected."

Later, as we stroll in the Botanical Gardens, I try to imagine the intensity of Connie's work. "Can you leave all of that behind when you leave the hospital?" I ask.

"I have a whole other life," she says, "and need to be present for my kids, my husband, my musical activities. I have a five-year-old and an eight-year-old at home. But my work really enriches the rest of my life. I tend to be a very quiet, patient person. It takes training to sit back, not control, let things happen. I'm good at that and carry it over to my children. I let them be who they are. I allow their differences to develop instead of yelling and controlling or saying this is the way it has to be. My work situation has allowed me to be very flexible in my life."

As a professional trumpet and cornet instrumentalist, Connie plays with several ensembles, a church baroque group, a woodwind group and a brass quintet. Working in the schools, she introduces kids to the various brass instruments. Her husband plays baritone horn, trombone and tuba.

Most summers, from Memorial Day weekend through the first week of August, Connie and her husband join in a Westchester County wind ensemble for two or three concerts a week. "In our White Plains concerts," she says, "we have no idea what's on the program until we meet for the forty-minute dress rehearsal. Luckily, everyone is an accomplished musician so we rehearse only the nuances with the conductor. I love playing all this music. The only thing I feel bad about is that my kids get bounced around a bit with both of us playing.

"Did I tell you," she asks, "that I got this really nice award? It's from a group called Women in Music. I was amazed. My mother and my older brother came to the ceremony. That was wonderful. I love all that I'm doing. People think I have absolutely everything, my doctorate, my kids, the music I perform, travel. I affect my patients profoundly and they affect me. I have a husband who makes sure the kids are fed. He's a great musician but we don't compete, and when I'm overwhelmed with my hospital work and haven't the time for the reading I need to do, he does a lot of my reading for me. I have a great family." She pauses and smiles. "I guess I do have everything."

Recently, Connie Tomaino was promoted to vice president for music therapy at the Beth Abraham Family of Health Services, in addition to directing the Institute for Music and Neurologic Function.

"We as clinicians observe responses which often can't be rationalized or objectified through scientific means," Connie says. "Only when technology improves will we start to know exactly what neural processes are taking place. But if we could better understand how music affects brain function, we could have a better window into brain function itself."

NEIGHBORS

DAVID WERNER

biologist, health educator

PROLOGUE

In spite of a lot of positive rhetoric that tries to be universally inclusive, international disability organizations are focused primarily on the world's middle class. The membership of these organizations is comprised mainly of middle-class people whose well-meaning efforts emphasize the issues they know and live, such as accessibility and equal rights, rather than meet the essential but very different needs of the world's disabled poor. Even when trying to help Third World populations, the management of these organizations pays inordinate attention to fixing up cities to make them accessible for wheelchairs because most of the disabled use wheelchairs, although in the world today 90 percent of those who need them don't have them and must function without them.

What is seen as essential here in the privileged First World is altogether different elsewhere. There is a cartoon in one of David Werner's books in which a UN supervisor arrives at a little village, comes up to a mother who seems very sad, and says, "I've got good news. We were finally able to get a hearing aid for your deaf daughter. And we're going to be able to get her into a school." And the mother says, "I'm sorry but she just died yesterday of diarrhea and hunger."

In this country, the struggle to achieve certain rights, more evolved attitudes toward disability and the distribution of some technologies, albeit mostly to middle-class clients, has come as a result of a great deal of toil on the part of the disability community in general and its activists in particular. The progress that has been made derives from unusual conditions such as great wealth, power and the concomitant feelings of entitlement. In many other parts of the world, high-tech innovations are not an answer. If one's life takes place closer to the ground than from chair level, mechanized wheelchairs don't help. A screen-reading computer program has no use where computers play no part in everyday life.

My own life began in Europe, and when as a little boy I came to America, I saw this country with a refugee child's worshipful eyes as the haven that in fact it was. Later, when as a young man I went back to Europe to live, my appraisal was mediated and broadened. Because of my early encounters with nationalistic and ethnic hatred, I found nationalism, parochialism, any kind of narrow, exclusionary views intolerable. My value systems had evolved not only in my politics but my art. Seeing art history through the lens of French, Italian or Spanish chauvinism gave me a better sense of proportion, hence a better platform from which to create my work.

Thus, seeing America from the viewpoint of elsewhere offers a certain perspective and clarity to our own reasonable expectations. It allows for a more evolved assessment of where we have come from, where we now are and the speed with which we are moving forward. Our affluence, privilege, power and entitlement take on a somewhat different value when considered from a global point of view.

Though being blind or paralyzed or deformed or mentally disabled is in itself the same wherever it exists, the attitudes toward those conditions differ greatly, and it is those attitudes that determine inclusion or exclusion, opportunity or the lack of it. It seemed central to the understanding of contemporary views of disability in the United States to have a look outside the country and then attempt to reconfigure the situation within it. Is the poverty of the Third World equivalent to the conditions of American poverty? Do the entitlements and use of resources by the wealthy nations further pauperize the Third World? Does our world export good attitudes, useful technology, or does an unregulated free market actually contribute to the creation and export of disability?

Among our exports to Mexico, according to international health worker David Werner, are highly explosive bullets, banned by the Geneva Convention for all domestic use but used indiscriminately by Mexican soldiers in their zeal to police insurgent populations. David described amputating the hand of a ten-year-old who was nicked by one of these bullets. Had it been a conventional bullet wound, it would have meant setting a bone, but here the hand was like hamburger. "It's not hard to see how these imposed global policies contribute to disability," he said.

Cultural differences between the United States and Africa or Mexico are immense, though not always totally contradictory. With a lot of the American population believing in angels, the view of nitty-gritty political issues may be no more dreamy than that of other cultures' belief in bad karma as an explanation for disability. Werner's friend Ralph Hotchkiss, who travels the world on a mission to provide wheelchairs for all twenty-five million people who need them, told me of the complicated attitudes of the people of Uganda, from which he had recently returned. In that country, there are forty-five thousand disabled elected officials, from the township level to the federal level. Disability, then, is well represented. On the other hand, to marry a disabled person is an embarrassment to the family. Ralph told me about Sharifa, a crippled woman he knew well, whose husband was blind. "Blindness was okay," Ralph said, "and being a man helped, but her inability to walk was considered intolerable." Because of pressure from his family, the blind husband improved his diminishing status by converting from Christianity to Islam, then taking a second, this time ablebodied, wife.

In many poor countries, people with spinal cord injuries are taken to the closest hospital, where surgery is imposed on them whether they need it or not. After that, they are allowed to stay only as long as their money lasts. Because of poor nursing care, they often develop pressure sores or urinary infections that can be lethal. When the family runs out of money, totally ruined, the patient is thrown out of the hospital to die.

With this sequence of events a reality in Mexico, word got out about David Werner's mountain village disability program, PROJIMO, where spinal-cord-injured people in Ajoya are recovering, learning skills, beginning to work again and, to the surprise of many, helping one another. Mostly, the helpers are other disabled people in wheelchairs or belly down on gurneys. They weld, do machine-tooling or carpentering in the prosthetics or wheelchair shop or make specially adapted toys for disabled kids. When a mother brings her disabled child into all this activity, her expectations and assumptions about disability are challenged by the sight of adults and children, many of whom are a lot worse off than her own child. Often the enormous weight of what she accepted as her lifelong burden dissipates.

One of the wonders of Werner's disability program, the basis of its uniqueness and power, is precisely the fact of its being village centered and client centered. In the United States, too, the independent living movement is essentially spearheaded by disabled people themselves, though too often the target of its concerns is primarily the middle class. The poor and rural disabled are relatively neglected, as are those with mental disabilities, although the disability rights movement continues struggling to improve those inequities. The structures that programs like PROJIMO are trying to avoid are those, like the ones set up by the World Health Organization, that promote hierarchies of supervisors who talk to other supervisors who eventually reach down to the disabled person, the low man on the totem pole. "Those organizations are not really listening to the disabled people themselves or to their families," Werner said. "Reaching the most needy and voiceless families is the key to community-based rehabilitation in the Third World."

"The most lasting thing David has done in Mexico," said John Fago, "is to give so many people skills that can be translated into higher-paid work. It's a bizarre, rather anarchical scene down there, but a world in which disabled people can have independent lives. The PROJIMO program has spawned many other programs. In its early days, word would go out and fifty disabled kids and their families would show up. It was an amazing, very inspiring scene, but when David Werner exits Ajoya, I think that things are going to change. He's the essential visionary center, the avatar, and when the avatar leaves, often there are corruptions and distortions. Who knows what will happen?"

As for me, I wondered if it was merely raggle-taggle scraps that socially conscious, driven professional volunteers were capable of delivering, or if their work and the programs and ideas they initiated made a real difference. I wondered what in the lives of people like David Werner, Ralph Hotchkiss and John Fago had compelled them to contribute outside the United States and to serve the less privileged parts of the world.

David Werner has written several books, one of which, *Where There Are No Doctors,* has been translated into eighty-six languages and has passed the three-million mark of copies in print. All five of his books, including *Nothing About Us Without Us,* are a blend of teaching manual and manifesto, illustrated with his own simple, expressive drawings and photographs.

Their influence is enormous, and the royalties are channeled back into his work.

I had heard stories about David Werner for close to thirty years, from two poet friends who had accompanied him on one of his first forays into a remote Mexican mountain village to help in the delivery of health care to a rural population whose very existence had been pretty much ignored. Over the years, he remained in my mind as an obsessed, saintly figure, the picture of the barefoot doctor on muleback, traveling from one end of Mexico to the other. I was delighted to meet an entirely approachable, funny, unsaintly man with admirable politics. I was to discover that David Werner's village-based, client-run disability program, PROJIMO, might well serve as a model for the empowerment of the powerless of the world.

NEIGHBORS

In his family's New Hampshire house, once a genteel, spacious summer residence on a pristine lake, now a bit down-at-heel after a long, hard, unheated winter, David Werner tells me about his life's work, which for the most part is rooted in Ajoya, a remote mountain village in western Mexico.

He is a biologist by training, though he has performed complicated surgeries, has treated hundreds of people in his clinics and has disseminated a host of village-centered participatory health and disability programs worldwide.

Every once in a while, David and I go out the back screen door to stretch our limbs and breathe the piney lake air while Tobias runs around the house chasing squirrels. David wears leg braces, and as I hang on to his arm I can sense his limp, the result of a congenital condition called muscular atrophy, which has left him with withered muscles from elbows to hands and knees to feet. "It's not much of a disability," he says. I experience his movement as an odd gait, a kind of *marche militaire*.

The day before I arrived, he climbed Mount Chocorua, a grueling all-day hike that he makes three or four times during his monthlong stay in New Hampshire. The climb is not intended as a macho challenge, nor does its completion represent a victory. Standing on top in the late morning, with lakes and mountains all around him, is pure pleasure. Still, physical tasks are not easy. In order to turn the key to the car, for instance, he has to clench his fist around the blade of the key, then twist his whole arm.

We settle down around his kitchen table and he reminisces about first encountering the village that was to become the center of his life. He had taken time off from teaching in an alternative high school in California to hike in the mountains of western Mexico, where he could spend long days surrounded by wild orchids, exotic birds and beetles, all the beauty and diversity he loved.

"At the end of one day in the wilderness," he says, "I was surprised by the sudden onset of darkness. I was sort of in the middle of nowhere, so I began moving fast, trying to get back to the village where I was staying. As I passed one little hut off on the mountainside, the people saw me and called out to say that, given the pitch blackness and the snakes along the trails, I'd never make it. They urged me to stay the night."

That night the weather turned bad, the cold so deep that David thought he'd freeze inside his sleeping bag. The adults of the family, on the dirt floor and with only a few deerskins for cover, held the children in their arms to keep them warm. In the morning he noticed that one little kid was limping, pus running from a wound in his swollen foot. He had stepped on a thorn three months before. "Something clicked at that moment," David says. He understood that with a minimum of care at the time, the boy would have been fine. The other kids in the family, ages three and four, were developing goiters from iodine deficiency. "I was overwhelmed with the warmth and friendliness of these people and the severity of their health problems. A little naively, I though that with a little bit of intervention, everything could change."

Back in California, he mobilized all the resources he could think of and, with his students, began a year of medical study, mainly of tropical diseases. "In those days," he says, "some of my doctor friends trained us in emergency care. No chance that this could still happen today." They studied and observed. They assembled medical kits in coffee tins. They made comic-book depictions of different medical conditions and amounts and frequencies of dosages for various drugs. At the end of the school year, they took off for Mexico.

"To put it mildly," he says, "it changed the course of my life." Some of the students from that initial trip went on to other forms of service work. David settled in Ajoya, where, on muleback, he began traveling from village to village, asked to do a lot more than he could handle. It didn't take long to fully understand that he needed to train village health workers and organize a village health program.

From very early on, David Werner dreamed of better worlds, better ways to live. Even as a boy in Cincinnati, he was a loner and a maverick. "I think my disability had something to do with needing to get out of there," he says, "but it was more than that."

When he was fourteen, he befriended a young naturalist who shared David's love of flora and fauna and also his strong political beliefs. "He pulled the wool from my eyes," David says, "opened up a whole new world for me." A Quaker and a conscientious objector who had spent five years in jail for his convictions, the young naturalist was involved with the Fellowship for Reconciliation, a group of socially progressive people who sought understanding in the realm of social conflicts. One of their earliest issues was racism, and to that end they supported Koinonia, a commune in Americus, Georgia. The mixed white and black commune was under attack by its neighbors. Not only were the races living together but the rampant anticommunism of the period made them a prime target for attack. "When I was sixteen, I jumped at the chance to go down there to help out. The rednecks would stretch wires across the roads," he recalls. "They'd let the cattle out so that they'd be hit by cars and they'd drive through the commune shooting shotguns. This was my first exposure to communal living, to people throwing in their chips together instead of living a life of dog eat dog."

His father was a lawyer, so Republican that David remembers his family cheering when Roosevelt died. But in spite of this conservative ambience, his mother had a streak of the rebel in her. She loved the poetry of Rabindranath Tagore. "When she read me his 'Crescent Moon' poems, she planted in me the notion of people living in a more connected kind of way. By the time I was finishing high school I had a social conscience that was different from other kids I knew."

David and his naturalist friend took a trip to Mexico, where they collected camel crickets in the Sonora desert and scorpions and plants for biologists in California and Arizona. "I wanted to get as far away as possible from both Cincinnati and the whole country. I felt out of place in both. Somehow I developed the image that on the other side of the world, people lived in a different sort of way, that they looked more inside the person rather than at the surface. So what popped up as fitting that bill? Australia. Australia was about as far as I could get and still stay on the planet, not to speak of its special interest for me because it had separated from the other continents and had an animal and plant life that was distinct in many ways. I wanted to become a self-made biologist."

He arrived on the doorstep of a small rural university in Australia and three years later got a degree in zoology. Seeking the interrelationship between things, their diversity and beauty, he was disenchanted with the way zoology was taught. He hoped to do a master's thesis comparing different ecologies, but because he was the university's top student in biology at the time, it wanted to use him for other purposes. He was pulled off his project and put on something that involved the soil of pastures, important to cattle ranchers but of no interest to him.

"Of all things, my two professors were the world experts on the regeneration of cockroach appendages. Their laboratory had thousands of little glass jars filled with snipped-off cockroach parts. The two of them would cut off the legs of the cockroaches at different segments and then note how much regeneration had taken place. That did it for me. If that was science, I wanted no part of it.

"It's strange to look back on all that now," he says wistfully. "It was a time when I questioned everything. The biodiversity I loved, the whole spectrum of birds, insects, trees, orchids, deserts and rain forests, the whole wonder and messiness of life on the planet, I guess all of it translated into the work I've been doing ever since."

After Australia, David was still not finished exploring the world. "I had a huge need to prove myself physically and spiritually. With the Tagore poems still resonating in my mind, its locus had to be India. I went on bicycle."

In late spring, he biked from New Hampshire to Montreal, then shipped out to Europe. He biked across Italy and Turkey and Iraq, nearly dying in the desert from dehydration. He was skin and bones when he finally arrived at an ashram in northern India.

"You must have been pretty damn strong to do all that bike riding."

"I looked like a stork," he says. "I have strong triceps and biceps and thighs, but from the knees and elbows out it's very atrophied."

"Were you trying to torture yourself? St. Anthony in the desert?"

"I was just trying to get there the best I could. And I had a passion to do it under my own steam. You're right, though, it was a spiritual journey."

"I'll say."

"When I finally arrived at the Shivananda ashram, I met the chief guru's representative. I asked to stay for a little while but the only thing he wanted to know was how much money I had. I thought, 'Oh shit,' and lied to him, saying I had none. Well, he said I could stay the night and leave in the morning. So much for Indian gurus."

David ended up staying at the ashram for four months. At his initiation ceremony, guru Shivananda, an enormously obese fellow, sat on his throne while everyone kneeled before him. David was asked to stand and say a few words about himself to the guru. He spoke about the importance of reaching people who looked inside as well as on the surface. The guru looked at him sternly and, in perfect English, asked what was wrong with David's hands.

"This sounds like a Peter Sellers spoof," I say.

"Well, yes," David says, "it was curious about this great big guru who was worshiped like a god but seemed very separate, very alone. It was hard to read his emotions. Frankly, I'm not sure he had any."

David was accepted into the community and, a couple of months later, guru Shivananda asked him to come to his private sanctum. "He asked me if I liked poetry. I said I'd written some here and there, not very good. He said he'd been looking for somebody to write his life story in poetry. I said I'd take a stab at it if he'd give me enough information. He said he'd had books written about him but none of them had said what he wanted to say the way he wanted to say it. So I agreed to do it. For the next several weeks I worked on what was essentially a tragicomedy."

"Not what he had in mind?"

"Not what he had in mind. Basically I portrayed him as an ordinary man who had somehow got caught up in this image he projected and had become one of the world's most revered and loneliest people because nobody saw him for what he was, nobody saw his humanity. So by candlelight I'm reading him the poetic history of his life and, about a third of the way through, he raises his enormous hand and makes a strange sound which apparently meant I should stop."

"It sounds like you should publish this poem," I say.

"I hope I have it somewhere," David says. "I haven't seen it for years."

"You seem to relish the ironies of your spiritual quest."

He smiles. "The next day the guru invited me again to his inner sanctum. He never mentioned the poem though he did say that several officials wanted me out of there, but as far as he was concerned, I could stay forever. I was eventually thrown out but for other reasons."

I urge him on.

"I was visiting a woman, an American actress who'd gone through enormous disillusionment with Hollywood and had ended up in this ashram. She had apparently divested herself of everything, changing her whole life, but now she was beginning to question everything that went on at the ashram. On hearing about this, the officials transferred her from the room they had given her to a very hot, tiny, triangular space under the stairs. She began to fall ill, unable to sleep or eat, unwilling to accept food of any kind. She got sicker and sicker, more and more dehydrated and black around the eyes. I was concerned about her and talked to some of the officials and told them that she was sick, but nobody paid any attention. Because she was a great believer in faith healing, I told her I knew a mantra that I'd learned in another ashram upriver. In fact, I created one for the occasion. I tried to convince her that I could bring her out of the state she was in but

I could do it only if she really wanted to live. She said she did. I put my hand on her forehead and said the mantra and told her that her pain would be transferred from her body to my hand. She said, 'Oh, David, don't hurt yourself,' and I told her not to worry, that I knew how to handle it. Though I was making this all up, I chanted the mantra. I could actually feel where her pain was by the tensing of her muscles. She hadn't slept for many days and nights. I said now the pain is going out into my hands. And she sighed and went to sleep. She woke up about twenty-four hours later, exhausted and hungry and thirsty but basically well. They threw me out because I wasn't supposed to visit her after hours."

In Mexico, David found that theater was often the only way to get through to people with urgent, lifesaving messages, as at the time when village midwives had learned that city doctors would speed up labor and minimize bleeding by injecting the mother with hormone products like Pituitrin, which can be fatal to the mother and the child, causing contraction of the blood vessels, which in turn causes spasms. If the baby isn't ready to be pushed out yet, the uterus can rupture and the mother can bleed to death. More than likely, the child no longer gets the oxygen it needs and can asphyxiate, resulting in either death or cerebral palsy, blindness, deafness or epilepsy, all because of the overuse of this drug.

The reasons why the village midwives wouldn't stop using these hormones were fairly obvious but the solution was not. Birthing mothers insisted that city doctors were using it, therefore it had to be good. They also believed that it gave strength to the baby. It was the modern way and if the midwife didn't use it, the mother would threaten to go to another midwife.

"The village health workers tried to talk with the midwives," David says, "telling them it's too risky. We couldn't budge them, so we created a theater in which we put a man on stage to play the part of the birthing mother."

"A man?"

"We had to use a man because no woman would pretend giving birth on stage. The first man we used was Miguelato, the village health worker who eventually became a doctor.

"In the first scene, the mother begins her labor pains, sends her daughter to get the midwife. The mother says, 'Oh, I don't think I have the strength to push this baby out. I want some of that medicine that will make it come faster.' The midwife injects the mother with the medicine. The baby is born dead and everybody in the audience cries. At that point, a health worker comes on stage and explains why the baby died.

"In the next scene a new midwife comes and both she and the mother are very cautious. They decide not to use the medicine. Things progress slowly and the mother says, 'Maybe I should use the medicine' and the midwife says, 'No, just let it happen naturally. If the baby comes too fast it can tear the tissue.' Then a bright, rosy baby is born. Somebody under the bed goes *waa* and at the end of the scene the health worker comes out with two babies. One is bright and rosy and the other is blue and dead. And the health worker asks why did that baby die? And they reply, 'Well, because they used that medicine.' And she asks again, and the audience answers. One more time she asks why, and this time the whole audience shouts, 'Because they used that medicine!' This participatory process is, in my experience, the only way to get the message across. It's no good to just talk to the midwives. It doesn't work. You have to involve everyone."

Nowadays, David lives about a third of the year in Ajoya, above the Río Verde. He used to drive down to Mexico, but, busy as he has become, he now flies to Mazatlán, where he is picked up by a friend and delivered to his village. I guess correctly that the car was once his and he had given it to his friend. He says simply that the man needed it more than he did. Ownership seems not to matter. It doesn't pollute his life. When he's in Palo Alto, his California home, he mostly bikes or walks. He spends a lot of time in many different parts of the world, giving workshops and teaching. To some extent the workshops finance the health and disability projects, though half of them have no money and thus don't pay.

With great diffidence he confesses to having gotten a MacArthur genius grant. "The money helps a lot with my upkeep and travels," he tells me. "I'm pretty independent because of that. Both the programs in Mexico and I have always operated on a shoestring."

At the beginning, more than thirty years ago, he lived in a house way up in the mountains, about ten miles on muleback from the village. "Now, that was basic living," he says, delighted to reconstruct those early days. "There was no electricity and the water had to be carried from a spring a few hundred yards away. But it was a beautiful spot at the edge of a pine forest, some four thousand feet above sea level. The villagers helped build it in the center of a circle of small communities, and people would come from all over to the house, which doubled as a clinic. I loved that house in the mountains and lived there for many years. In spite of real loneliness, it was the happiest time of my life.

"During the rainy season the rivers would flood and there was no getting out. If there was a medical emergency, forget it. You were at the mercy of the elements and I really loved that. I need and enjoy solitude."

Eventually, he had to move from his idyllic mountain retreat because the village below was a lot more accessible to many more people, but while he lived there no one was charged for any of the health services he provided. People brought him barter, food or flowers, or they would plant or build or carry water, but there was no exchange of money. "People just gave what they had," he says.

"Would the word *monkish* describe this life?"

"I wouldn't say monkish," he laughs. "Maybe monkeyish. As in monkeys living off the land. It was lovely and simple. Sometimes I had to go see someone in the middle of the night, traveling for six or eight hours on muleback. I got to know all the mountain trails probably better than anyone else around there. Everywhere I traveled, I was welcomed. People would always run out to greet me. It was a wonderful feeling."

David just recently moved into a village house of his own. It has one large long room over a storage space. There's no kitchen so he eats most of his meals with a family next door. If he didn't, he'd have to carry water up to his room bucket by bucket.

The room is filled with artwork, most of it created for him by the communities of people he has served. On his walls are tapestries with woven inscriptions, honoring him. On the few available flat surfaces stand wooden sculptures, decorated gourds, artifacts from Africa, Asia, India, South and Central America. "It's my own little museum," he says.

The population of Ajoya has shrunk from one thousand to seven hundred, largely because of drug-running and the violence that accompanies it. Once a traditional mountain village, it has entered the new century via this unwanted intrusion. The houses are close together, the poorer houses on the periphery. It's probably the only village in Mexico that is wheelchair accessible. Virtually all the village stores, the plaza, all the public places have ramps. For this reason, David sometimes refers to it as little Berkeley.

PROJIMO, which means neighbor and fellow man and whose initials translate to Program of Rehabilitation Organized by Disabled Youth of Western Mexico, is housed in six adobe and brick buildings, functional though hardly quaint or beautiful. The cluster of houses includes a consultation area, the women's and men's dormitories with their kitchens and dining rooms, the workshops for making wheelchairs, prosthetics and children's toys, a physiotherapy area, a carpentry shop and storage rooms. Down one village street, a single bar has survived many actions and demonstrations mounted against alcohol and drugs, which have been responsible for so much misery, social dysfunction and disability in the area. "We are undoubtedly the biggest employer in town," David says. "It makes me feel good. It's a haven for a lot of people."

The unique wonder of a place like Ajoya reminds me of my last visit to Poland, a year before the end of communism. A couple of days before leaving the country, I asked our driver to take us to Laski, a school for blind children some twenty miles south of Warsaw. He was more than perplexed: He was in shock. "Mr. Andy," he said, "are you really sure about this? Laski is full of blind children. It is too awful."

My guide dog Dash was at my feet in the man's car. "Do I depress you, Mr. Marek?" I asked.

"Oh no, not you," he assured me, "but why go out of your way to be depressed? The world is full of beautiful things." Though he cheerfully tagged along with us wherever we went, including the death camps at Auschwitz, Treblinka and Majdanek, he wouldn't get out of the car at Laski, choosing instead to bury his face in the newspaper.

Inside this school for blind children, we were met by a bouncy young nun who danced us into the house, down a long narrow corridor, and into a large room decorated with kindergarten furniture, stuffed animals and huge beach balls. Two nuns floated in at the head of a chattering line of little kids and I was sure I had walked into a sequel of *Madeline.* My kid-loving dog was thrilled, his tail wagging furiously. One kid at a time was good fun, but fifteen? One of the nuns gathered the kids, all of them holding hands. "The gentleman has brought a dog," she said, "a dog who guides him when he walks. If anyone is afraid of dogs, please stand behind the table. Everyone else can line up to pet him." Most of the children lined up, breathless with anticipation, then, as Dash tried to sit without moving, one by one they touched him. Convinced that there was no danger in this dog adventure, they lined up for a second touch. When everyone was touched out, they ran around, playing games, climbing up the jungle gyms and rolling on top of the enormous, bright beach balls with the joy and security of the very fortunate.

I tell David about Laski. "Anywhere, a place like that would have been a pleasant experience," I say, "but in Poland, where everything was crumbling and hopeless, Laski was like a beam of sunshine."

"That's how I feel about Ajoya," David says.

Our Polish driver could not get out of Laski fast enough. He wiped his wet cheeks. "Mr. Andy," he said, "I have never seen anything so sad in my life. I watched these children walk into the woods, all of them holding hands. They see nothing, they are helpless, but do you know what they were doing?" He dabbed at his eyes. "They were singing songs."

The original idea for the Ajoya disability program was to serve the mountain area where there were literally no doctors, no professional services of any kind. PROJIMO attempted to break down the walls of professionalism and give a voice to disabled people. Its strength has been helping those people who have most often fallen through the cracks.

Word got out about PROJIMO, causing an influx of people from the cities. "We were overwhelmed," David says, "but it showed us what a tremendous need existed all over

Mexico." Most of the people came from poor families who couldn't afford whatever services did exist, but it was getting some patients from well-to-do families too.

The facility also had links with Project Interplast, started by Don Laub, the doctor who trained David in emergency medicine at the beginning of all this. David got a lot of professional help from people like Laub, mainly from the United States, but also from Canada, France, India and Africa. They came to teach, give advice, share expertise. Bruce Curtis, a quadriplegic who was active in starting the Independent Living Program in California, taught peer-counseling skills. Ralph Hotchkiss taught people how to make cheap wheelchairs, believing that each individual can contribute to the design of his own chair. John Fago came to teach the making of prosthetics.

PROJIMO expanded and grew to a level never anticipated, but the program slowed because the government had come into the mountain area with its own programs, run by its own doctors. "We're the only place in Mexico where five different government programs were introduced," David says, "the main purpose being to get rid of our villager-run programs, which are politically threatening. When people began to organize and take responsibility for their own health, when they began to learn skills which the professionals see as their monopoly, the Mexican government felt it had to do something about it. Then when village workers began to organize farm workers and educate them about their constitutional land rights, huge landholdings being constitutionally illegal, when the villagers began to go to Mexico City to protest the lack of land reform, that was truly threatening."

"You're a dangerous man," I tell him. "Haven't they come after you personally?"

"We've been raided by a combination of doctors and soldiers, looking for drugs. I've been arrested, health workers have been thrown in jail."

"I should think so."

"Especially since our program went from curative to preventative to the sociopolitical, into the redistribution of land."

"But I take it that they haven't come after you seriously. They haven't broken your knees."

"Well, there was a time when I was warned by the drug czar in Mexico, who told me to leave the country and never come back because my life was in danger. I think the reason that they haven't done me real harm involves different factors. For one, I've had really strong support from the larger community, and the second is that I'm a gringo and they don't want an international scene, and the third thing is that even within the government there are people who are supportive of our program and would take a stand for us."

PROJIMO started with a focus on physical disability because, particularly in a rural area, this was the greatest need. In the mountains, where life depends so heavily on physical abilities and on hard physical work, a physical disability is a greater handicap than elsewhere. In the urban areas, mental disability tends to be more debilitating. In Ajoya, a kid with Down syndrome can often do his share of physical work and be really appreciated for doing it. Because the citics weren't doing very well dealing with their physically or mentally disabled, PROJIMO reached a point where it saw more children with both physical and mental disabilities brought in from the cities than from rural areas such as theirs.

"A number of the health workers who were chosen by their village communities happened to be disabled," David says. "It wasn't so much that the people thought the disabled would make better health workers, it was that they were the only people available. Everyone else in that community, as in all poor farming communities, was doing heavy physical work. The men were in the fields, the women tending to their large families. In a way, it was fortuitous, because the disabled people ended up being great health workers. For them, it wasn't only a job. It meant gaining respect and appreciation of their community, where they'd been largely thought of as useless. And because they'd been marginalized in the past, their hearts would go out to others with special needs."

"How do you sustain all your energy and passion? Do you get burned out?"

"Well, I never married. I never had any children. I think that if I had a family of my own, I couldn't be this involved with other people."

At times it's hard to keep David on the topic of David. He is the instigator of all this, the energy behind it, but he is also a born teacher and needs to give constant credit to those he has taught, who, he says, are carrying the ball all over the world. The real heroes, according to David, are Roberto, Marcelo, Maria, Conchita, Ralph, John, Don, a whole host of others.

"One of these disabled village health workers, Roberto," David says, "became a leader of the program. He was first brought in as a kid of thirteen completely frozen up with juvenile arthritis. He had a hard time growing up. He was shunted off to the grandparents because he couldn't be productive. One night when it was really cold, his grandmother came and took the blanket off Roberto to put it on another kid. It was triage. He was being given up. The disabled are the first to go."

"How different is the concept of triage, of who should live and who should die, in Mexico from what it is here in the United States?"

"My personal view is less fanatical than what I know of the American disability movement's position, which is driven to save absolutely every infant no matter how dire its condition. I take a more flexible stance. I think there's a legitimacy to different points of view about all this. Still, I see it as a very difficult decision, playing God against your own will. I've been caught in the middle of that debate and can easily understand both sides. Even in Mexico, there are ample resources to save any life if that's what they want to do."

Ralph Hotchkiss told me of the time he was visiting the PROJIMO program and a baby was born with spina bifida. Mexican doctors refused to implant the shunt to drain the fluid from the brain, meaning the child would die. If it had been born to a rich family, the doctors would have saved the baby. "I could in no way appreciate that perspective," Ralph said, "but the others, like David, who had been in Mexico a lot longer, understood these terrible dilemmas better than me."

"I questioned what kind of a life this kid was going to have but Ralph was adamant," David says.

Questions of who should be allowed to die are, of course, not limited to rich nations. Everywhere, there is a huge spectrum of feeling about who should be kept alive, who better off dead. In the United States, there is a difference in opinion between organized disability groups like the independent living movement who feel that every effort should be made to save every single child, no matter the severity of a disability, and some of the health professionals and perhaps a large segment of society who question this.

Roberto, who was saved in spite of his grandmother's unhappy triage, had been brought to David's program on a stretcher before PROJIMO had even been started. The health workers had no experience with juvenile arthritis, and did their best with a combination of drug therapy and physiotherapy and what some people would call psychotherapy, though they called it love. Roberto became a leader of the program, doing everything from operating its donated X-ray machine to delivering babies. He became one of the founders of PROJIMO. Another was Marcelo, whom David saw for the first time in a very remote village, a three-year-old sitting in the dust, paralyzed by polio. They brought him down to

Ajoya, got him on crutches and braces, then into school. Eventually, after he became one of the founders of PROJIMO, he went back to his own village to work as a health professional.

Even though poverty in Mexico is absolute compared with the relative poverty in the First World, barriers to health care in the United States are also enormous. "Let me tell you what's been happening recently with my brother in New Hampshire," David says. "Last year, he was hit by a car and lost a leg below the knee. We've had a terrible time getting adequate attention for him. If he had money, things would have happened very quickly, but he's land-poor, his land beset by all kinds of mortgages and debts, and thus he can't get county or state assistance. The unbelievable part is that he has both Medicare and supplementary insurance, but because of bureaucratic idiocies like waiting periods, delays in payments for adjustments to a prosthesis-in-progress and for rehabilitation, the confusions of local providers about my brother's other medical problems and the hardships of living in a trailer in New Hampshire—all add up to his falling between the cracks and not getting what he needs.

"Anyway, we're taking him to Mexico, to the village disability workers who will make him a proper prosthesis, then all the necessary adjustments, rehabilitate him and I'm sure send him back home walking better than he did before his accident. And the whole thing will cost him less than it does to heat his trailer for the winter. My brother is not an easy case, but he shouldn't be left out in the cold like this."

I am stunned by the irony of this and, as it sinks in, I begin to enjoy the thought of a man from the most affluent nation the world has ever known, going to a small impoverished mountain village in western Mexico to get a proper prosthesis, care and rehabilitation.

David too is laughing. "It's like what happened to me many years ago," he says. "From the time I was a little boy, orthopedists and orthotics experts have been making me a variety of braces and other devices to help with the atrophy problems of my legs and ankles. Each device they created made the situation worse. I could hardly walk and the pain was horrible. It wasn't until Marcelo, the crippled kid we saved when he was little, started PROJIMO with me and began considering how to help me that we solved my leg problem.

"How did we do this? For one, Marcelo included me in trying to solve the problems and create proper leg braces, experimenting, adding, subtracting, adjusting until it was right. I waited thirty years for relief, and it came not from the interventions of orthopedic specialists in the United States, but from a disabled village brace-maker who worked closely with me as a friend and equal."

Stories about the personal and social evolution of Roberto and Marcelo are in no way unique. Two of the leaders of PROJIMO's disability program are spinal-cord-injured young women. Both had attempted suicide before they joined the program. One of them refused a wheelchair because she didn't want to be perceived as being disabled, but finally realized that without a wheelchair she couldn't accomplish much. She accepted her wheelchair, got married, had a kid and started a disability program of her own.

Out of all these workers' concerns about disabled children grew a child-to-child disability program. The people of Ajoya put together a building, and some of the village children made a rehabilitation playground with the understanding that the nondisabled kids could use it together with the disabled ones.

"A person who is completely normal and then becomes disabled goes through a tremendously difficult period of acceptance," David says. "And as we both know, there's a whole collection of medical hornets who try to bleed the disabled for everything they possess. People use up the money the family might have with phony cures, and they get no better and sometimes suffer further damage. It's very hard to get people to just accept their disability, but one of the nice things is that the leaders of our program are paraplegics who rediscovered life by working with other disabled people. They've become wonderful peer counselors, who try to dissuade people from dreaming of impossible cures and to get them to accept what there is."

"In Mexico, is disability believed to be a function of God's will?"

"At times," David says. He tells me the story of a big storm and a flash flood that carried away an entire family who lived way up in the mountains on the edge of an arroyo. The father tried to save his seven-year-old daughter but she was torn out of his arms by the rushing water. He lost all of his children, his wife and his mother. He was thrown into the torrent, ended up about two miles downstream and crawled back to where his house had been. When people found him, almost all the skin from his body was ripped off, and so they sent for David.

"I really didn't know what I was getting into," he says. "I wasn't well equipped for it, but we managed to give the man emergency treatment. He already had gangrene in his leg. It was gruesome but we cauterized the cut, without anesthetic, with a wire which we heated in the fire. Anyway, we saved him. Afterwards people wondered why this tragedy happened to this particular family. Basically, they said, this was a good family, so why would God do this to them? Then they started inventing bad things that the family had done. They finally came up with reasons why God punished that family. To blame God for doing this terribly bad thing was unacceptable. In India, of course, it's different. There, the cause of illness or disability can just as easily be pinned on karma."

David and I take a walk in his New Hampshire woods, Tobias bringing us sticks to throw every few steps we take.

He tells me that the lack of resources, superstition or the neglect of crude and corrupt politics and politicians aren't the only obstacles to a Third World health and disability program. When he begins talking of U.S. interference and particularly the North American Free Trade Alliance, his cheerful mood vanishes. "NAFTA has caused an economic disaster for the poor in Mexico," he says. "The spinoff is that there are now a lot more street children, a lot more crime and violence and a lot more disability from gunshot wounds. We've had over four hundred spinal cord injuries come into this little village program, all in the last five years or so. There's more drug traffic in the city but there's more drug-growing in the mountains.

"We've had problems with a lot of these kids because they're often macho, violent, drug-running, alcoholic street kids. Just because they become disabled doesn't mean they leave their habits and lifestyles behind. We've even had a couple of attempted killings, another outcome of the dissolution of these communities."

In preparation for NAFTA, the United States got Mexico to annul the agrarian reform laws in its constitution so that American agribusiness could come in. Before, there were very strict limits on how much land an individual could own. "All of this has made for a huge exodus of farm people into the growing slums of the cities," David says, "causing enormous unemployment, causing real wages to drop by forty percent, all since NAFTA."

A few years back, the United States estimated that 70 percent of the repayment of the huge Mexican debt was paid through drug money. "Knowing that," David says, "why would they want to demolish the drugs? They don't. The war on drugs is a farce. And as for this little village, we're at the end of a dirt road going back up into the mountains. It's a kind of Dodge City of that area of Mexico."

The drug traffickers began to come to the mountain villages of Mexico to buy *goma,* or raw opium, to take up north on their way to the United States. South American cocaine traffickers had discovered that taking a side trip to Mexico's Sierra Madre could be highly profitable. First the dealers hook the young mountain villagers on cocaine, then they swap them cocaine for raw opium from locally grown poppies. Through this clandestine barter, the dealers increase their earnings tenfold. Village health workers have estimated that some 70 percent of youth in the mountain area have at least tried cocaine. The profits are very small for the growers compared to the middlemen. A kilo of raw opium for which the campesino is paid only four hundred dollars sells on American streets as adulterated heroin for over a million.

For a long time, David would spend half of every year in Mexico. "Now with all the globe-trotting," he says, "life is too busy. It's interesting but not as pure, not . . ." he searches for the proper word, "not as spiritual. There was a kind of purity then in helping one another without expecting something in return. That was part of the traditional culture. It's the way I really believe people ought to live but not too many do anymore. The kind of cohesion that used to exist no longer does.

"When I first got to Mexico, people believed it was a sin to own a Bible. The priests said that *they* were the intermediaries, thus the only ones who could possess the word of God. It's interesting that both doctors and priests struggle so desperately to keep their particular knowledge as their exclusive right.

"A lot of these village people are very humble but I think that, primarily because of their television and radio contact with the outside world, they have gotten a very low opinion of themselves. They are constantly being hammered with false moods and images in commercials and sitcoms that lead to success and happiness, while they perceive themselves as not only poor but without the resources needed to feel good about themselves. As health workers, we've had to break through their negative self-image of stupidity and inability to learn.

" 'We need the doctors, the professionals, the city people to tell us what to do, how to get well,' all of them felt. To get around this, we used to play a game with people, saying: 'Suppose there was a disaster in Mazatlán and one of the doctors from there arrived in this village with just his clothing and family but with no money, no tools, nothing. He needed to stay and live here. Could he do it?' So people said, 'Well, he could do what we do, clear a piece of land, plant corn.' 'But,' we'd say, 'he doesn't know what trees to save, which to use. Not only that but when he starts to cut the wood, his hands would get full of blisters and what would he do? You've seen doctors' hands and they'd have a real hard time. So,' we'd ask, 'what would you do about it?' 'Oh,' they said, 'we'd see that the family had enough to eat, we'd help, we'd teach them.' 'Oh, you would? Well, how much would you charge them?' 'We wouldn't charge them anything. How could we? They arrived with nothing.' 'Okay,' we'd say then, 'what if you went to the city with a sick or dying child and you went to the doctor, what would he do?' 'Well, if we have money, he'll attend to the child. If we don't, the child would be allowed to die.' So they then begin to compare their values, their lives, their knowledge with those of the doctor. It's a real awareness-raising exercise.

"To me," David says, "if humanity is going to come out of all this greed and violence without destroying itself, we need to relearn the processes of caring and sharing, community and reciprocity."

BROTHERS AND SONS

JAY NEUGEBOREN

writer

MONA WASOW
ANNE LARKIN

teachers

SAM TSEMBERIS

agency head

PROLOGUE

Who or what determines which life is not worth living? It might be the genetic counselor or doctor, it might be the politician, the ideologue or, as events of the twentieth century made clear, the spirit of the time. There is a persisting seductiveness to the idea of improving the human race by selective breeding. In the Germany of the 1930s and '40s, not only the majority of the population but the vast majority of the doctors pushed toward a "pure" master race, free of the physically and mentally disabled, free of Jews, gypsies and homosexuals—a concept that loomed so large as to justify, in the minds of this majority, the right to determine who is fit, who is not, who survives, who needs to be wiped out. Just as the urge to get rid of "defective" citizens or patients is not confined to any one nation or ideology, so it isn't limited to naive or incompetent professionals. Leading academicians, physicians, psychiatrists, geneticists and biologists, individuals intellectually immersed in fields that endorse the concepts of normalcy, deviance, abnormalcy and pathology in person-fixing rather than context-changing, seem particularly prone to the kind of thinking that privileges certain behaviors, certain ways of being, functioning and looking.

In all this, there is an uncomfortable similarity to American managed-care programs that focus on the young and healthy, often denying services to the old and disabled. This time the intent is not to produce a master race but to bow to a cost-benefit analysis. Still, the same questions are being confronted: which life is without quality, who is worthy of further treatment, who is not. One of the present dangers, as it has been in all eugenically active times, is that the fate of patients is decided from a bureaucratic distance by healthy, able-bodied professionals in teams, thus shielding single individuals from the responsibility of delivering life-or-death sentences. Once, this power was in the hands of doctors. With managed care, it has shifted to insurance company functionaries.

Eugenics—this "science" of improving humanity—is the concept of defining fitness in human beings and engineering its survival by enhancing the chances that the fittest will produce more offspring than the less fit. Because of evolving eugenics theories and deeply ingrained popular beliefs regarding the hegemony of "normalcy," the mentally ill have long been looked upon as among the most threatening of the "imperfects" and thus are easily judged to be living a life not worth living.

It would be convenient to say that it was just the Nazis who pursued this, but, though it became state policy in Germany, its attraction and at times implementation existed everywhere, in the so-called underdeveloped world as well as the so-called developed one. The susceptible mind is always there, ready to act in the name of an ideology, or God's will. When people can be convinced that whatever happens to be the reigning social order is the natural order—that the inevitability of things as they are, the existing rank and privilege around them, derives from the will of God or the intent of nature or both—it is a prescription for justifying the annihilation of everything that does not conform to that order or those beliefs.

During the second half of the nineteenth century, race began to be cast as the primary moving force of human history, racial vitality seen as the essential ingredient leading toward world primacy. As science became increasingly important in European culture, the justification for this no longer needed to come from religion. Biology could then be counted on to prove the intellectual inferiority of any number of groups: Jews, blacks, women or the physically or mentally disabled. Biology rationalized the belief that criminality is inborn, or that schooling of women would shrink their ovaries, or that the social station of certain groups, such as those reduced to slavery or peonage, is natural and inevitable.

"Feeblemindedness" defined a wide range of mental deficiencies and deviant behaviors, not only among the people with schizophrenia, manic-depression or epilepsy but among the depressed, among prison inmates and residents of homes for wayward girls, among truants, paupers and prostitutes. Immigrants everywhere were considered as root causes of this menace, threatening the rapid decline in the quality of a nation's genetic stock. It was claimed that feeblemindedness, alcoholism, poverty and criminality were transmitted by heredity and were uncommonly prevalent among immigrant ethnic groups with their shiftlessness or volatile tempers. Unless immigration was limited, it was claimed, the American population would become "darker in pigmentation, smaller in stature, more mercurial." Even Margaret Sanger, mother of family planning, wrote that it was especially the poor and foreign-born who needed contraception, so as to reduce their "inferior" births. For her, "feeblemindedness" was a fertile parent of degeneracy, crime and pauperism. She warned that those who were least fit to carry on the race would increase more rapidly than people of quality and would divert funds from nobler causes to those who should never have been born.

American social Darwinists saw, and often still see, in evolution by natural selection a scientific guarantee of cosmic optimism, where those who survive are by definition those who are also most fit. Those who are alleged to be weak or different, physically or mentally, are expendable, unworthy of equal opportunity or, at times, of life. Darwin's work is thus seen to justify the moral superiority of industrial capitalism and the competitive entrepreneurial spirit. Economic competition is considered a natural form of social existence, a law of nature and a law of God. In the 1930s, going further, the Germans stressed the need for state intervention in an effort to stem the degeneration of the human species. Because it was feared that the poor and the misfits were multiplying faster than the talented and the fit, medical care for the former was seen as destroying the natural struggle for existence, so medical intervention was often denied those segments of the population. In promoting the good of the race, the Germans felt they had to put an end to allowing weak and inferior elements in society to prosper and procreate. Intelligent "racial hygiene," they thought, should eliminate the need to struggle for existence. The mentally ill were first among the undesirables. This, of course, led to mass annihilations in hospitals and concentration camps.

People found in Darwin what they wanted to find; thus racial hygiene became recognized as a respectable part of German biomedical science. The idea saw no ideological bounds, crossing easily into the progressive as well as the reactionary camp. Among American eugenicists, hardly out of step with the public at large, the sterilization of psychiatric patients was avidly supported, as it was by the German Communist party. A long collaboration between American and German scientists thrived before, during and after World War II, with American eugenics societies favoring Nazi biomedical policies and giving them substantial support. Even after the war, American eugenicists came to the aid of their murderous colleagues in Germany, helping with de-Nazification and finding jobs for them, the whole lot no longer answering to "eugenicist," now calling themselves human geneticists.

A biomedical vision of national hygiene may begin with the killing of faulty infants, as in Germany, and as has also been suggested by Peter Singer at Princeton, but it can, and has, ended with the killing of any life deemed unworthy of living. It is also interesting to consider this rage for cleanliness and "purity" in light of the human genome project, which dreams of perfectability, a disease-free, disability-free humanity, a more efficient and happy workforce, the conquest of death.

Even if the genesis of mental illness should turn out to be primarily genetic, it is the product of many genes whose locations and interactions are largely unknown. Schizophrenia has been thought to be located on this or that chromosome, each site proving to be wrong. Indeed, it may be that its genetic component has been woefully exaggerated, the multifarious environmental causes largely unstudied. For all the hope and hoopla that have been given the human genome project, its actual usefulness in putting an end to mental illness as well as physical illnesses with a genetic component is considered distant at best. Even the most optimistic studies admit that the interconnections among the genes presumed to be involved with heritable conditions may never be known. Certainly current scientific research is nowhere near knowing them. A lot of the optimism about the human genome project comes from the fact that one disease, Huntington's disease, seems to have a single gene causing it. But all the either/or questions deny the truth which is that life is usually very complex, there are no easy decisions or answers, there's not much that's predictable, and every human being is different.

For many people, confronting a mentally ill person is a dreadful prospect. It's hard to resist the impetus to flee, to marginalize or dismiss or to look from a safe clinical distance. Our built-in early-warning system alerts us, making us suspect anyone who is not like us. Many of us cross the street, turn our heads, do anything so as not to engage. We are alarmed by slurred words, tics, by the terror in another person's eyes. These signs tell us not to bother, to turn away, to flee. We know we won't understand and the effort to do so seems herculean. Not only that. Many of us have a secret terror that some form of mental illness lurks deep within ourselves, at times appearing in our nightmares, in our manifestations of irrational rage or hatred. The abyss that stares at us when reason vanishes is atavistic, terrifying. The separation between "us" and "them" is not as wide as we had hoped.

Jay Neugeboren, who until recently lived and taught in Northampton, an idyllic, progressive, enlightened college town in rural Massachusetts, told me about a group of townspeople who had demanded that the city stop a local human services agency from renovating a dilapidated building under a $600,000 grant from the Department of Housing and Urban Development. The money was intended to transform the building into six one-bedroom apartments for people with psychiatric disabilities.

The local newspaper noted that news of this had inflamed people in the neighborhood. A city councillor from the ward was quoted as saying that people were so angry that they began organizing a property-tax strike. "I've never seen neighbors so upset since a 1977 rock concert," the councillor said. "My neighborhood and ward feel betrayed by the city."

"Social programs," one woman said, "must not be allowed to come in and basically rape our neighborhood." Another resident had consulted a lawyer about putting his taxes in escrow until he could be assured the apartments would not be built. He and other residents of the ward formed a committee to raise funds, hire a lawyer, file complaints in superior court, meet with their representatives in Congress, even publish a newsletter. As a result, HUD had second thoughts about the suitability of the project.

The strong feelings against group homes are all about a feared decrease in property values and an increase in crime rates, though studies conducted to determine the validity of these fears have shown that no change in either rate has been found to exist. "If we were really interested in reducing violent crime rates," the head of the social service agency told the Northampton city council, "we should restrict the number of unmarried males under the age of twenty-five. That's the only group one can say is more violent than any other in America. It is certainly not mentally ill people, who as a group have little or no correlation with violent crimes."

BROTHERS
AND SONS

Even though Jay Neugeboren has a rich and busy family and
social life, though he is kept busy teaching and, more than anything, writing, he devotes a tremendous amount of time, energy and love to being the advocate and chief support to his
brother Robert. For forty years he has been monitoring his
brother's often short-lived, sometimes catastrophic therapies,
pushing the mental health system toward more humane responses to the needs of people with severe mental illness. For
all that time, Jay has been trekking to a seemingly endless number of institutions in and around New York City, to wherever
Robert happened to be housed—to Hillside, Creedmoor,
Elmhurst, Gracie Square, Bellevue, King's County, Riker's
Island, Mid-Hudson Psychiatric Center, South Beach Psychiatric Center among others.

"Given the forty years of psychiatric illness and the horrors that the mental health enterprise has inflicted on my
brother," Jay Neugeboren says, "the true miracle and mystery
is that he has survived with his humanity intact. After all the
failed therapies, the shotgun drugs, the punitive incarcera-
tions, I don't know what has enabled Robert to retain his
generosity, warmth, intelligence and humor.

"Recently," Jay tells me, "the psychologist from Bronx
State Psychiatric Center called me to say that people are

cracking up about Robert, who was asked to bring in a urine sample. He filled up the little cup, started to give it to the nurse, then took it back and said, 'I'd like a receipt.' It's extraordinary that given what he's been through, he can retain a sense of humor about the very conditions that have been the cause of his pain all these years.

"My interest in Robert will only increase," Jay says. "It isn't based on the sadness of his life but the wonder of it and the depth of his resiliency. I came to feel this partly as a reaction to the stereotypes. It was my anger at the world's notion of what it means to be mad, the way the world treats people who have been labeled as schizos, nuts, head cases, lunatics. You say those words and then nobody has to think any more about it. It puts the person into another, an unthinkable, category. So I respond by identifying with Robert. He's as interesting, complex, as *human* in every possible way, from the most trivial to the most profound, as anybody on the face of the earth. He has a very unenviable life, that's all."

Jay Neugeboren is a teacher and writer, most of whose thirteen books are novels. The last two, however, are nonfiction, *Imagining Robert,* a memoir of his schizophrenic brother, and *Transforming Madness,* a broader look at psychiatric illness. *Imagining Robert,* his eleventh published book, reached the biggest audience of all his books, but before it found a home it was turned down by forty-one publishers.

"I've always been a fighter," Jay says. "My mother was a bear, wouldn't take no for an answer, persevering, determined and willful, while my father was the opposite. I didn't want to be like him so I do everything not to fail. Fear of failure keeps me going."

"But forty-one rejections," I marvel.

"I've always enjoyed the fight," he says. "Nowadays the reaction isn't as fast, I won't pop up the moment after I've been knocked down, I'll wait for the count of seven. Still, I have a basic faith in my talent, my gift, my work. Also," he adds, laughing, "it's the song of the Jews. They can try to stop us or get rid of us but they won't get us all."

Judaism has played an important part in both brothers' lives. Because they were brought up together in an observant Jewish home, it gives them common ground regarding things like food and holidays. "Robert often says, 'Let's say Kaddish for Dad,' and he gets all teary," Jay says. "It's one part of our childhood we can go back to and share. Observing the Sabbath still means a lot to both of us." When Robert visits Jay on a Friday night, they light candles together. It conjures up not religion but aspects of family life, what it was, what it wasn't, what they wish it could have been. Judaism is a religion that is celebrated mostly in the home, not the church. "Since I'm not a believer in God or prayer," Jay says, "it's been a gratifying part of my life, something I connect to easily. In short, it's a world we share, and by the way, being Jewish has taught me a lot about oppression. It's not a leap for me to understand the oppression of the mentally ill.

"In writing *Transforming Madness*, one of the humbling things was meeting so many people who remind me that being distinctly privileged, whatever I've been through is nothing compared to the dark nights of the soul these people have to face all the time. How some of them have recovered is very inspiring. Meeting them, I've come to realize how far down people can go. I marvel at how in their despair, while having the shit kicked out of them, sometimes even collaborating in their own failures, they can survive, get back on the road and have a full life. I don't know where this comes from but it's remarkable."

Robert's diagnosis has changed frequently over the years, depending largely on which drugs have been successful in keeping him calm and compliant. His diagnosis was schizophrenia when enormous doses of thorazine and Stelazine calmed him, bipolar when, for short periods of time, lithium worked. He was manic-depressive with psychotic symptoms, or hypomanic, when the anticonvulsants Tegretol or Depakote, or some new antipsychotics or antidepressants like Trilafon, Adapin, Mellaril, Haldol, Klonopin or risperidone showed promise of making him cooperative; and he was schizophrenic (again) when various doctors promised cures through insulin-coma therapy or electroshock therapy or a long menu of psychotherapies: group, family, Gestalt, art, behavioral, milieu, psychoanalytically oriented psychotherapy and more.

Most often, the more chronic his condition, the more he was treated solely with drugs and received no therapy at all. "The history of the ways in which this past century has dealt with those it calls mentally ill has, for forty years now, been passing through Robert's mind and body," Jay says.

Robert has been in and out of the locked wards of hospitals where he was straitjacketed, four-pointed, confined in bare rooms on sheetless beds. Telephone privileges, outdoor privileges, smoking privileges and visitors have been sporadically denied him as punishment for his "crazy" behavior. The behavioral, punitive model of limits and boundaries, which included beatings, was largely relied on for teaching compliance, punishment for mental illness rather than therapy for it. "And the prescribing psychiatrists knew nothing or little about Robert's history or feelings," Jay says. "This is not enhancement but containment, infantilization and neutralization. What drives me crazy is that the feelings, thoughts, memories, fears and hopes forming Robert's character and identity exist but that these professionals know nothing of his evolving and becoming. They know only the chemicals, the dead end of a scientific materialism. They deprive Robert of his humanity. What kind of madness is it to throw a bunch of

drugs at somebody and hope that some of them will work?"
Jay asks. "How different from witchcraft is this?

"They do all of this partly for housekeeping purposes but
I know they also hold on to the nagging concept of cure in
the back of their minds. Don't they know that, no matter
what they do to him, Robert will not get well? The fact is
that practically none of us get well. Don't they know that's the
human condition?"

Adaptations that enhance mobility and independence exist
for most physical disabilities. A prosthetic leg can get a person
moving again, a cane or guide dog open the world to the
blind, as do screen-reading software and braille. Though economic opportunities are scarce, most of us who are physically
disabled have the technical possibility for an independent life.
But unless one is a particularly high-functioning person with
schizophrenia, autism or other serious mental illness, chances
are that he or she will not only never get well but will be
functionally dependent on a network of families, case managers and attendant care throughout life. Still, whether schizophrenic or quadriplegic or blind, it's highly unlikely that any
of us will "get better."

I tell Jay the story of my first book's encounter with Hollywood. The producer, Art Linson, said he loved *Ordinary
Daylight* and wanted David Mamet to write the screenplay,
but Mamet doubted that Linson could inveigle the money
from Warner Bros.

"Okay, let me get this straight," Mamet said. "You are going to march into Warner Bros. and say, I want to make a
movie about a guy who goes blind and doesn't get better."

"Yes," said Linson.

"Make sure you mention that he doesn't get better." Mamet
was sure Linson was going to get tossed out of the office.

"I will," Linson said.

"Believe me, they'll never get it. One more time," he said. And in unison they repeated the pitch, "He starts to go blind and he does not get better."

Though Mamet wrote the screenplay, the movie of *Ordinary Daylight* was never made. And I kept going blind without getting better.

Brothers and madness appear frequently in Jay Neugeboren's work, as do all kinds of family insanities. Most of his novels deal with people on the margins, blacks, Latinos, gays. "Demeaning someone for something not in their control has always made me furious," he says. "I even have trouble using the term disability. To me the spectrum from so-called ability to so-called disability merely points out aspects of the human condition. The only real difference is that some of these lives are more difficult to endure than others."

When I first began talking with Jay, he had just come back from Israel, where biblical brother themes haunted him. Cain and Abel, Jacob and Esau, Joseph and his brothers, Moses and Aaron, David and Jonathan, the complexities of love and hate, of envy and affection, were everywhere. "Though the brothers theme is a large presence in my life, it took me twenty years to finally write Robert's story, though I've used some of this material in my fiction. Since I'm a writer," he says, "I'm going to use all that I know."

"Artists aren't well known for being caregivers," I tell Jay, knowing it well from my own life. "What made you such an exemplary one?"

"I have a craving that's never been satisfied," he says. "It feels that if I do a good enough job taking care of Robert and my children, someone will come along who will do the same for me." He laughs at this confession. "I love Robert and I'm a person who, for ethical and cultural reasons, believes in taking responsibility. But I would cut through all that obvious stuff to say that my impulse to caregiving and nurturing of Robert and my children comes from my desire to give to others what I never got. There's a deep wound in me for not having had unconditional love, which I'm convinced should be every child's birthright. I know what it feels like to be abandoned, to be left hanging, to not be appreciated when you need appreciation, comfort and care. In Robert's often frightening and miserable life, it is good to be known, and Robert and I know each other better than anyone else in the world knows us. I would especially not want Robert, who is so vulnerable, to be lacking these things."

He sometimes wonders if his own survival has been bought with Robert's madness, if someone had to pay and it just happened to be Robert rather than Jay. Searching for answers back there, he recalls a litany of awful possibilities, their parents' own brand of insanity, the use of the brothers as allies for one parent or the other, but there is no answer, no gene or obvious early incident, no telling why Robert, why not Jay, why not one or another of us who come from our own brand of family madness to face a cold world alone? In some lives, abuse, neglect, abandonment, childhood memories of parents quarreling, beating on each other or the children, all the possible horrors of family, lead to big-time payments throughout life, a continuation of abuse, spoiled and wasted lives, years of psychiatric horror. Others who emerge from the same circumstances exploit the madness, turning it into less antisocial, more productive, even artistic drives.

Given my own experiences of war and displacement, I don't know why I chose or happened to become the nice boy who adopted a numbing strategy to get through, while another child might have more appropriately adopted rage and violence, some kind of acting-out rebellion. Like Jay, having had only bad models of family life, I have no idea what prevented me from allowing my nightmares to take over, from hearing voices, from slipping away from sanity.

Even though there is a huge difference between sporadic brushes with depression and severe, chronic psychiatric illness, the one time I landed in the psychiatric ward of a hospital, panicked about blindness and obsessing about loss, gave me some indication of the utter impotence of being that kind of patient, ashamed of being there. Though there was nothing romantic about it at the time, and as terrifying as the panics and obsessions then were, time has allowed the experience to become tinged with irony, even farce.

At the time, overwhelmed by waves of unbearable darkness, I groped my way to my desk, got on my atheist knees and prayed. I put my head on the swivel chair in front of my computer and, bathing in my hypocrisy, I begged for help. When none came, hyperventilating, I picked up the phone and called Bruce. "Give me an aphorism, a maxim, anything," I begged my friend, who had survived his own brushes with madness.

"Breathe into it," Bruce, now a yoga teacher, said. "It's moment to moment."

"Bruce, I'm smothering."

"Smother," my friend repeated, "sss*mother*," he said, rhapsodizing on the connection as he sometimes did with his favorite etymologies. "Spirit, conspiracy, breath, breathing together," Bruce said in capital letters. "One day at a time," he said.

Ed, a poet, called. "I just have a second," he said, "but I want to remind you that yours is a *spiritual* crisis, an existential quest for soul. Don't lose sight of that. Remember you're a writer. Another writer would kill for the opportunity to live your anguish right now."

In my hospital room, a nurse frisked me, then looked through every bag, making a pile of my wallet, nail file, nail clipper and a penknife. Even though I understood the absurdity in their effort to disarm me, I was able to forfeit rights to myself by creating a certain distance between me and them, a space for irony, self-mockery. The nurse next wanted the couple of Xanaxes I carried everywhere. Deep inside my pocket, she found and confiscated a Tums.

I settled into a chair to answer questions, exuding sincerity now, a will to please. It felt like my book tour. I was full of charming, sober, cynical observations about my condition, about life. "I've never been hospitalized before," I boasted. At my age, after all, this was a reason for congratulations. "I try to keep myself in shape," I said. "My years are just a number." I waited for some sort of appreciation but no one spoke. What did they want anyway? Joseph Heller? Robert Lowell? They left my room.

I looked for my Talking Book machine and my tapes. I didn't want to think, just to listen to a chirpy Dawn Powell novel. After a few minutes of *The Golden Spur,* I hungered for Kafka or Dostoyevsky or Styron's book on depression. I craved a story of a man turning into an insect, then dying from the sheer neglect and hatred of his loved ones.

Nurses brought me sleeping pills and antianxiety pills, antidepressants and lithium, in tiny paper hats. I took it all, hoping that I'd be a candidate for electricity. I wanted my brain recircuited, numbed, fried. Whatever the logjam of wildly firing neurons, I wanted them zapped, excised, made into a heap of ashes.

When the whole ward met daily with our "team," the psychiatrist lectured about the importance of our meds, then asked each of us to set goals for the day. That night, unable to sleep, I found the nurses' station. "You're in the right place," Nurse Sandy said. "You'll be well taken care of here. You're safe. You won't harm yourself."

"I wouldn't have done that," I told her. "My threat was a call for help," I said from the book of suicide clichés.

"Do you want me to bring you some material about grief? Loss is difficult," she said, and I wanted to marry her right then and there, Joseph Heller and I both falling in love with our hospital nurses. "I'll read you the stuff on grieving when I'm off duty," Sandy whispered.

Though possibly of some use, the shotgun administration of medication also turned out to be powerfully destructive, leaving me with years of side effects. The music therapy and the yoga were boring if not insulting, the sessions with the team vacuous. But Nurse Sandy taking the time to talk to me almost every evening for two weeks helped give me back my life.

And as for my friend Bruce, his advice was wiser than I'd thought. No matter the high-tech interventions, it all boils down to just getting through it one day at a time. And as for Ed, there turned out to be a lot to write about.

In *Transforming Madness,* Jay quotes Moe Armstrong, a patient turned advocate. "They won't pay people to talk with us and it breaks my heart," he said, "low-tech solutions such as talk being infinitely preferable to high-cost, high-tech medication." A veteran of every antipsychotic medication, he maintained that medication is only the beginning of what works. People with psychiatric disabilities helping others with the same problems—that seems to be missing. "We are a people with a history," Moe said, "we are a resource to the world. Because our lives and our brains work differently from those of so-called normal people, we can enlighten others about the human mind and the human condition."

Moe doesn't go out after dark for fear of confusing the reality of the streets with the hallucinations in his brain. When he's alone in his apartment at night, it's only when his dog doesn't bark that he can be sure that the voices are in his head.

When I was young and feared that my art was banal, uninteresting, the lack of madness in my life seemed the obvious reason. Back then, I flirted with insanity as if it were a sexy and romantic alternative to boredom, a way one could choose to be as an antidote to the good behavior required by my family. Being untouched by obvious pathology felt like being exposed as a pretender. An artist, I knew, had license to be outrageous. Society was willing to overlook his vulgarity, paranoia, obsessiveness, his monstrous ego. Even though the history of art is populated by as many bourgeois, anal types as wild, unruly desperados, my notion of creativity was defined by self-absorbed maniacs. And I thought I understood why some seriously ill artists, especially those diagnosed as bipolar, refused to take their lithium, choosing the horrors of their deep depressions in order to keep their incredible manias intact.

But my fantasies of romantic madness had no resemblance to the pitiful, mundane mental illness in those hospital rooms. The lives of most of the people in my group were marked by poverty, and, having been readmitted over and over again, most were certainly not an advertisement for the help offered. Still, human contact in the form of witnesses or fellow sufferers or experts in the use of one therapeutic technique or another, plus medication, often relieves the terrifying demons that plague us.

When I tell Jay about my early romantic views of madness and art, he says that he doesn't subscribe to any of this neo–R. D. Laing stuff that ennobles the mad as prophets. "It's a wild view of madness," he says. "It's grim, terrible garbage." He himself is driven to deal with his fears of insanity by writing clearly and lucidly. "This is crucial for me," Jay says, "though sometimes I wonder if writing is not as insane an enterprise as Robert's madness. I wonder about my intense desire to make sense of life through words and stories, along with the violence and madness I sometimes conjure up in my books. Madness plays somewhere around the edges of my concerns as a writer in my desire to be free. I have always envied Robert his lack of censoring devices. Whatever goes through his mind comes out. This is a great freedom if you're not in the life he has, in which case it becomes a terrible enemy. So I'd like to be freer imaginatively, to follow a thought wherever it will go. The other thing is that thoughts of madness have made me affect a very plain style, an effort to avoid all confusion. I don't want there to be the kind of madness that makes us lose our way. If I can find the right thread, the right word to name something, I can relax."

It is quite obvious that Robert's life would have been a lot more threadbare without Jay. "Robert knows that he can count on me no matter what," Jay says, "and that gives him a little purchase on this world."

Jay has overseen all of Robert's moves, all his therapies. Over the years, he has pleaded with administrators in the hospitals and in state government, writing letters, lodging complaints, reasoning, begging. Through all this, the brothers have talked almost daily, even though the timing of telephone calls has had to be carefully planned to avoid Robert's smoke breaks. If they didn't, Robert would scream, "Never call at smoke break again, Jay!" and slam down the phone. "Funny thing," Jay tells me, "but they've found that nicotine is not only calming to many schizophrenics but it counteracts some of the ghastly side effects of the medications.

"Still," Jay says, "I'm not the only variable. If a person other than Robert had someone like me, there's no telling what would or wouldn't have happened. Robert has a very strong will, which some psychologists would say is from identification with the aggressive mother and that's what keeps him going, but who knows? If he had less will, I might not be making a difference. He doesn't have a great life but he has a life. I certainly have been instrumental in that."

I ask if his closeness to Robert has taught him other lessons.

"Among many other things," he says, "I've become a better parent. I've learned patience. I've had to hold off being offended or enraged or whatever the feeling of the moment. When Robert gets angry and says vile or stupid things, I could pummel him, but I've learned how to draw limits because I don't want to let him abuse me, which wouldn't be good for either of us. I don't want to empower an unhealthy part of him.

"A while back when we had supper together, he was at me the whole time, the way he often is. It may be pleasant for him but it's never easy. He's constantly asking if it's okay to go to the bathroom, to use the toilet paper, to turn the light on, to sit here or there. Finally he looks at me and says, 'I'm very demanding, aren't I, Jay?' I said, 'Robert, you are very demanding.' So he starts about his fiancée Sophie, an elderly woman who was his neighbor when he was in a group home on Staten Island. He's telling me how they're going to get married someday and I say to him, 'But, Robert, you like guys.' 'Jay, that's just for practice,' he says, and we both crack up. As you can see, it's not all giving. I get a lot from Robert. He's charming and he's exhausting but he has a life. This is a miracle."

"How different would it be being a parent rather than a sibling of a schizophrenic child?" I ask him.

"I think it's enormously different. It's much easier being a sibling," Jay says. "I used to worry about my own kids. If something were seriously wrong with them, it would have been very hard to extricate the guilt. The responsibility would have been a lot more intense. I can only begin to imagine the feeling of helplessness and the fear of having done something wrong or of not having done something right. You're only as happy as your least happy child, and if you have a child who is never happy it must make for enormous sadness.

"In the case of the mentally ill guy who pushed a woman

into the subway tracks, everyone was sure that it could have been averted if caring parents had prevented him from leaving the house or had just loved him more. I disagree, because by virtue of being the family, you're already incredibly overburdened. What the family needs is a system that will support it and help deal with the child.

"Some parents walk away from kids, some brothers from brothers. I tried to survive by differentiating myself from Robert but the feeling of responsibility will never go away. For instance, I put aside money for him from the book. It's his money but it was in an account in my name. I've signed it over to Robert and he's going to work with the network of people who will assist him to learn how to become responsible for his own finances. What a lovely moment! Robert's my brother so I don't want to be in a position of a parent. When other people help take care of him, this allows me to be just a brother, which is what I like. I never have to fantasize about the Robert who might have been. Who knows what that would be like for a parent?"

"As far as being able to be only as happy as the least happy child," says Mona Wasow, the mother of a forty-four-year-old schizophrenic son, "if I lived my life that way, I would be a constant basket case. It's a never-ending, unresolvable grief. It's below the surface and it doesn't, thank God, keep me from having a good life. I'm not that wrapped up in it though the sadness is always there.

"My David's life is a misery but I've been feeling relatively good about him for the past several years. He has his first job, he's kept it for two years now, he's never late, he never fails to show up. But what he's doing is washing a stove in a restaurant. If this were one of my other kids I'd be devastated. Then the other thing I try to do is to focus on how much David has accomplished with his music, his pottery and his staying a nice person. It's all relative.

"One of my coping modalities is counting up the statistics for developmental disabilities or extreme physical disabilities, to say nothing of drug abuse. You've got conservatively one out of four families in misery. The thought cheers me. I tell myself that I was not singled out for damnation. There are lots of other miserable people. I comfort myself with that."

Mona Wasow has, for many years, been heading up the concentration in severe mental illness at the University of Wisconsin at Madison. Almost all the students she's been teaching will end up working with the severely mentally ill—including the homeless.

"Who do you think most students in the helping professions want to work with?" Mona asks. "It's people like themselves, the worried well. And after that, cute little children. And who is at the bottom of the list? People with serious mental illness. And after that, old people." Mona works hard at interesting her students in working with just that shunned and terribly underserved population. Her program emphasizes values, knowledge and skills. "A deep respect for these people can only lead to compassion and commitment," Mona says.

Her students spend a great deal of time doing frontline work with the seriously mentally ill elderly, including those who are homeless. Her students are taught to reach into the lives and spirits of disabled men and women—people who do not get cured, who sometimes get worse, who may try to avoid them, who might die—and they learn to do this work without judgment or fear. "There are human beings behind these crippling disabilities," Mona says, "and most of them are longing for human interaction. Good books, classes, field placements help, but I suspect that it's students' contact with elderly people who have serious mental illness that does the most profound teaching."

According to Mona, there is a direct connection between a person's inability to come to terms with what she calls "the random hit of catastrophic events" and her inclination to enter the "helping field." "I do the work I do totally and entirely because of David," she says. "Why else would one do it? Surely there are better things to do. But some of us have no choice. I do it to cleanse myself of guilt, of anger, of the immense sadness that accompanies having a mentally ill child. For those of us who don't have conventional religion, we struggle looking elsewhere to find meaning in it."

One-third of her students have mental illness in their family and are dealing with overwhelming grief and anger. "If you don't do anything with it, it's going to eat you up alive," she says. "Working in the field is a rechanneling of the anger and the grief. The compassion these students find is comforting to them. Also, kindness generates kindness, plus the fact that the status one gets from altruism is not to be sneezed at."

A colleague in her field said her reason for being involved was that she's painfully shy, thus was able to identify easily with the shyness and loneliness of the mentally ill. "I suppose that anyone who goes into social work is also motivated by social injustice," Mona says. "Every once in a while I get a student who says she has a calling, but I don't have a notion where that kind of thing comes from."

What Mona teaches has very direct consequences on her son's life. Her students provide David and others like him with assisted living situations in their communities. These professionals work with them in their own environments, doing laundry with them, shopping, going out for coffee, showing them how to live, rather than talking about their conditions. "That's what I've been teaching my students to do for the past twenty years," she says. "Because David's health care team is so good now, I'm free to be Mom, free to make cakes, to nag him about his fingernails, as well as to make music together and laugh."

It wasn't always like this. Mona tells me about the time of David's first schizophrenia diagnosis some twenty-five years ago, when the psychologist told her that it would be best if she didn't expect him to go to school or work. "It was very bad advice," she says. "He went to pieces when I took all the expectations off. He knew then that the jig was up. But I stopped the frantic trying to make him normal and gave in to the horror of the diagnosis.

"I have known people who were relieved when a label was put on their behavior or illness. I argue this point with my students when they talk about the stigma of labeling. It can be a stigma but for some there is relief in knowing that a name exists for what is going on. As for me, I didn't know what schizophrenia was so I went to the library and started reading. Now I know that it's a neurobiological brain disorder, which is some progress from the days when they talked about schizophrenogenic mothers and double-bind communication, but really not much is known about it, *schizophrenia* being a generic term for many different illnesses, like *cancer* is."

But before the first diagnosis, there was a devastating misdiagnosis. "My son was very likable, sweet and charming," she says, "so the psychologist who prescribed what we as a family should do misread him totally. As a matter of fact, he decided that there couldn't be anything that wrong, that all David needed was a kind of cold shower that would help him grow up. Well, that was a time of family bashing, and this idiot psychologist told him he should break off all relationships with his family. Imagine a kid seventeen years old being told that. And imagine us listening and kicking David out of the house, allowing him to live by himself at the YMCA." She has a very hard time recalling this horror. "Mother bashing was in its heyday and I accepted for a while that it was all my fault. But the separation really broke him. Before that he had spirit. He was feisty. Even now I have to tell him to say what he wants to say, not what he thinks I want to hear. He still asks me if he can have a glass of water in his own house! He's still terrified of offending anyone.

"He had all the symptoms and it was a great sin on their part for not seeing the schizophrenia earlier. I don't forgive them their ignorance. There was no excuse for it. It's like misdiagnosing a cancer. How dare they be in the field and not keep up on the research? How do I feel about that person? If I met him on the street, I'd kill him.

"It's different now than it used to be," she continues. "The emphasis of David's care is to make sure he gets to his guitar and pottery lessons. Nowadays they rightly want to concentrate on his strengths, not the interior voices he still hears. I have to lecture myself that he's forty-four and I have to let go. It's hard to let go. My well children are now as competent and mature as I am, so when I get sick, they want to help me, to tell me how they think I should take care of myself. It's easy to let go of them because they're my peers. David will never reach that point.

"I began to change a little about all this some ten years ago when David was put into a foster home. Until then he'd been in hospitals, group homes, on the street, in a hundred horrible crises. When we found the foster home and foster mother, I could again be a mother and not a case manager. The burden was off me, and David got a lot better in foster care. All in all, social workers have improved, letting families be families.

"Even though his foster mom had said to me that he could do more than I'd thought he could, there's a natural tendency with a fragile kid to overprotect. So it's important to try to find out how much he can do and to learn to back off.

It's also important to know your own limitations, to know what you can't make better, what you can't change no matter what you do."

I tell her what I know about some people within the disability community despising the idea of aborting a fetus solely for reasons of disability, and ask her what she would have done had she known David's future diagnosis while she was pregnant.

"I would have had an abortion and wouldn't have given it a second thought," she answers without skipping a beat. "The pain I have over him far outweighs the pleasure." She tells me about first meeting Ann Deveson, an author and mother of a schizophrenic son. "It was fifteen years ago," she says, "so the thinking about psychiatric illness was somewhat different." In the first hour of getting to know each other, the two women admitted that their kids suffered so much, the situation and treatments were so hopeless, that they hoped their sons would die. "Even though Ann and I wished our sons dead," Mona says, "we were both doing everything in our power to keep them alive and to make their lives okay.

"Two years later, Ann called me from Australia to tell me that her son Jonathan had died of a drug overdose as he was trying to admit himself to a hospital. In light of our earlier conversation, I asked how she felt about this, expecting her to say that she was glad it was over. I actually felt envious of her. Well, she bowled me over with words I didn't expect. 'I'd do anything to have Jonathan back,' she said."

Recalling this, Mona stops, then begins to cry. With some difficulty, she continues. "The situation has improved in the last few years in terms of David's getting better care, and he's having some kind of a life so I guess I don't feel that way anymore. Still, if anything happened to my well children I don't know if I could bear it, yet I'm pretty sure I wouldn't feel that way if David died. There'd be a lot of sadness as well as

closure. Our culture doesn't give us much permission to acknowledge the fact that you may love somebody and also
wish them dead, wish that they would not have to continue
living their unbelievably difficult lives. Many parents of the
mentally ill are shocked by my attitude, but there are also
many who nod and know exactly what I'm talking about. But
I always recall Ann's words, and I have renewed respect for
how we don't know how we're going to react to certain
things until we're facing them.

"Look," she says, "it's so muddy and complex that I am
absolutely thrilled with the dentist who gives so much loving
care in trying to save some of David's teeth. I go in two directions at once: I wish he were dead and I love it that his teeth
are being saved."

Even today, when David's life is somewhat better, his expression always shows intense anxiety and depression. He has
a routine now. He does nothing in the mornings, goes to a
club for the mentally ill for lunch, then goes to work for an
hour cleaning a restaurant oven, then wanders around town
and goes to bed early. "I don't think he gets any pleasure from
life, but I don't know him that well anymore," Mona says.

David has more than a glimmer of his previous, healthy
self. He watches his siblings and some of the people with
whom he grew up with what seems to be great agony, a very
pained nostalgia. "He's very much alone," Mona says. "He
hasn't had a single friend since eighth grade. When he was
quite young, he read Plato, and now, aside from cigarettes and
orange soda, which are his two great loves, he still goes into
bookstores to buy yet another copy of Plato, which he can no
longer read. Who knows what compels him to keep buying
it? When he has to go to the hospital, he packs his pajamas,
his toothbrush and his Plato. Even though he's functionally
retarded now, he's trying to hang on to an old dream of himself as an intellectual."

When I tell Mona of Adrienne Asch's strong feelings about disability being no worse, no more difficult, than anything else, Mona says that to her, mental illness and mental retardation are entirely another sphere of disability, one that doesn't compare with physical disability. "It's our minds, our brains, that make us distinctly different," she says. "With blindness or paralysis, people may be taken aback at first encounter, but then they relax and relate. At those times I can forget the disability, but I can't forget the mind's dysfunction. It's unpredictable. It makes us less human."

Mona tells me that her most dramatic moment as a grandparent came when she and her two granddaughters, ages five and eight, were in the park and a woman came by in a wheelchair pulled by a dog. A retarded man with a dog showed up and his dog attacked her dog. The woman in the wheelchair panicked, told him to get his dog back, and he screamed at her, "I got as much fucking right as you do!" Then he looked panicked and said how sorry he was that he'd lost control.

"My grandchildren wanted me to say that everything was fine," Mona says, "but I started to cry. They were puzzled. I told them that some people in this world have it so much harder than we do, that they can't think or walk straight, that they have a lot of problems and we have to be especially nice to people like that. My granddaughter picked a flower, handed it to the retarded man. I was proud of myself for passing on the mantle. I loved her, I loved myself, and I shook hands with the retarded man, to whom I said, 'Yes, you lost control but you got it back again, and good for you.' As Margaret Mead said in one of her books, it's the grandmother's role to hand down the family culture. I think about that a lot. For generations, my family has been very involved in music. Handing down feelings about mental illness is as important to me as handing down a feel for music."

She recalls that when she asked David to do something in

the past, she would always end the request with "if you feel up to it, dear." At Mona's retirement party, for the first time she put it in other terms: "If you would make music with the rest of our family, that would be an incredible gift to me." And he did. Happily.

One of the more important problems for a parent to solve is how to provide ongoing stability, including oversight of financial security, for the future of a mentally ill child, how to assure a continuing management of needs such as housing and health care. Who can ever love them as the parents have? Who can know the basic personality that lies behind the illness? And how can one depend on maintaining the former quality of service? These are the primary worries of many if not most parents of seriously mentally ill children.

Case managers come and go, staff in supervised housing may be poorly trained and horribly underpaid and government funding might easily be cut. For everyone who must deal with these questions, there is enormous frustration with the available social services, a lack of housing options and the insensitivity of professionals to parental needs.

Anne Larkin, the mother of an autistic son, works very hard at finding such solutions not just for herself but for all parents of disabled children, whatever the family's finances. One of the most important programs she and her husband helped create is called PALS, Personal Advocacy of Lifetime Support. Hoping to lighten their other children's future care-taking burdens, as well as looking ahead to their own diminished abilities in old age, the Larkins modeled their efforts after an existing Canadian program that develops networks of volunteers, supervised by a paid facilitator, to serve each disabled child. The volunteers take over different facets of the person's day-to-day existence, such as home life, work life, social life and medical needs. The aim of the program is to encompass not only autism but all kinds of disabilities.

"There is no doubt in my mind that when we get our first network off the ground, the program will soar. The need is enormous," Anne says. "The problems are so overwhelming that it's taking us a lot longer than we thought to get it all in full swing. It happened much faster in Canada," she says, "where they've already initiated over a thousand networks. We will get there too, but slowly.

"When Tom and I got married," Anne says, "we simply wanted to have a family, certainly never anticipating that we'd have a child with a disability. But after John was born, I knew that if these were the cards that were dealt, we would have to move forward from there." Her voice is Boston tough, a gravelly, no-nonsense voice. "Even though we knew nothing about autism," Anne says, "we knew something was very wrong. John wasn't going through the normal developmental stages but we couldn't get the problem diagnosed until he was three years old. From the beginning, he was way beyond hyperactive. He never napped. He hated cuddling, became rigid every time we tried to hug and kiss him. You can't imagine how hard that is. My twins were a piece of cake compared with this. I could have raised quads."

Seeing to John Larkin's education as he was growing up called for constant vigilance, having to push schools and others to make unheard-of allowances, to take risks, to try harder. When John reached adolescence, Anne and her husband Tom finally put him in a residential program. Because he was home only weekends and vacations, it gave them a break, gave their twins, five years younger than John, some time of their own, and gave John a structure he desperately needed and, they realized, couldn't get at home. "Parents tend to become overly protective," Anne says, "making their needy kids very dependent."

The Larkins, who seem to have left no stone unturned, have investigated, imported or otherwise examined many different programs here and abroad. They have found that what separates most of the foreign programs from the American ones is that the former promote a very disciplined approach to learning, well balanced in academics, performance, physical education, music and art. In these programs, every aspect of a child's behavior and learning is carefully guided, leaving little to chance or accident. Even though in the best of them, expectations are very high and the children do very well with the structure, the rigorous exercise, the control, the sameness every day from morning till night, when they leave, unless a lot of care has been taken to integrate them into the community as well, they tend to fall apart. "As parents," Anne says, "we have to struggle to keep informed about things like this, actually about absolutely everything that is known about autism."

The severity of autism runs the spectrum from being indistinguishable from a learning disability to manifestations of extreme aggression toward one's self and others. It can be defined as a combination of problems with communication, social interaction and sensory intake. People are no longer buying into thinking that a majority of kids with autism are retarded, rather that their behaviors and developmental delays resemble retardation because of serious flaws in their processing mechanisms. It's now recognized that their cognitive levels are unknown and can change daily.

Since the time of John's birth thirty-five years ago, the most drastic and effective change in the field of autism has been very early intervention. At three years old kids are now bombarded with all kinds of stimulation, with language therapy, communication skills, social and sensory integration and behavioral programs.

As other people with autism might have difficulty processing sight or touch, John Larkin is hypersensitive to sound, reacting to it as if there were a sensory overload, a cross-wiring in the brain. Information floods his senses, overwhelming them, sounding like static. "As a child, John liked to spin and twirl things," says Anne. "He was very echolalic, repeating phrases in an effort to understand something one step at a time but unable to grasp the concept. Now he's perseverative, stuck on a memory, repeating it over and over, wanting others to repeat it too, and if they don't he gets extremely agitated. He loves music but wants to listen to the same phrase over and over. Certain words are particularly pleasant to him. He would say, 'Mama, say beautiful,' then keep telling me what a wonderful word 'beautiful' is.

"John is very lovable," Anne continues, "though that isn't easy for most people to appreciate. He's very good-looking, almost six feet tall, with thick black hair, big brown eyes and an olive complexion. He's always in motion. His anxiety level and his perseveration get in the way of anyone's knowing who he really is. He has very few inhibitions and is certainly the loudest and most active man in his group home.

"Though I wouldn't have missed having John for anything," she says, "I tell prospective parents who are debating whether or not to keep a pregnancy of a disabled infant that they should be as informed as humanly possible and make their own decisions. No one knows what kind of a life their child or that family will have. Some families can't deal with a mentally disabled child and they know up front that they can't. I don't think anyone else—not a doctor, not a genetic counselor—should make that decision for them. Having lived through all the pain as well as the joys, all the issues John brought with him, I would never tell another parent to do the same thing we did. It takes a lot of patience, love, adjustment and a lot of sacrifices. Some families fall apart. When I hear people complaining that another family doesn't treat their autistic kid right or they never come to meetings, I get angry because no one should make such judgments. If you don't have a network of people who'll support you, you can't do it alone. But those of us who have the energy have to confront the bureaucracies, develop political relationships, keep plugging away at all that. One needs to be political, resourceful, assertive and very aggressive."

Anne and her group of parents are constantly in the faces of their governor and state representatives, a presence at all relevant legislative meetings. "I would guess that Massachusetts is a more responsive state than most," she says, "and we feed them our concerns, making them aware of our issues. I just returned from a legislative breakfast at the state house, where we discussed the wages for direct-care staff workers. We will not give up until these important workers are making a decent wage. I don't nag, but they all know I'm not going away until I get what is needed and what our kids and their providers deserve. Most of the parents have become very politically active, realizing that it's important for the future of their kids regarding housing, trusts, wills, their financial and social security."

Anne organizes many conferences throughout the state, teaching other parents and guardians about these issues and the importance of future planning. "I've become well known. People there respect my tenacity and willingness to press hard for the rights of the underserved. I personalize everything. They will know who John is and what he needs in order to live a happy and productive life."

"How were your life plans altered by John's autism?"

"I'm a teacher, which is what I always wanted to be, the only difference being that because of John I moved into special ed." Aside from her daily involvement in John's life, Anne works full-time at Lesley College, where she is a reading specialist and where she directs a scholarship program called Say

Yes To Education, which takes inner-city kids from a very young age through college, guiding and supporting them in every way possible. She also teaches courses on autism and on the issues of inclusion of special-ed kids into regular classrooms, training students and teachers on the graduate and undergraduate levels as well as within the local school system.

"The focus of my work is to explain autism, discuss the educational, social and emotional issues involved, review all the interventions, the methodologies, the theories, and the latest research. I try to explain the role that these future teachers will play when children are integrated into their classrooms. We review adaptations and modifications to the curriculum as well as behavioral and social skills.

"It's a very full life," she says.

Mona Wasow has actively exposed her classes to the national shame of homelessness and many of her students go on to work specifically among this population. And Jay Neugeboren, both in *Transforming Madness* and in his conversations with me, talked about the extraordinary plight of those who are dealing with both severe mental illness and homelessness.

Jay pointed me in the direction of an organization that deals with New York's mentally disabled homeless, a special population that the city won't touch, people who don't meet the usual prerequisites for eligibility, people seen as unmanageable, treatment-resistant, not ready for housing. "You want to see some real cutting-edge stuff?" he asked. "Talk to Sam Tsemberis, who runs an outfit called Pathways to Housing."

In fact, Pathways to Housing has had unbelievable success by finding housing first, doing the rehabilitation and support work later. Following this radical sequence, they've had an 85 percent retention rate in the apartments they find for people with major psychiatric diagnoses, homelessness, poverty, malnutrition, sexual abuse, substance abuse, child abuse, crime, alcoholism, lack of education, lack of decent medical care and lack of hope. "Though they are a population as difficult as any in America," says Sam Tsemberis, "they refused to consider themselves victims. Instead, they take responsibility for their own lives."

Sam, a soft-spoken man, runs this whole amazing show. "I'm not actually sure how I got into all this," he says. "I haven't really stopped to think about these things. Some people have a sense of what they want to do early. That was not my case."

I ask Sam to describe himself. He tells me he is six feet tall with dark hair and a beard beginning to gray. A friend recently sent him a birthday card saying she loved his "fierce gentleness." He sees himself as passionately compassionate, the embodiment of that exciting tension.

Coming from a little village in Greece, eleven kilometers outside of Sparta, without running water or electricity, Sam loved the intimacy of readily available aunts and uncles, grandparents, godfathers and godmothers. Everyone's being related to him was cozy and safe until his family decided to emigrate to Montreal, where he had to remake himself.

"From the beginning, I was attracted to people's stories," he says. "In college I majored in literature and psychology, then started teaching in a New York City school where the kids had just come off the boat from small Greek islands. I felt really useful, helping them with their adjustment. After three years I went back to graduate school in psychology, even though I was sorely tempted to study drama at the Circle in the Square. Even now I make videotapes of our program, loving the chronicles of people telling their experiences and stories.

"When I was learning about mental illness, I have to say that I never fully understood why people were locked up in wards. The first time I went to visit Creedmoor Psychiatric

Hospital, I had an interesting exchange with a patient. I had been going through a period of changing from Canadian to American cigarettes. I was smoking Marlboros one week, Pall Malls the next, trying to find something that tasted like Rothman's. So I'm talking to this guy locked up in Creedmoor and he's saying, 'I like Pall Malls, sometimes I like Camels, sometimes I need Marlboros,' and I'm thinking that this guy's got the same problems I have." Sam laughs. "And he's locked up! What's wrong with this story? I've always thought there was some misunderstanding going on in those psychiatric hospitals. To just sit and talk with a person, about their life, how it came to be that they are where they are, makes perfect sense to me. Even now, with all my training, I haven't lost that perspective. The institutions and the system try to professionalize you into a disconnect with the people you're dealing with. It's not because people aren't well intentioned. They just make a lot of wrong assumptions about what really helps.

"I think we all have pockets of disability. People get stuck emotionally, they get enraged or depressed. For some it's brief, more manageable, for others it lasts longer and we need more help. We all know the geography, all of us are human. The way each of us navigates is a little different."

"So why homelessness and why Pathways to Housing?" I ask.

"First, I was a street outreach worker in the city, dealing with the homeless, which I thought to be the most visible and compelling public health social issue. It was a city project that took mentally ill people on the street to a psychiatric hospital, against their will if necessary, if they met the legal and clinical criteria of being dangerous to self or others. The idea was that no one was going to die on the streets of New York City. It was always wonderful to pull people out of the cold but always very painful to bring them to a psychiatric hospital."

Most of the people he picked up had enormous physical

and mental health problems. More than anything, they needed a home, but he had to take them to Bellevue. In New York City, when a person with mental illness is homeless, the entire mental health system focuses on the illness, not the homelessness.

"But these people didn't want to go to Bellevue," Sam says. "They wanted what every other homeless person wants, a place of their own. As much as we tried to cajole, the system was locked into treatment first, then housing. So we had to create an agency that would accept referrals from the street. In 1992, I ended up starting our nonprofit Pathways to Housing, and we took the risk of transferring people right from the sidewalk into apartments of their own, just as they wanted."

Other city programs reject clients for not taking their medication. With Pathways, whose aim is to separate homelessness from treatment, people lose housing only by acts of violence. Unlike those of the city, Pathway's requirements aren't draconian. With them, it is housing first, and only then does the rehab process begin. Their workers are out helping people in their new apartments, in the courtrooms, in stores, on job sites, in schools, medical centers and doctors' offices. Many of the peer specialists have experienced similar problems themselves and are now providing models of recovery. Ironically, the cost of this seemingly exorbitant program is less than the cot provided to some of the homeless by the city. The price of such a municipal shelter is about $25,000 a year, while a Pathways apartment together with attendant care is $20,000, half of which goes to the rent, including furniture, half to support and clinical services. This latter half is each client's share of the salary of the service coordinator, the psychiatrist, the nurse practitioner and others. Thus, for each hundred clients, a million dollars goes to staff salaries. Each service coordinator, for example, is responsible for some ten people. Each client has his own service person available seven days a week, twenty-four hours a day, though there's a wide range of need for contact, from daily to every other week, and this need changes over time.

Because of recent statewide pressure to empty psychiatric facilities in New York, where the annual cost per patient is as-tronomical—more than $120,000—Pathways signed a con-tract with the state office of mental health to place its outgoing patients, many of whom had been hospitalized for years. "They knew us," Sam says, "and knew we would take anyone. As for us, we thought that after taking people from the streets, this would be a piece of cake. But the people com-ing out of the hospital were much more labor-intensive than we anticipated, which makes sense when you consider that in the hospital these people needed permission to do anything, to take a bath, have a meal, take their medication, go to bed, get up. When we left them alone in an apartment, they be-came terribly anxious. They needed a person nearby all the time and we ran into a very significant financial problem. It proved to be quite a demonstration of the destructiveness of institutionalizing people."

Pathways is a small agency of about fifty-five people. So far, they've had little time to fund-raise, but they're about to start looking for private donations to supplement the city, state and federal funds. "Initially there were just five of us," Sam says, "and I was the only licensed clinician. I still get calls at two in the morning from one of the tenants in our program, saying, 'Sam, I came back from my walk and found a pencil mark on the wall near the light switch in the kitchen and I don't think it was there before. Do you remember it being there when I moved in? If it wasn't there, someone's been here and I'm leav-ing to go back to the shelter.' So I say of course that pencil mark was there.

"When we sit down and talk to a diagnosed person, we get the rhythm of their language, the frame of reference, where they're coming from," he says. "I used to interview everyone who came into the program and I never found anyone who didn't make sense to me. Over the years I've seen people struggling, relapsing, coming back, getting to a new place in their lives. There are heroic things going on every day."

Recently, Pathways was invited to submit a proposal to Westchester County, eliciting a front-page story in the *Westchester Journal News* announcing that "the County plans to introduce a mental health program that will put mentally ill drug addicts into apartments without therapy." "How are people supposed to react to that?" Sam asks. "They're coming to your neighborhood. They're going to walk the same sidewalks as your daughter. Boy, did that ever cost us! But reading all this garbage, I wonder if anyone realizes that mentally ill people are no more violent than any other segment of the population. A tremendous amount of harm is done by events such as the *Wonderland* TV program or by Andrew Goldstein, the man who pushed a woman into the subway tracks. It just perpetuates the lies. Studies have shown us that if you have a good case manager, you will do well, regardless of whether the process is voluntary or involuntary. But the minute Goldstein pushes the woman into the tracks, $125 million goes into the involuntary program. *Why?* It doesn't work. What works is considered, compassionate, continuous care, but that doesn't sell as well politically.

"It's horrendous, this representation of violence and destruction associated with mental illness. A tremendous number of column inches in the press are given to violence when it's committed by a mentally ill person as opposed to anyone else, while crimes inflicted on people with disabilities are notoriously unreported. Violence against the disabled, particularly the mentally disabled, occurs at rates that some say are nearly ten times higher than violence toward the general population. In this country, more than five million disabled people are victims of serious crimes every year."

The provider community itself is at best skeptical about Pathways, even though it has been in business for seven years and its housing retention rate is a lot better than that of other providers. "It's so amazing," Sam says, "the difference we're making."

In some communities, like East Harlem, Pathways workers would drive or walk around the neighborhoods and go inside the abandoned buildings, cars and subway stations describing the program to homeless people, who, more often than not, are in total disbelief about it. The workers go in teams, traveling in a van clearly marked with the organization's name. "One of the issues of street survival is people trying to figure out who you are," Sam says. "Are you safe? Are you a threat? Do you conduct yourself in a social-worker manner? Are you really here to help?"

Not everybody working for Pathways wants to walk the streets and do outreach but it's appealing to some. "And it's hard to tell who would like it, who not," Sam says, "like Jane, a fabulous worker, who back home in England used to be a governess. Everyone either is or quickly becomes very streetwise. We learn how to approach a person, and if they say no it means no, though we have this concept of the soft refusal. When somebody snarls at you, wanting you to go away, we figure, well, they're not in the mood today, it's not a good day for them, and we'll probably try to come back another day. The job does require persistence."

Pathways workers ask where people want to live, then hit the streets like anyone else, looking for affordable housing. Because some 40 percent of the staff are people who have themselves been homeless, in psychiatric hospitals, in drug rehab programs, they believe deeply in what they're doing.

"So what happens to people once you find them a place to live?" I ask.

"After they're settled in, we begin taking care of their other needs, like supervising their medication or therapeutic programs, helping them look for work. Some people eventually leave the program because they've found work or they move, celebratory things. A very few people are asked to leave, mainly because their apartments are overrun by drug dealers. We've had characters with guns come to the office looking for people on days the checks come in."

Sam tells me about Ed, one of his workers, who was in Robert Neugeboren's unit in Creedmoor thirty-five years ago. "The state-of-the-art at that time was insulin shock treatment," he says. "Can you imagine? They put people into a coma, not too deep or they'd kill them." He trembles with outrage. "In Creedmoor, Ed and Robert used to play chess together. Thirty-five years later, Ed was showing Robert one of our apartments."

"Is Robert a more serious schizophrenic than Ed?" I ask. "What made their lives so different?"

"Ed had been told by the psychologist who was treating him at Creedmoor that he must escape, that his life depended on it. He took this to heart and got out of there, struggled, was married for a while, had a daughter, a lovely teenager now. He's been working for the last twenty years. Ed's and Robert's experiences of family, their different personalities, the blind luck of running into one person rather than another, a whole series of varied life events took each of them in a different direction.

"Even though Robert became a celebrity in the world of mental illness because of Jay's books, Robert isn't going to change much from being Robert, a man with thirty-five years of institutionalization, which makes anyone extremely dependent. We talked about our program with him but he didn't like any of the apartments and ended up in a community residence with much more support, a better fit for him."

"How do mental health organizations look on your work?"

"Folks such as the National Alliance for the Mentally Ill like some things about us," Sam says. "They admire the fact that we never give up on anyone ever. We're a nice replacement for family in that respect and they feel reassured, but the idea that we don't require medication before we find people housing is definitely one of the more controversial aspects of our work. They don't like that. They must like us for getting people off the street but they definitely see the hospital as a friendly ally. We definitely do not.

"There is a tension between the consumer movement and NAMI, the former wanting choice, the latter insisting first that everyone take his medicine. Ideologically, we fall much closer to the consumer voice," Sam says.

For Jay Neugeboren too, the National Alliance for the Mentally Ill has historically been overly preoccupied with cures and, in his judgment, too focused on mental illness being a biologically based disease, which propels it to support a cure that is chemical. Jay believes that NAMI is too wedded to drug companies, and that even though it does excellent work as well—advocating, lobbying for insurance parity, campaigning against stigma, providing families with groups where people can talk to one another—it tends to mistrust the judgment of people with mental illness and thus favors hospitalization over other, less paternalistic solutions to everyday care.

"However," Jay says, "little by little, NAMI is beginning to favor programs rather than pills. The philosophy of going for the cure implies that you're an imperfect human being, in the garbage, until a cure is found. The most egregious, well-known examples of this wrong-headed thinking are Christopher Reeve and Michael J. Fox."

I know this all too well. Going for the cure has always been the focus of the foundation which, from its beginnings in the early 1970s, took blood oaths that it would not rest until it found a cure for retinitis pigmentosa. Decent people, some of them affected by the disease, and dedicated researchers insisted that the large amounts of money raised go exclusively into research and the administration of fund-raising, rather than into the support of retraining and the establishment of therapeutic and educational systems that can offer the kind of day-to-day help that far outweighs the benefits of waiting endlessly for a magic bullet.

Obsessing on the search for a magic bullet alone is as destructive in mental illness as it is in the case of cancer, diabetes or heart disease. Cures are stupendous when they happen, but until they do, those who suffer the long-term devastations of mental or physical illness don't easily survive the lack of human attention to their ordinary needs. A megalomaniacal drive for cures often forgets how the illness is experienced by the ill and those who care for them. This does not contradict the fact that research in brain chemistry, technical advances in diagnostics, new knowledge of any kind can lead to better medication and better care. Certainly antipsychotics and lithium have proved to be dramatic in easing the torment of some psychiatric illnesses and have allowed some people to function who would have otherwise been unable to do so. But it is also true that a seriously mentally ill person, just as anyone seeking relief from any illness, needs a certain amount of luck to find effective medication as well as beneficial psychiatric or medical care.

"Note that on the doctor shows on TV, it's always a crisis," Jay Neugeboren says, "with bells ringing, everyone running, reinforcing the notion that medicine is strictly heroic, only about lifesaving procedures. The truth is that saving lives is a last resort, usually meaning that the professionals haven't dealt with the patient's well-being until that point. They'd need that heroic stuff much less if they just went about making people's lives better."

At the beginning of Robert's illness, Jay was told by the head psychiatrist at Bronx State that the unanimous prognosis of every professional who had contact with Robert was that he would never be able to exist in any other environment than a hospital. It's now two years that Robert has been successfully living in supervised housing in New York.

"If I hadn't written the book," Jay says, "if I hadn't pushed, he would probably not be out of Bronx Psychiatric. There may be some people who, not having these advantages, would have the resilience to say, 'Fuck you bastards, I'm going to get out of here anyway,' but from my experience visiting the wards over the years, I would say that those who have been abandoned by their families do very badly. They languish and die. Robert has been greatly helped by the book because now that he's a famous mental patient, people want to show that they can do a good job with him."

These days, Jay lectures widely on mental illness. He accompanies doctors on rounds in hospitals. Many psychiatrists have written him to say that he has reminded them of the larger familial context. And he seems to have had some influence on public policy as well. His books have made the rounds of state and congressional representatives when relevant bills needed to be passed. They understand that his books are serious critiques of a ghastly mental health system. "As individual citizens we can push in the right direction," he says, "but I'm not a doctor, not a therapist. I'm a writer and a brother, which perhaps gives me the credibility that professionals don't have.

Now, wherever Robert goes, people are going to give him good treatment. They're afraid I'll write about it, which is fine. I'll take what I can get."

It's impossible to calculate the effect of books and teachers on public policy or health delivery systems. One can count the number of the blind given mobility via Pete Lang's dogs, the number of the comatose given moments of life via Connie Tomaino's accordion, the thousands worldwide given access to decent work via Ted Henter's software, the hundreds or so each year given artificial limbs by Dave Loney. Nevertheless, it's clear that the writings and teachings of Jay Neugeboren, Mona Wasow and Anne Larkin have penetrated the mental health establishment and have begun to change attitudes toward serious mental illness. It is true that their models are different in kind than the one offered by Chai Feldblum in changing the world one word at a time, or by David Werner initiating programs and teaching the disabled to work with fellow disabled all over the world. But one common thread they all share seems to be the exchange of warmth and love, the struggle to preserve dignity and the passion for building a just society.

In *Transforming Madness,* Jay cites several programs that help people with serious mental illness successfully maintain productive lives outside of institutions. "The one thing these programs have in common," he says, "is their reliance on providers who have been through mental illness themselves. Once you've had your own lifelong battles with mental illness, including countless hospital admissions, you tend to be very respectful to others going through the same experiences. These programs are easily replicable, as long as you can be nonjudgmental and nonauthoritarian. This doesn't sound so difficult, does it? If it happened more, I'm convinced that many people, certainly not all but many, could be leading happier and more productive lives."

When I ask Sam Tsemberis if Pathways can be a template for other mental health programs, he says, "Look, assertive community treatment and supported housing exist in every mental health department in the country. All we've done is rearrange the sequence of those services. It requires a certain shift in the way people see mental illness, but if they're capable of that, the whole mental health system would change."

Except for the fact that mental health caregivers get woefully inadequate wages and no benefits, there is no uniformity in each state's delivery systems. There is no national policy on the quality of care. Robert Neugeboren lives with fifty-six other mentally ill people in supervised housing funded by the city and state of New York. David Wasow, who had been living for many years with a foster family, has moved into a boardinghouse with three other mentally ill men. Though he receives no help with meals, hygiene or socialization, a building manager alerts appropriate social service agencies in case of need. When it comes to caring for the seriously mentally ill, according to Mona Wasow, Madison, Wisconsin, is one of the more enlightened communities. John Larkin and three other autistic men live in a group home built by their parents on donated land in their own neighborhood. But even though Social Security Disability Income or Supplemental Security Income, which includes Medicaid or Medicare, is the right of all who are seriously disabled, the people who are not well represented by families and social workers can and often do fall through the cracks, sometimes landing in the streets or in jails.

One of Jay's recent talks on mental illness was delivered at a conference on the Swiss-German border. From a window on the conference site, he noticed that the lawn was covered with markers. It turned out to be a memorial for the 560 mental patients the Germans took from this very place to the death camps. Before they fully organized the destruction of the European Jews, they took the mentally ill.

At times, the struggle is for quality of life, for dignity. There are times, though, when it's for life itself.

"What does one do to change things?" I ask Jay.

"As writers, we try to make sense of the world in words, like the famous story of the Jewish historian on his way to the death camp saying, 'Write it down.' You can do nothing else except witness and say the truth."

EPILOGUE

In the last twenty-five years, the lives of many disabled people have improved considerably. Thanks to the labor and activism of the disability community, many disabled people are no longer looked upon as hopelessly different, no longer shunned. At times, the effort to include the disabled in the mainstream of society has paid off, leading to improved access to education, employment, housing, transportation and dignified participation in a community's social life. The individuals who talk about their work in the preceding pages have been instrumental in the struggle, contributing mightily, mostly in quiet, loving ways.

But all those wonderful things like progress in medicine and technology, the mapping of the brain and the human genome, the evolution of laws protecting human rights, the dissemination of new ideas and more evolved attitudes, do not benefit everyone. Far from it.

New technologies such as text telephones for those with hearing impairments, computer access via screen readers and braille displays for the visually impaired, lighter wheelchairs and artificial limbs, infrared pointers for people who can't use their hands—all the things essential to disabled people's productivity and autonomy—are often not available to them.

To achieve the independence that the nondisabled take for

granted, a disabled person must be able to afford certain adaptive equipment. For the most part, however, these devices are out of financial reach. With disability unemployment numbers stagnating at about 70 percent, and with most disabled people relying on Supplemental Security Income (SSI) at an average monthly stipend of $372, or on Social Security Disability Income (SSDI) of $786, the money for all those wonderful technologies at market prices is simply not there.

The vast majority of disabled persons can and want to work, but the disincentive of losing health insurance often prevents them from seeking employment. The presumption all too often is that those with disabilities will be a burden, either unable to do the job adequately or in need of costly workplace adaptations. Without affirmative action, employing the disabled remains voluntary, a nice thing to do, a charitable deed. Though our society expects and rewards an individual's lifelong productivity, the right to a job is not seen as one of society's obligations.

In some enlightened states, Vermont among them, the blind are favored because the mandate of the agencies providing services includes the goals of vocational rehabilitation and of independent living, meaning not only a push toward employment but toward autonomy. Oddly, however, this does not improve the overall unemployment figures of the blind, in part because of the catch-22 nature of work disincentives, in part because of many employers' assumptions that workplace adaptations will be burdensome.

I am still naive enough to be shocked that most of the agencies providing services to people with disabilities are not preoccupied with their clients' quality of life. Because funds are limited and shrinking, the dispensing bureaucracies are required to narrow the definition of who is eligible. Thus, Medicaid providers seek reasons to deny wheelchairs rather than furnish them. Trapped in the economy of scarcity that the society chooses in providing for the poor, Medicaid will usually not finance a wheelchair for use outside the home, home models being considerably cheaper, even though most work opportunities are not to be found in one's living room.

Of course, for those of us who are privileged by education and money, by access to legal clout, the whole situation changes. As Mary Lou Breslin said about her "magnificent" lightweight, mechanized wheelchair and modified van: "All it takes is money." Though guide dogs and canes are provided free of charge, and though the state of Vermont has contributed generously to my technological functioning, I am able to hire readers at will and buy the equipment necessary to scan the books of my choice into my talking computer. In Mary Lou's case, as in mine, privilege enables our work and our livelihood.

Seeking rational behavior within government bureaucracies or profit-oriented enterprises as it relates to disabled people can be a maddening pursuit. Mary Lou Breslin's Disability Rights Education and Defense Fund is suing to halt the rebuilding of the huge Laguna Honda Hospital and Rehabilitation Center in San Francisco. DREDF's lawsuit, in the name of a large group of institutionalized disabled plaintiffs, is seeking relief from their unnecessary isolation in this giant nursing facility. Because federal law requires that individuals be given services in the most integrated setting appropriate to their needs, the suit claims that these plaintiffs are being unwarrantedly segregated from the larger community and therefore that funds are being inappropriately provided to this construction project.

It's not hard to convince the public at large that everyone would be better off if the severely disabled were in a nice, clean lockup of their own, so a huge bond issue to rebuild Laguna Honda passed easily. Ironically, it had the backing of labor unions, which were protecting a thousand well-paid jobs inside the facility while ignoring and further devaluing miserably paid similar jobs in the community. The entrenched way in which the society undervalues the independent long-term-care community worker is not confined to San Francisco. These attitudes are endemic nationwide and it will require rethinking social policy and priorities to change them.

It's also perplexing to try to understand the fiscal logic of Medicaid's preference for places such as Laguna Honda, where the average yearly expense per patient is more than $23,000, as compared to $7,000 for community-based services. This logic is as skewed as New York City's preference for institutional confinement of the mentally ill homeless rather than for Sam Tsemberis's cheaper and more humane Pathways to Housing. But the deck is stacked against the rational, nursing homes and hospitals being an entitlement under Medicaid, while community services are only an option.

How then is further empowerment of the disabled to come about? The gaps between them and the nondisabled in income, employment, education, political participation and community social life are formidable, and to level the playing field will require equal access and thus equal opportunity. For all that has been accomplished in law, in the academy, in technology, in social-policy thinking, it's essential to protect those hard-won gains and to consider them as only a beginning.

In this book, I sought not only to explore the disability community and my relationship to it but to find people who engage in what Pete Lang called "an honest day's work." Those portrayed in these pages are rare individuals working in large part against the selfish grain of the time, a time in which attention to respectfulness and dignity seem revolutionary. It became my good fortune to witness their unflamboyant, unshakable conviction that what they are doing is an essential human obligation.

There are, of course, many others in the disability community who are engaged in equally important work, some in similar areas, some in a host of diverse fields: in theater, dance, movie-making, photography, in the training of athletes, in rehabilitation, in medicine and other sciences and technologies. Although the work explored here focuses largely on those of us who have disabilities, it seems clear that everyone, disabled or not, benefits from such work. It is rewarding not just to witness people at their best but to be enriched by the cross-pollination between the disabled and the ablebodied that occurs in scholarship, social activism, technology and ways of caregiving.

From its beginnings, this book was a personal journey through my complicated feelings about myself as a disabled man trying to come to terms with my reactions to others who were blind or otherwise disabled, with a friend who had no notion that he was wounding me when he pointed to a quadriplegic in a wheelchair and mumbled, "There but for the grace of God go I," with being an inspiration to some, a fearful blind man to others, with a woman who couldn't stop referring to my blindness as "Andy's tragedy," clearly not understanding that tragedy is inseparable from the human condition.

"Doesn't this work make you sad?" most of the people who work with disability have been asked at one time or another. "Wouldn't you prefer to work with people who are, you know, normal?"

Pete Lang, for one, is very clear in his answer: "I get a lot more out of it than I can ever give."

Though many people are baffled by the lack of remedies to life's essential problems, this attitude misunderstands what makes life worth living. Surely, in part, it's life's many forms and shapes, its surprises, including the certainty that things don't always come out well in the end. "Chaos should be regarded as extremely good news," a wise man has said.

The good people who agreed to be part of this book can't by themselves change the world. Still, I think it increasingly apparent that Chai Feldblum's hope of changing the world one word at a time is not to be taken lightly. If you want to move the mountain, carting it off one basketful of dirt at a time will be slow, very slow, but eventually the mountain will be moved.

ACKNOWLEDGMENTS

Many of the people interviewed in these pages have not only given generously of their time and hospitality but have contributed greatly to my understanding of the world of disability through their writing and lectures. Books, articles and class notes by Mary Lou Breslin, Chai Feldblum, Mark Jeffreys, Adrienne Asch, Rosemarie Garland Thomson, Paul K. Longmore, Connie Tomaino, David Werner, Jay Neugeboren and Mona Wasow have inspired my progress through this field.

Among other writers whose ideas on disability have very much influenced mine are Joseph Shapiro, Hugh Gregory Gallagher, John Hockenberry, Robert F. Murphy, Leonard Kriegel, Nancy Mairs, Simi Linton, Lennard J. Davis, Oliver Sacks, Michel Foucault, Erving Goffman, Kenny Fries, Henri-Jacques Stiker and Richard Scotch.

I am extremely grateful for the support of the Division for the Blind and Visually Impaired of the State of Vermont. Without their help, my transition from visual artist to writer would have been much more difficult.

I am grateful for the expert counsel as well as friendship of my editor, Ann Harris, and my agent, Phyllis Wender. As for the constant reading and rereading of my text, I depended wholly on the marvelous voice inside my computer (whose stern and well-inflected voice sounds very much like NPR's Carl Kassell), my two excellent readers, Barbara Carnes and Ethel Bower, and on the voice and judgment of my wonderful wife, Loie.

Please remember that this is a library book,
and that it belongs only temporarily to each
person who uses it. Be considerate. Do
not write in this, or any, library book.

DATE DUE